Almost a Girl

Male Writers and Female Identification

Alan Williamson

And it was almost a girl and came to be
out of this single joy of song and lyre.

—Rilke, *Sonnets to Orpheus*

University Press of Virginia   *Charlottesville and London*

The University Press of Virginia
© 2001 by the Rector and Visitors of the University of Virginia
Printed in the United States of America
First published 2001

♾ The paper used in this publication meets the minimum
requirements of the American National Standard for Information Sciences—
Permanence of Paper for Printed Library Materials, ANSI Z39.48-1984.

Library of Congress Cataloging-in-Publication Data

Williamson, Alan (Alan Bacher), 1944–
    Almost a girl : male writers and female identification / Alan Williamson.
      p. cm.
    Includes bibliographical references and index.
    Content: Jarrell, the mother, the Märchen—Rilke's solitude—Lawrence and the
"Oedipal riddle"—Pavese's despair—Questions of autonomy : two European novels—
Male sexual prophecy : Blake to Bly.
    ISBN 0-8139-2039-6 (cloth : alk. paper)—ISBN 0-8139-2054-X (pbk. : alk. paper)
    1. Femininity in literature. 2. Male authors—Psychology. 3. Literature, Modern—Male
authors—History and criticism. I. Title.

PN56.F4 W55 2001
809'.933052041—dc21

                                                                        00-51255

For Richard Wertime

Contents

Acknowledgments

THIS BOOK is dedicated to the one male friend who has remained, for forty years, close enough to discuss these issues with in full candor; and who has read most of these chapters with keen perspicacity. Next, I would thank the three women friends who have not only given much good advice, but made me feel that gender criticism was a conversation I could participate in, not a prosecutorial brief I had to answer: Joanne Feit Diehl, Sandra M. Gilbert, and Elizabeth Tallent. I would like to thank the following for reading one or more chapters in manuscript and/or for steering me to the right book at the right time: Mandy Aftel, Susan Balee, Paula Friedman, Robert Hass, Patricia Moran, Carol Siegel, and the anonymous first reader at the University Press of Virginia. I am grateful to Jessica Benjamin for discussing this project with me, and looking at two chapters, during her visit to the University of California at Davis in 1997. Both Joseph Aimone and Sean McDonnell were everything one could wish for in a research assistant. I must thank Belle Huang and, especially, Joyce R. Tedlow for keeping me thinking about these issues in my own life. I thank Jeanne Foster and my daughter Elizabeth for love and tolerance, and for years of thoughtful conversation.

Two of the chapters in this book appeared, in much earlier form, in journals: "Jarrell, the Mother, the Märchen" in *Twentieth Century Literature,* and "Rilke's Solitude" in *Michigan Quarterly Review.* Both are reprinted by permission of the editors of those journals.

The following poetry excerpts are reprinted by permission of Farrar, Straus & Giroux: excerpt from "The Bronze David of Donatello"; "The Death of the Ball Turret Gunner"; "Eighth Air Force"; "The Face"; excerpt from "Hohensalzburg: Fantastic Variations on a Theme of Romantic Character"; excerpt from "The House in the Wood"; excerpt from "The Lost World"; excerpt from "The Night Before the Night Before Christmas"; excerpt from "A Pilot from the Carrier"; and excerpt from "A Quilt Pattern," from Randall Jarrell, *The Complete*

ACKNOWLEDGMENTS

Poems, copyright by Randall Jarrell © 1969, renewed 1997 by Mary von S. Jarrell. Excerpt from "No Messiah," from Robert Lowell, *The Dolphin*, copyright © 1973 by Robert Lowell.

Excerpts from *The Selected Poetry of Rainer Maria Rilke*, edited and translated by Stephen Mitchell, copyright © 1982 by Stephen Mitchell, are reprinted by permission of Random House, Inc. "Oh, misery, my mother tears me down" and "Again and again, though we know the landscape of love" are taken from *An Unofficial Rilke*, translated by Michael Hamburger and published by Anvil Press Poetry in 1981. "Grapes," "Humiliation," "She Said as Well to Me," "Snap-dragon," and "Wedlock," are from *The Complete Poems of D. H. Lawrence*, edited by V. de Sola Pinto and F. W. Roberts, copyright © 1964, 1971 by Angelo Ravagli and C. M. Weekley, executors of the estate of Frieda Lawrence Ravagli; they are used by permission of Viking Penguin, a division of Penguin Putnam, Inc.

Pavese, *Hard Labor,* pp. 9–11, 17–19, 35, 39, 53, 63, 97, 127, © 1979, is used by permission of Johns Hopkins University Press.

Excerpts from *The Bonds of Love,* by Jessica Benjamin, copyright © 1988 by Jessica Benjamin, are reprinted by permission of Pantheon Books, a division of Random House, Inc.

Almost a *Girl*

Introduction

IN A LATE poem by Robert Lowell, we come upon the following lines:

> I come like someone naked in my raincoat,
> but only a girl is naked in a raincoat.

Certain emotions, certain basic human motives (including those that Lowell's lines rather movingly combine—narcissistic display, intense awareness of one's own body, tender self-surrender, vulnerability) are typed by our culture as "feminine." So the man who experiences them— or, especially, who finds them predominant in his own psychic makeup —may face a crisis of gender identity. Still more so the man who ideo- logically finds himself on the wrong side of the reason/containment versus emotion/intuition dualisms that have been gender-typed, in Western culture, at least as far back as the Pythagoreans, for whom *female* was on the same side of the dichotomies as *unlimited, curved, darkness,* and *bad.*[1]

If even so conspicuously male a writer as Lowell experienced this sense of unnatural limit, what of the legions of men who have had to learn, from the schoolyard on, that they simply cannot fit the received definitions of maleness? Such men may be homo- or bisexual; but they are at least as likely to be obsessively drawn to women, at a level of longing where lost part of self is hard to distinguish from erotic other. If they are writers, they may specialize in dramatic monologues in female persona; or concentrate on minute renderings and analyses of the psy- ches of their heroines. They may come to feel that creativity, even in men, is innately feminine: a psychic pregnancy.

I became interested in writing a book on this subject partly because elements of it fit me personally, my own character, and perhaps for that reason I had long wanted to write essays on several of the writers taken up here. But I was also responding to a sense that gender criticism has for too long been shaped by a dogmatic separatism (this includes even the criticism that focuses on men, since it tends, overwhelmingly, to focus on gay men). In *His Other Half,* Wendy Lesser calls for a new kind of gender criticism, one that would at least be open to the possibility of genuine empathy, and beneficent influence, between the sexes:

> On a practical level, the gender-separatist stance is self-defeating. But I also think it is wrong. The rich world of men's artistic visions of women cannot be summarized with a mere reference to the artists' sex. . . . There is no single meaning that women have for men, no single manner in which men use the feminine in their art. . . . There was something compelling and moving, I felt, in the way certain male artists portrayed women: a kind of longing that was not just an expression of the erotic (it's not, certainly, erotic attraction as we usually think of it, since one thing these artists do not share is sexual preference), a desire to *be* the other as well as to view her, and at the same time an acknowledgement of irrevocable separation.[2]

Not surprisingly, perhaps, no fashionable movement of thought, at least until very recently, is entirely comfortable with the feelings, or the kind of men, Lesser and I are interested in describing. Feminist criticism has felt the need to emphasize how hard it is for men *really* to imagine what women experience. It has been quick to smell preemption, rather than legitimate empathy, whenever male writers attempt to represent a female point of view. The fear is that they will perpetuate stereotypes, offer up straw men, or rather straw women, so that the patriarchal side can have the last word, or, at best, steal insights women writers deserve the chance to express for themselves. So Adrienne Rich, in "Paula Becker to Clara Westhoff," has Becker anticipate Rilke's famous "Requiem," written for her after her death, and emphasize that she was really Clara's "friend," not Rainer's, and that Rainer has treated her, as the ostensible subject of his poem, "like a guest / who comes on the wrong day."[3] The sophisticated application of this stance to literary criticism may be seen in Sandra M. Gilbert's essay on William Carlos Williams's use of the Cress letters in *Paterson.*[4] The unsophisticated version can be encountered in any creative writing class, whenever a male student dares to present a piece taken from the female point of view.

Beyond even this, I think, feminism has been suspicious of all ideas of a positive femininity coming from men. They savor too strongly of the idealizations that, through the centuries, have served as propaganda to keep women in their place. "Up from the Pedestal" went a famous slogan of the 1970s. In particular, the praise of women for thinking or creating on a more intuitive level, for existing, in Sartrean terms, *en soi* rather than *pour soi,* is seen as a subterfuge for denying women intelligence, agency, and anger.

And so we find that even as subtle and adventurous a book as Kaja Silverman's *Male Subjectivity at the Margins,* seeking to define, even to "eroticize or privilege," those "kinds of male subjectivity . . . which open in a variety of ways onto the domain of femininity" can only define "femininity" in negative terms, as "castration, alterity, and specularity." The primary lesson that male subjectivity can learn from female, it would seem, is the Lacanian lesson that "what the subject takes to be its 'self' is thus both other and fictive."[5]

But I think our culture as a whole knows better. Consider the popularity, a few years ago, of the transvestite movie *The Crying Game.* Critics attuned to Theory made a good deal of "the phallus as signifier" in this film. But the experience of this viewer, at least, was that the "phallus" seemed unimportant in comparison with a femininity so positive—in its grace, in the authenticity and expressiveness of permitted emotional lability—that one man would choose to become it and two others would fall in love with it in "her"—all this in defiance of biological "nature." The physically attractive female character, on the other hand, is rejected or devalued, ultimately, by both men, because she has adopted stereotypically "male" values—ideology, brutal pragmatism, and the use of sexuality as a form of power.

If feminism tends to treat female identification as suspect, unreal, unless it is an acknowledgment of "castration" and lack, we find quite an opposite diagnosis outside the academy, in Men's Movement thinking. For Robert Bly and his followers, female identification is all too real, but unfortunate. Our culture, over the twenty-five years since the Vietnam War, has produced "soft males" who, taking the lead from feminism, "become more thoughtful, more gentle," but not "more free."[6] The root of gender problems, according to Bly, is absent or remote fathers, because "only men can initiate men" (16). The association of feeling and sensitivity with the feminine alone is a false one, engendered by too-exclusive mother-son bonds: "When the son is introduced primarily by the mother to feeling, he will learn the female attitude toward masculinity. . . . Some mothers send out messages that

civilization and culture and feeling and relationships are things which
... the mother and the sensitive son ... share in common, whereas the
father stands for and embodies what is stiff, maybe brutal, what is un-
feeling, obsessed, rationalistic: money-mad, uncompassionate. 'Your
father can't help it'" (24).

Bly and his associates have a favorite word for men who remain
sons of the mother: *naive*. Such men, Bly acknowledges, are capable of
extraordinary achievement, but an achievement always compromised
by character defects. These are, basically, the defects of the Jungian
puer aeternus archetype: "Flying people, giddily spiritual, [who] do
not inhabit their own bodies well ... and are averse to a certain boring
quality native to human life" (57). I defer my own analysis, and critique, of Bly's position until my final chapter. But I think the very presence of this position, and its invisibility in academic theory, indicates
how much narrower the academic debate about gender has become—
to its cost—than the debate among educated people at large.

Where I finally did find real help in thinking about female-identified
men, not as misguided but as in some sense venturesome and heroic,
was in the object-relations psychoanalytic tradition. Object relations
acknowledges that the strongest experience of merging, mutuality,
and inter-identity, for both men and women, is the infantile relation
to the mother, and that the requirement that men, in particular, leave
this behind has to be traumatic. Even Kaja Silverman observes, "Much
has been made of the difficult erotic itinerary of the little girl, who is
asked at an early age to surrender her first object of love for another,
and not enough of the tortuous identificatory itinerary of the little boy,
who is expected at an equally tender age to relinquish one identity for
another."[7]

Jessica Benjamin, in *The Bonds of Love,* calls this "tortuous identificatory itinerary" the "Oedipal riddle," because the boy must lose
his mother twice. He must not only renounce her as an erotic object,
but must also reject his early commonality with her in order to become
like the father and so, eventually, have access to the mother's surrogate.
"After Oedipus, both routes back to mother—identification and object
love—are blocked. The boy must renounce not only incestuous love,
but also identificatory love of the mother. In this respect the contradictory commands of the oedipal father—'You must be like me' and 'You
may not be like me'—unite in a common cause, to repudiate identity

with the mother. The oedipal injunctions say, in effect: 'You may not *be like* the mother, and you must *wait* to love her as I do.'"[8]

The violent repudiation of "feminine" traits that can be seen in little boys after the oedipal period is, Benjamin suggests, partly a reaction formation against real grief for the loss of the mutuality of the earliest bond. The "feminine" comes to mean, not the mother's actual traits, but the characteristics of the preoedipal bond itself: nurturance, empathy, dependence, acknowledgement of weakness. "The whole experience of the mother-infant dyad is retrospectively identified with femininity, and vice versa. Having learned that he cannot have babies like mother, nor play her part, the boy can only return as an infant, with the dependency and vulnerability of an infant. Now her nurturance threatens to reengulf him with its reminder of helplessness and dependency; it must be countered by his assertion of difference and superiority. . . . This is why the oedipal ideal of individuality excludes all dependency from the definition of autonomy" (162).

Benjamin goes on to observe that "emotional attunement, sharing states of mind, empathically assuming the other's position, and imaginatively perceiving the other's needs and feelings, are now associated with cast-off femininity" (170). The boy will even lose faith in innerness as a dimension of his own personality, because his sense of it has developed in the intersubjective play with the mother: "The identification with the holding mother supplies something vital to the self: in the case of the boy, losing the continuity between himself and mother will subvert his confidence in his 'inside.' The loss of that in-between space cuts him off from the space within. The boy thinks: 'Mother has the good things inside, and now that she is forever separate from me and I may not incorporate her, I can only engage in heroic acts to regain and conquer her in her incarnations in the outside world.' The boy who has lost access to inner space becomes enthralled with conquering outer space" (163). These disidentifications, Benjamin rightly perceives, have enormous social consequences. Such political attitudes as "contempt for the needy and dependent, emphasis on individual self-reliance, rejection of social forms of providing nurturance," while "not visibly connected to gender," have their roots in "the mentality of opposition which pits freedom against nurturance" (171–72).

But the consequences for personal relationships are equally disastrous. When the "exclusive identification with the father" involves "disavowing all femininity," then any later experience of empathy or likeness with a woman threatens to draw a man back into the black hole of preoedipal helplessness. Heterosexual love becomes at once compulsive, being the only way back to the original "good things," and denigrating, since it is too dangerous to allow the woman "equal subjectivity" and "mutual recognition" (164–65).

Benjamin's theory powerfully refutes Bly's view of the stereotypes of male limitation as simply the "messages" that "some mothers send out" and suggests why some men might find it necessary, at whatever cost, to resist those limits. It also provides a basis for theorizing male writers' inhabitation of female characters, not as wish fulfillment or preemptive strategy, but as the recovery of an attunement that was once literally real.

Moreover, Benjamin's theory also suggests that the power and goodness that men (even conventional men) attribute to women, the longing they feel, and their rage when that longing is frustrated, cannot be reduced to subterfuges of patriarchal domination. They are either the result of grief at what is lost with the preoedipal bond or, more deeply, of the preverbal memories and ambivalences all mother-raised children carry toward the female—the "envy," despair, guilt, as well as ecstasy, in relation to her initially charted by Melanie Klein in *Envy and Gratitude*.

The latter possibility is explored at length in another book oriented toward object-relations that has greatly influenced my thinking— Dorothy Dinnerstein's *The Mermaid and the Minotaur*. Dinnerstein, who is earlier and more flagrantly speculative than Benjamin, goes farther in her analysis of the preoedipal roots of some of the cultural images of woman noted by Simone de Beauvoir and others—the association with nature in its ambivalence and capriciousness, the "carnal scapegoat-idol," the "dirty goddess." In particular, Dinnerstein gives an etiology to the identificatory Muse figure, which many feminists simply castigate—to the conviction, found even in women, that "female sentience . . . carries . . . the atmosphere of an unbounded, shadowy presence"; that "'She' designates the borderline between the inanimate and the conscious."[9]

From Benjamin and Dinnerstein, I made my way back to the thinkers who shaped them: Klein on envy, splitting, the good and the bad breast; Winnicott on the good-enough mother and the transitional object. The influence of these thinkers will be evident throughout this book. I must also acknowledge a debt to the first book I read that saw parent-child relations from the point of view of inter-identity rather than oedipal conflict—Alice Miller's *The Drama of the Gifted Child.* Though much criticized, Miller's portrait of the "narcissistic" attunements between mothers and children—their creative consequences and their tragic dimension—still seems to me right on target for several of the biographies examined here.

PERHAPS IT is in the images of poetry that the vicissitudes of identification can be traced most clearly; so my book will begin with poets. It then expands to novelists, whose works represent interpersonal reactions as well as the interior of the psyche; and finally it takes up men who have themselves tried to theorize the rights and wrongs of gender. It will cross national and cultural boundaries, testifying, I suppose, to a belief in the relative universality of certain psychic configurations; but it will not go outside Euro-American culture or the past two hundred years, the era in which gender roles have been self-consciously under debate. Unlike Wendy Lesser, I have concentrated on hetero- or bisexual men because to me they seem to be the test case. Our culture acknowledges, even expects, that gay men may be female-identified; Queer Theory is, rightly, offended by this expectation, since it seems to undermine the independent validity of male-male desire.

This book will have a good deal to say—following on Benjamin—about how ideas and feelings about gender come into being in individual lives. It will have nothing to say about where those ideas come from in human history—how far from biology, how far from culture. I remain agnostic on this very subtle question, which many of my colleagues in the humanities pronounce on far too glibly, it seems to me, without the detailed knowledge of anthropology, genetics, neurology, primatology, and so on that it would take to have an informed opinion. I suspect that the real reasons for making a dogma of "social construction" are often shallow and time-serving. The fear is that scientific evidence, if allowed in at all, might undermine cherished beliefs or political projects (which of course is not necessarily the case: in a recent issue of the *London Times Literary Supplement,* I read about the bonobo, a little-known great ape whose social structure is based on polyandry and female bonding and that has not developed human, or chimpanzee, habits of violence).

Be that as it may, I think psychoanalytic criticism has a right not to try to answer such questions, but, for a reason eloquently stated by Jessica Benjamin in *Like Subjects, Love Objects,* to look from within the perspective of individual experience:

> Psychoanalysis has to retain some notion of the subject as a self, a historical being that preserves its history in the unconscious. . . . Even if the subject's positions are "constructed," psychoanalysis must imagine someone who does or does not own them. . . . And precisely because psychoanalysis claims that something else that is not-I (not ego but *It*) speaks, that the self is split and the unconsciousness is unknown, It must also be considered to belong to the self. And this idea of an otherness within, an unconscious, unavoidably both transforms and preserves *(Aufhebung)* the idea of a transhistorical, essential self.[10]

The psyche has an ongoing history, wherever its images and assumptions originally come from; and that history deserves our attention, if only because it is, ultimately, our own.

Briefly, in conclusion: I could wish that the stories that follow were happier ones. The most female-identified male writers have often been obsessively ambivalent toward, and unhappy with, the actual women in their lives, for reasons Benjamin and Dinnerstein anticipate. Often such men will remain psychically "stuck," demanding the nourishment, the mirroring, of the preoedipal phase, unable to accept the give and take of more limited relationships. To this extent, Bly has a point. But such men, of course, also suffer from a culturally induced shame that they have not grown into "real men." That shame may merge with infantile frustration, rage, and fear of abandonment or engulfment to produce a covert misogyny as powerful as the overt contempt felt by "patriarchal" men. Such men may move restlessly from woman to woman, as Rilke did; others, like Pavese, seem fated to encounter the woman who seeks a "strong" man, and does not care for the kind of oneness men like Pavese can offer.

But then, few significant stories about gender in this century are happy ones. That our lives are often experiments, now, is neither our fault nor our silliness. What would be the solution? A New Jerusalem, in which traditional monogamy came back, purged by fierce personal loyalty and candor of all its bad roots in economics and power, as

Lawrence believed? A life suspended among friends and lovers, accepting loneliness as the price of authenticity, such as Rilke ended up living? Most of us, probably, have tried to live some variation of one of these; and we have not failed to discover the faults, in the premises and in our own characters, that Rilke and Lawrence discovered. And yet, I am grateful to have lived in an age when human identity became so much more flexible, when many women pursued their visions with a "masculine" exactness and firmness of purpose, when "the son," as Auden said in his elegy for Freud, was allowed to regain "the mother's richness of feeling." And I am grateful for the far more nuanced, multifaceted relations and candors between men and women that came into being with these changes. I hope that gratitude will show as the ground emotion behind this book, however much pain is also recorded.

Jarrell, the Mother, the Märchen

"THERE IS one story and one story only," Randall Jarrell was fond of quoting, from Robert Graves, about those poets whose enabling obsessions he felt he had penetrated to their depths. It was true of many of them, but truest of all of himself. Appropriately, since he was the most consciously psychoanalytic even of the poets of the "confessional" generation, his is a story that resonates with the earliest, most forgotten experiences of life and with the senses of identity, relationship, and gender that begin to be formed there. To understand it is to understand why Jarrell's poetry has been accused of sentimentality, and why, at its most incandescent moments, it completely transcends that accusation.

Jarrell's story is, first and foremost, a story about our loneliness in the world, or about the world's failure to keep us: how to see things is not to be joined with them; how close, beyond the little circle of warmth our bodies cast, begins the unimaginably dead space that does not know us; how all the beauties, the fables of return, the talking animals, are a web of illusion cast over these unacceptable, irrefutable facts. The aging Marschallin, looking at her own face in the mirror, says, "If just living can do this . . . / It is terrible to be alive." The bomber calls *"Little Friend!"* to the fighter it can already see going down in flames. The adolescent girl in "The Night before the Night before Christmas," falling asleep "under the patched star-pattern / of the quilt,"

> warms a world
> Out slowly, a wobbling blind ellipse
> That lengthens in half a dozen jumps
> Of her numb shrinking feet.

But, beyond that world almost assimilated into the self, she feels the other "world . . . no longer hidden . . . / By the day of the light of the sun," where

> nothing moves except with a faint
> Choked straining shiver;
> Sounds except with a faint
> Choked croaking sigh

and where "There is not one thing that knows / It is almost Christmas."[1]

Even a seemingly reportorial war poem like "A Pilot from the Carrier" derives much of its strength from these underlying preoccupations. The airman, having ejected from his burning plane, finds in his narrow escape, its renewed guarantee of a complete future, a momentarily "steadie[d]" relation to reality. He

> falls, a quiet bundle in the sky,
> The miles to warmth, to air, to waking:
> To the great flowering of his life, the hemisphere
> That holds his dangling years. In its long slow sway
> The world steadies and is almost still.

Though still "[s]light, separate, estranged," he experiences the mastery of "[r]eading a child's first scrawl." But what he reads are, in fact, the signs of something he does not see and cannot control, that can still destroy him—first "[t]he travelling milk-like circle of a miss," then the "little blaze" of the carrier's guns,

> Toy-like as the glitter of the wing-guns,
> Shining as the fragile sun-marked plane
> That grows to him, rubbed silver tipped with flame.

The beautiful world is, read correctly, the malign or indifferent one; toy-scale to the ego's false perspectives, it will soon reduce the ego itself to the dispensable toy.

The other story Jarrell tells obsessively—really it is only a variant of the first one—has to do with our failure to keep each other: our inability to find, even in our loved ones, even in ourselves, a trustworthy "good" that can be categorically opposed to evil. It comes up in the war, as the poet looks around at the lovable, frightened men who have destroyed cities:

> If, in an odd angle of the hutment,
> A puppy laps the water from a can
> Of flowers, and the drunk sergeant shaving

Whistles *O Paradiso!*—shall I say that man
Is not as men have said: a wolf to man?

It seems almost part of the nature of things that there are only semantic solutions to these problems: a "puppy" is good, but a "wolf" is evil; and there are only "men" to say which of these it is that "man" resembles. The problem comes up earlier, in childhood, in one of the most memorable scenes in Jarrell's poetry: in "The Lost World," the grandmother "looks with righteous love / At all of us, her spare face half a girl's," then goes into the chicken coop and wrings a chicken's neck. As the chicken's body tries "to run / Away from something, to fly away from Something / in great flopping circles," the grandson thinks, "Could such a thing / Happen to anything?" And the grandmother, the "farm woman," has to

tr[y] to persuade
The little boy, her grandson, that she'd never
Kill the boy's rabbit, never even think of it.
He would like to believe her.

Without diminishing their reality as stories about the world, these are all, I think, in a sense stories about childhood. They take us back to the very earliest stages, when the knowledge of separateness does indeed bring "death into the world, and all our woe," but is necessary for the very existence of an individuated self. And then they take us to the complex angers of separation, as psychoanalytic writers from Melanie Klein to Jessica Benjamin have charted them: anger at the parent for abandonment; anger at the parent for being so powerful to begin with; anger coming from the parent but inextricably confused with the anger coming from the child—all that the "good" and "evil" of fairy tales try so hard, and unsatisfactorily, to sort out.

Jarrell knew his Freud thoroughly—and intuited much that object-relations theory was only beginning to explore—and I think we can see him, consciously or unconsciously, returning to these primary feelings for his deepest sense of the crises or the potential horror in life. Looking back at "A Pilot from the Carrier," we see how inescapably "And falls, a quiet bundle in the sky" suggests birth; similarly, "In its long slow sway / The world steadies" suggests the sensuous blurring, and precarious triumph, of learning to walk. Or take Jarrell's most famous single poem, "The Death of the Ball Turret Gunner":

> From my mother's sleep I fell into the State,
> And I hunched in its belly till my wet fur froze.
> Six miles from earth, loosed from its dream of life,
> I woke to black flak and the nightmare fighters.
> When I died they washed me out of the turret with a hose.

This poem may have succeeded so well as an elegy on the indifference of war precisely because it is really an elegy for the primal separation. The "State" itself is only a hopeful, if colder, womb (a fact, of course, that totalitarian states have known very well how to manipulate). But by the third line, the metaphor has become cosmic: Earth itself, in its capacity to support life, is, from the point of view of outer space, only another womb, another contingent "dream." Nothing ultimately cares for us; so that the waking to inevitable mortality, when it comes in the fourth line, is only the last in a series of destructive births. It is the grief and anger about this that give to the brutal, journalistic details—the loss of the shape that constitutes an *I*, the body reduced to a thing—so much more power than the detailed brutalities of many war poems. The feeling about death, technology, the state, the universe becomes the primal angry grieving of Stevens's great poem "Madame La Fleurie": "His grief is that his mother should feed on him, himself and what he saw."

In the German fairy tales, of course, Bad Mothers do eat their children. Jarrell was fascinated with the märchen partly because they recall a harsher time in the history of the species, when we were more at the mercy of the surrounding forest, the conditions of being (see the poem "The Marchen"), but even more because they recall a harsher time in the history of the psyche. The child driven into exile or setting out on a heroic quest—it hardly matters which: at age one or two they are so profoundly the same event. The Good Mother, the stepmother, the Witch—that triangulation that so clearly suggests the way of handling very early feelings of anger that Melanie Klein calls "splitting." I quote Dorothy Dinnerstein's beautifully succinct summary of the Kleinian concept: "[The child's] hateful feelings are sharply dissociated from its loving ones; the menacing, vengeful aspects of the mother (as she exists in the child's mind) are walled off from her comforting, providing aspects. The child comes to feel 'that a good and a bad breast exist.' The good breast remains intact, unsullied by badness, but it disappears from time to time and a bad breast is there instead."[2] "Splitting" applies to the child's own feelings as well as to the image of the mother. As Klein writes, "love and hatred as well as the good and bad aspects of the breast are largely kept apart from one another"; and "[t]he urge to idealize both the self and the object is a result of the infant's need to split good from bad, both in himself and in his objects."[3]

The Hansel and Gretel story was Jarrell's favorite of the märchen, I think because in it the mechanisms of splitting are so perfectly articulated—as, too, is the transformation of the lost oral unity into an engulfing horror. Jarrell draws on the loneliness of the story for the girl's predicament in "The Night before the Night before Christmas," and in "The Marchen" he makes Hansel a type of questing humanity. It is in "A Quilt-Pattern," however, that we find the quirky locus classicus for his psychoanalytic understanding of the story.

"A Quilt-Pattern" is taken from the point of view of a sick child—threatened with the ultimate abandonment of death, but also subjected to a level of maternal ministration that, in his healthy state, he would have outgrown. He falls into a troubled sleep and redreams the fairy tale. The dream shows, among other things, how strong his longing is for the lost infantile unity:

> Here a thousand stones
> Of the trail home shine from their strings
> Like just-brushed, just lost teeth.

"Home" is the place the milk teeth lead back to, the original undifferentiation. The witch's house is the place where we go when that is not only no longer available but has become a threat. There, to need the mother is to eat the mother—a guilty, dangerous act that the child must deflect onto something smaller and weaker: "'It is a mouse.'" But to accept that the mother wishes to feed is equally dangerous: no doubt she is fattening him up, to eat him in turn. Her yard is full of rabbits in cages. The reader who knows Jarrell's later work—as the initial readers of this poem could not—will immediately make the connection to Mama's rabbits and chickens in "The Lost World." Thus the childhood issues open directly onto the largest moral issues, even those of the war poems. Where does one find goodness in this world of eaters and eaten? "His white cat eats up his white pigeon."

And so, both mother and child are split, in the child's mind. The "dead mother"—the unambiguously good mother of infancy—is buried underneath the witch's yard, her face "scaling." The twins of the story become the compliant "good me," who represses his pain ("All small furry things / That are hurt, but that never cry at all"), and "bad me," whose oral aggressions are punished in kind: "'My mother is basting / Bad me in the bath-tub.'"

Finally, splitting apart "good me" and "bad me" is not sufficient to contain these conflicts, and the terrible "Other" is born. This is what consciousness cannot acknowledge at all—both the murderous mother who deserves to be killed and the child who wants to kill her.

> If something is screaming itself to death
> There in the oven, it is not the mouse
> Nor anything of the mouse's. Bad me, good me
> Stare into each other's eyes, and timidly
> Smile at each other: it was the Other.

"A Quilt-Pattern" is a disturbing poem, not least because the sources of the hatred of the mother remain mysterious. Jarrell himself, in a letter trying to explain the poem, seems unreasonably angry with her: "she is demanding and completely possessive and awful to him and he hates her."[4] This is so out of keeping with the data within the poem that one is tempted to put it down either to some unexpressed personal memory or to the ready availability (as many writers have noted) of misogynist mother-hatred in the culture in prefeminist days.[5] Within the poem, the worst thing the mother does is to wash the child's mouth out with soap—not good, but hardly enough, in the context of the 1910s, to qualify her as "awful to him." What we hear most about is her intrusive tenderness. Her "humming stare" becomes the "hum[ming]" voice of the "house of bread"; "mouse" turns out to be her nickname for the child. But the child's reaction is as extreme as the poet's: hearing her voice outside his door,

> He says to himself, "I will never wake."
> He says to himself, not breathing:
> "Go away. Go away. Go away."

> And the footsteps go away.

In D. W. Winnicott's terms, he has killed off his True Self, or at least its outward manifestation ("'I will never wake'"), to put it forever out of reach of the mother's infantilizing care.[6]

"Never trust the teller, trust the tale," as D. H. Lawrence said. What Jarrell has written is not a story about an objectively "awful" mother but one about a child's fear of (and nostalgia for) maternal engulfment. For Melanie Klein, such fears are nearly universal: the preoedipal mother is simply too powerful, the strength of the child's dependency on her, and consequent guilty anger—or, as Klein would say, "envy" of a goodness felt to be outside him and only unpredictably accessible to him—are too great. But for later thinkers, from Winnicott to Alice Miller to Jessica Benjamin, there are less universal causes for the need to distance the mother so drastically.[7] What is crucial, they argue, is that the child should feel loved and "recognized" as he or she moves into, and acts on, the sense of being a separate self. When this link is not maintained, then the theme takes on the full, terrible force we have seen in Jarrell's work generally. Separation is cosmic lostness; unity is engulfment, loss of self. This happens, Jessica Benjamin argues, through a failure of the "paradox of recognition," the need to enjoy another's independent existence in order to receive their confirmation of one's own, which can so easily be thrown off by too much, or too little, control on the parent's part. Alice Miller, in a more famous, drastic formulation, speaks of the "narcissistically deprived" parent who needs "a specific echo from the child" because she experiences herself, still, as "a child in search of an object that could be available to her."[8] Such a parent, too involved in his or her own internal dramas to see the child as an other, unconsciously forces the child to assume a role in those dramas—often with exquisite attunement, since it is the only way for the child to get the parent's recognition at all.

Did Jarrell have such a childhood? William Pritchard's biography, though resolutely antipsychoanalytic in tone, does provide some suggestive evidence. There was, first of all, the trauma of the loss of Jarrell's father, when his mother moved back from California to Nashville after the divorce. ("Presumably there is no father in this family," Jarrell writes in the letter about "A Quilt-Pattern."[9] This in itself might, in the Kleinian formulation, intensify resentment of the mother's power, by cutting off one of the traditional avenues of escape, identification with the father.) Pritchard's characterization of Jarrell's mother, though sketchy, does fit the broad outlines of Alice Miller's "narcissistically deprived" parent, needing always to "feel herself the center of attention":

Anna Jarrell was not only young but pretty and petite, with dark eyes, curly hair, and a skin so sensitive she needed to wear silk next to it and used only non-allergenic soaps and creams . . . furniture and rugs, draperies and dishes were constantly replaced, and no leftovers were allowed to accumulate in the icebox. When she made her angel cake, said to have been delicious, she flushed a dozen egg yolks down the commode. But [Jarrell's father] Owen's salary as a photographer's assistant was unequal to such extravagances. . . . With money tight and no family of her own or Owen's to turn to, her health suffered and she became, in the ladylike phrase, "delicate."

Pritchard applies the adjectives *sensitive* and *histrionic* to her and suggests that the "recurrent . . . scene called Mother Has Fainted," from the late poem "Hope," is autobiographical.[10]

It does seem clear that the happiest phase of Jarrell's childhood was the year he spent away from his mother, with his paternal grandparents. Pritchard quotes a long, quite literary letter from that year, in which Jarrell seems to be trying at once to convince his mother both that "I wish I could see you" and that California is very "exciting" and he should be allowed to stay: "We sure did see lots of buzzards on our trip. On one detour we saw four great big ones right in the road eating a dead chicken. They just stalked to the side of the road when we passed and then stalked back again. They sure are mean, ugly-looking birds. They just sail around in the sky, looking for some carrion to eat. They seem to say, 'We'll get *you* someday, get you get you. We'll getyouyet, getyouyet, getyouyet.['] Just like choruses of songs that seem to run together."[11]

To Pritchard, this letter, "natural, untroubled, happily alert to this or that circumstance and expressive possibility," is evidence against "the assumption that Jarrell endured a lonely, unhappy childhood." But, as Alice Miller points out, the need to perform in this way for a parent is not necessarily evidence that the child feels accepted as and for his or her self; often, quite the reverse. The adult Jarrell is described —by students, friends, readers, even wives and lovers—as a continuously, and consummately, brilliant performer. We hear from Robert Lowell of an effervescent, almost manic Jarrell, who once shocked the president of Kenyon College by announcing, while skiing, "I feel just like an angel!"[12] But the voice of unexpressed grief, the voice of the buzzard saying "getyouyet," is heard obsessively in his poetry, and seems to have dominated in the desperation of his final year.

If Jarrell did, in fact, feel the ambivalence toward his mother that "A Quilt-Pattern" and some of the biographical details suggest, it is an interesting question why he was so obsessively sympathetic to women in his poetry, writing so many poems either in female persona or essentially from the woman's point of view. Undoubtedly, he projected the fragile, wistful side of himself, inclined to blame the universe when its absolute yearnings were not met, onto female characters partly because these traits were simply not acceptably "male" in the climate of the 1940s and 1950s. (Indeed, Mary Jarrell has said as much: Jarrell's decision to change the speaker's gender in "The Face," she writes, "rescue[d] the poem from the maudlin effects of a man's self-pitying confessions.")[13] But we need to remember, also, another insight of Alice Miller's: that the narcissistic mother has, helplessly, the same kind of fragile, wistful personality that she generates in her child, and that her child is used to, having spent much of childhood "understanding" it. In projecting the "inner woman," the son is projecting both a feelingful self *and* a feelingful mother, who can be rescued together. This element of pure wish fulfillment I think accounts for the sense of sentimentality and lack of depth of character that many readers have when faced with such famous, because very clear-cut, persona poems as "Next Day," "The Face," or "The Woman at the Washington Zoo."

But could Jarrell write for very long about adult women without dredging up some of the resentments, the harsh judgments, directed toward, say, the mother of "A Quilt-Pattern"? The ungiving characteristics of this "real" mother will often reappear, subtly understood and apparently forgiven, in the inner woman of the poems. If the speakers of "Next Day" and "The Woman at the Washington Zoo" seem wounded innocents in their expectations of life, what of the mother in "The Lost Children," whose sense of loss leads her to make no distinction between the child who has died and the child who has had the opportunity to distance herself in the normal way by growing up? Is there no murderous undercurrent in this poem, simply because its manner is passive, wistful, metaphysical, the manner of the Marschallin saying "It is terrible to be alive"? Is it entirely an accident that in "A Girl in a Library" both the bovine Home Ec. major and the hypercritical, imagined "Tatyana Larina" are embodiments of female narcissism? and that it is the task of the male speaker to mediate between the two of them with compassion?

It is in these tensions, I would argue, that Jarrell's poems pass beyond sentimentality to profound psychological truth. The person who experiences herself—or himself, since it is so clearly the poet—as weak and yearning, never getting enough from life, is the same person who will be perceived by others as self-involved, lacking the resources to give. One of the great moments of moral insight in Jarrell's poetry, therefore, comes in "The Lost World," when he perceives himself as capable of inflicting the same kind of damage on the child-selves of others as they have inflicted on his. The story is, in a way, a classically Kleinian one— the Good Object punitively repudiated because it cannot be controlled. When Jarrell was forced to leave his grandparents and his great-grandmother to return to his mother in Nashville, he simply erased them from his memory: never answered their letters, never communicated with them again. In the poem, this memory intrudes into the present time of writing, just as he has finished recounting the story of how his great-grandmother was frightened by a Union captain during the Civil War:

> She cries. . . . As I run by the chicken coops
> With lettuce for my rabbit, real remorse
> Hurts me, here, now: the little girl is crying
> Because I didn't write. Because—
> of course,
> I *was* a child, I missed them so. But justifying
> Hurts too.

And so, when, a few lines later, the "rabbit" becomes the potential object of his grandmother's murderous indifference, the speaker himself is implicated in the crime, in the universal cycle of victimizers and victims.

The way of handling these problems that is suggested by the persona poems has potentially tragic consequences if carried over into life. The man who comforts his own weaker, yearning side by projecting it onto a woman—thereby failing to recognize its destructive potential— may find himself back in the same situation of not being heard, not being understood, facing insatiable demands, that created the sense of weakness to begin with. Jarrell's love letters to Elisabeth Eisler and, particularly, to Mary von Schrader have at once a teacherly, protective quality and a sense of twinship, almost of alter ego, paralleled only in Rilke's letters to Benevenuta. "Truly we are one and were always one. *As* you know, there is no difference between us," he writes to Mary; and repeatedly addresses her as "sister."[14] But in lasting relationships, he never seems to have been quite sure whether he had gotten the Good Mother or the Witch. In his last year, he apparently turned vehemently against Mary, wanting to divorce her, as he had his first wife, and to marry a younger woman. It is one of the grim, but not unfitting, ironies of his life that today we are left to choose whether to believe Mary's conceivably self-serving account—that they were happily reconciled and that he fell in front of the oncoming car by accident—or to believe, with his close friends, that he chose to die.

There is one fairy-tale poem, "Hohensalzburg," that particularly explores the dark side of alter ego relationships and the underlying identity of the wistful and the destructive selves. Jarrell tried to distance himself from this poem—by the subtitle ("Fantastic Variations on a Theme of Romantic Character") and by all the jokes that remind us he is writing about German culture, tourist response. Yet its composition was intimately intertwined with the unconsummated affair with Elisabeth Eisler; that, and the sheer intensity of the writing, suggest that it may tell more of the truth about his inner erotic life than he was used to telling, or entirely comfortable with.

"Hohensalzburg" is a variant of the vampire story. The (female) vampire is imagined with great sympathy, as a tomboy who does not want to grow up, knowing that gender, sexuality, and relationship will compromise her freedom. She does not want to be the object of perception, of desire. When the old woman who serves her tea chides her for having "run, all evening, by the shore / Naked, searching for your dress upon the sand," and then asks her "What would you be, if you could have your wish?" she answers, *"I would be invisible."* And when the old woman says,

> "What you do will do,
> But not forever . . .
> What you want is a husband and children"

her reply speaks for all of the Jarrell characters who despair of, and therefore mystically see through, the world that would in any way delimit their yearnings: *"They will do, / But not forever."*

Yet, for the male speaker of the poem, this elusive woman is so profoundly an alter ego—"Pure, yearning, unappeasable"—that she becomes the vehicle for a more primary, preoedipal, even Wordsworthian experience of cosmic interfusion:

> I should always have known; those who sang from the river,
> Those who moved to me, trembling, from the wood
> Were the others: when I crushed on a finger, with a finger,
> A petal of the blossom of the lime, I understood
> (As I tasted, under the taste of the flower, the dark
> Taste of the leaf, the flesh that has never flowered)
> All the words of the wood but a final word.

What both the speaker and the girl have in common, in short, is the impatience with phenomena, the longing to gain access to the essence beyond, the "final word" that includes all other words. But in relation to a finite other, this longing has a vampiric potential. That this potential belongs to him as well as to her is made beautifully clear through the imagery of "taste," here and later in the poem:

> Your cold flesh, faint with starlight,
> Wetted a little with the dew,
> Had, to my tongue, the bloom of fruit—
> Of the flower: the lime-tree flower,
> And under the taste of the flower
> There was the taste of—

The unfinished sentence has to be completed, in the light of the earlier passage, by "the dark / Taste of the leaf," the "final word" it represents. But surely there is a burden of terror, guilt, repression in the incompletion. The reader who knows "A Quilt-Pattern" will remember that, there, where virtually the exact same phrase was broken off, it asked to be completed with "his mother." Jarrell's canon remembers, if this particular poem does not, the connection both of the desire for oneness and of the guilt of vampirism to the infantile relationship.

The guilt of consuming the mother is, it would seem, both expiated and acted out by submission to the other person's "unappeasable" yearning. The broken sentence cuts directly to

> I felt in the middle of the circle
> Of your mouth against my flesh

> Something hard, scraping gently, over and over
> Against the skin of my throat.

It is a deeply disturbing scene, for more than just the obvious reasons. When he realizes that his blood is being sucked, he feels such a sense of sacrificial union, perhaps of goodness restored through punishment, that he assumes the posture of the crucified Christ:

> I used my last strength and, slowly,
> Slowly, opened my eyes
> And pushed my arms out, that the moonlight pierced and held—

And this very action awakens his sexual desire, for the first and only time in the poem—a desire that the girl, in her perpetual virginity, must of course refuse.

> I said: "I want you"; and the words were so heavy
> That they hung like darkness over the world,
> And you said to me, softly: *You must not so.*
> *I am only a girl.*
> *Before I was a ghost I was only a girl.*

But if his desire is bound up with the need to consume or be consumed, hers, for all her elusiveness, includes the desire to be recognized—for Miller and Benjamin the fundamental desire of the narcissistically deprived child. She wants to be found out in her invisibility; and she despairs that it can never happen. "What shall I call you, O Being of the Earth? / *What I wish you to call me I shall never hear.*"

Why did Jarrell refigure the alter ego relationship of his Salzburg period in terms of the vampire story? Perhaps he intuited (it is a common enough psychological insight) that the very sense of lack that made the two sympathetic could lead to forms of dependence destructive to each other's autonomy. In the poem, "[S]omething light, a life / Pulse[s]" in her face only after she has absorbed his blood. Perhaps, too, he understood that to try to make up for childhood is always, in some sense, to repeat childhood. But beyond this, the vampire story is itself, in its odd way, a love story. Because the vampire has never learned how to connect with the earth, in mutuality, without loss of self, she/he can never leave the earth behind, like the souls that go on to heaven or hell. That is why her only accessible name is "a dweller of the Earth." And she/he kills, in part, to create another vampire, an immortal/earthly companion.

23

Strangely—and yet not so strangely, since the female voice, in Jarrell, is always the voice of grieving—in the poem it is the woman who sees through the limitations of this project: *"In the end we wake from everything."* And it is the male voice that continues to ignore its darkness in favor of its transcendent potential:

> And yet surely, at the last, all these are one,
> We also are forever one:
> A dweller of the Earth, invisible.

IN A SELF as profoundly female-identified as Jarrell's, and as affirmative of its own wistful, yearning side, the relation to the social definitions of the "masculine" must have been problematic. Jarrell was an immensely self-confident, intellectually aggressive human being; yet, as his father was absent from his early life, a traditionally male solidity seems to have been absent from his demeanor. Even his friends agree that his aggressiveness was not Hemingwayesque belligerence; rather, it fit the stereotypes of "female" cattiness and malice.

The poems are, for the most part, conspicuously silent on these issues; Jarrell even joked that all his adult male characters had been killed off in the war.[15] The one exception is, like "Hohensalzburg," a poem of myriad screens. "The Bronze David of Donatello" is a genre piece, a painting-poem; moreover, like Lowell's "Florence," which it may have influenced, it is framed as a moral poem, questioning our automatic preference for the hero over the monster. Yet David—with his history of absent or evil fathers, his beauty, his precocious triumph, his ability to fulfill the earliest dreams of narcissistic singularity—is a perfect vehicle for the mode of male selfhood Jarrell must have seen in himself. He emphasizes David's alienation from the masculinity his deeds bespeak: "The sword alien, somehow, to the hand." Above all, he emphasizes the androgynous, homoerotic, exhibitionistic quality of the statue:

> The boy David's
> Body shines in freshness, still unhandled,
> And thrusts its belly out a little in exact
> Shamelessness. Small, close, complacent,
> A labyrinth the gaze retraces,
> The rib-case, navel, nipples are the features
> Of a face that holds us like the whore Medusa's—
> Of a face that, like the genitals, is sexless.

Though the poem insists that these qualities are disturbing because they are "sexless," all the rhetoric tells us they are feminine; and in doing so the poem calls up a whole gamut of misogynistic feelings. To be feminine, in the way David is, is to be a "whore"—to instrumentalize the world in a horrid self-consciousness, to "take, use, notice"; above all, it is to be narcissistically remote, "close, complacent." It is as if all the hatred of the feminine, or the maternal, that is half repressed in the other poems, is here visited on the femininity within the self. But, as Jessica Benjamin has pointed out, rejection of the maternal usually also involves rejection of the preoedipal "narcissistic" self, dependent on the mother, not yet dragged into the hard-knocks oedipal world of the father. The acculturation into traditional masculinity "ratifies that repudiation [of the mother] on the grounds that the maternal object is inextricably associated with the initial state of oneness, of primary narcissism. In this view, femininity and narcissism are twin sirens calling us back to undifferentiated infantile bliss."[16] So the target of Jarrell's rage is not only the feminine but the self-satisfaction and self-display of a very young boy, the "unhandled" body that "thrusts its belly out a little in exact / Shamelessness." What is most detestable in this David is, ironically, the impulse Jarrell has given in to in poem after poem: the impulse to keep the self pure, to see to it that the self, if it cannot be perfectly taken care of by the world, can be separated from the world, like the "invisible" girl of "Hohensalzburg" or the boy who will "never wake" in "A Quilt-Pattern."

> Centering itself upon itself . . .
>   this offending
> And efficient elegance draws subtly, supply,
> Between the world and itself, a shining
> Line of delimitation, demarcation.
> The body mirrors itself.

How, one might ask, is a body that "mirrors itself" different from the body that finds the whole world beyond itself frightening and dead in "The Night before the Night before Christmas"? Jarrell seems unaware how much of his own emotional temperament he is calling into question in "The Bronze David," how deeply he has internalized social judgments on it. Yet surely he is right, and displays, once again, his genius and honesty, in connecting his more savage forms of aggressiveness to that temperament.

Perhaps the deepest source of anguish in the poem is the fear that, no matter how much aggression, how much "victory" there is, this version of selfhood can never equal, or include, the traditionally masculine one. Goliath's head, under David's foot, is undamaged, though *"The stone sunk in the forehead,* say the Scriptures." Moreover (Jarrell's description is absolutely accurate, here, to one of the most disturbing elements in a disturbing work),

> The head's other wing (the head is bearded
> And winged and helmeted and bodiless)
> Grows like a swan's wing up inside the leg;
> Clothes, as the suit of a swan-maiden clothes,
> The leg. The wing reaches, almost, to the rounded
> Small childish buttocks.

It is hard to escape the passive sexual implication here: that if David, the "swan-maiden," has taken on his victim's strength at all, it is by being anally penetrated. No wonder Jarrell goes on to imagine that Goliath is still the real presence, even in death, and David is reduced to Goliath's dream:

> Strong in defeat, in death rewarded,
> The head dreams what has destroyed it
> And is untouched by its destruction.

If it is fair to take "The Bronze David" as deep self-portraiture, Jarrell would seem to express a particularly self-defeating version of what Jessica Benjamin calls "the Oedipal riddle"—the male child's need to lose the good side of early oneness with the mother, long before he can hope to be truly like the father.[17] Jarrell must devalue the part of himself that identifies with the feminine; yet he cannot ever feel he truly incorporates masculine strength. The self's victories therefore become hollow, factitious, almost a form of defeat, as well as immoral. The concluding lines seem, in context, a moral judgment against "Victory" itself. But even in a superficial reading, their nihilism is abrupt, extreme, unmotivated by what has preceded: "Blessed are those brought low, / Blessed is defeat, sleep blessed, blessed death." In a deeper map of the poem, these lines might suggest the despair, even the suicidal impulses, brought on by the self-defeating nature of the inner conflict.

*   *   *

DESPAIR—BOTH the despair of the boy who will never feel truly independent and, I think, that of the young girl who will never feel truly connected or named—resonates through the last poem Jarrell wrote about the Hansel and Gretel story, "The House in the Wood." It is perhaps the only poem that gives us an idea of how unendurable the depression of his last year must have been. It is a poem about the taking back of projection; the moment when we see through the screens, splittings, and denials that enable us to tell stories and live lives.

> At the back of the houses there is the wood.
> While there is a leaf of summer left, the wood
>
> Makes sounds I can put somewhere in my song,
> Has paths I can walk, when I wake, to good
>
> Or evil: to the cage, to the oven, to the House
> In the Wood.

But when the leafless winter wood "begins / Its serious existence," that has "no path . . . no story" and "resists comparison," the speaker makes the fundamental psychoanalytic discovery that the fairy tale was constructed to prevent:

> If I walk into the wood
>
> As far as I can walk, I come to my own door,
> The door of the House in the Wood.

Such recognitions—in which there is no more Good Me and Bad Me or Good Mother and Witch—should be the beginning of psychic health. But, as E. M. Forster said in another context, wait till you have one, dear reader! In this poem, consciousness is not strong enough to endure either the horror of the discoveries or the implication that one has lived—and might live forever—in a solipsistic universe:

> On the bed is something covered, something humped
> Asleep there, awake there—but what? I do not know.
>
> I look, I lie there, and yet I do not know.

Instead of finding health, the self seems to fall out of adult time and space into a primal amorphousness in which it is at once infinite and infinitely helpless:

How far out my great echoing clumsy limbs

Stretch, surrounded only by space! For time has struck,
All the clocks are stuck now, for how many lives,

On the same second.

If this sounds like descriptions of infantile consciousness—in particular, the boundlessness, the seeming permanence, of infantile rage and despair—it is no accident.[18] For what is discovered on the bed ("covered," "humped"—deformed, copulating, and pregnant) is not just the self but the merging, both oedipal and preoedipal, of the self and the mother—what the self fears and, at some level, has never stopped desiring. The last line of the poem makes this explicit: "In the House in the Wood, the witch and her child sleep." In this boundaryless state, monstrous crimes occur—monstrous actualizations of (and confusions of sexuality with) anger and pain—but neither their agents nor their victims can be located:

> [S]omeone screams
> A scream like an old knife sharpened into nothing.
>
> It is only a nightmare. No one wakes up, nothing happens,
> Except there is gooseflesh over my whole body

All-powerful in one sense, the self is in another sense infinitely cut off, both from the male phallic identity that might enable it to rise above the preoedipal needs and fears and from the Good Mother, whose almost organic continuity with the self could assuage them: "I lie here like a cut-off limb, the stump the limb has left." The continuity is rather with the Bad Mother, who, as so often in Jarrell's poetry, becomes reality itself, the reality that has permitted all this to happen:

> Here at the bottom of the world, what was before the world
> And will be after, holds me to its black
>
> Breasts and rocks me.

Perhaps it is only in hindsight that this union with the Dark Mother seems, as in Sylvia Plath's poems, a premonition of suicide. (Although, in the passage that, of all Jarrell's work, is the one that most chillingly prefigures the actual circumstances of his death, it is when, in "Thinking of the Lost World," the driver-poet turns around to look into the eyes of the "mad girl" in the back seat that he is killed.) In any case, the deathly implications of that concluding "sleep" are strong. The grim lesson of this poem seems to be that splitting and projection are necessary to life itself; their distinctions give the adult ego its existence and its powers.

Here we would have to leave Jarrell, were it not for the strange fact that, at almost exactly the same time in his life as "The House in the Wood," he wrote his own fairy tale in which these dark forces are conquered, in which mutuality between formed personalities does, just barely, hold the infinite expectations and fears at bay. His great children's book *The Animal Family* is a parable of what Jessica Benjamin calls the pleasure of recognizing the irreducible otherness of other people.[19] A hunter courts a mermaid, eventually persuades her to live with him on land, and they adopt first a bear cub, then a lynx, then a shipwrecked boy. A great deal of the fun of the book lies in resolving the comic, but potentially harrowing, mistakes creatures make about other creatures' worlds. The mermaid wants to pick up a coal from the fire, thinking it a pretty shell; the "parents" fear the bear is dying, the first time he hibernates.

No doubt it is significant that what Jarrell imagines is almost, but not quite, a fully human erotic family. There is plenty of sexual, and even oedipal, tension in the book; but the fact that none of the characters has actually emerged from the body of one of the others gives them an ontological equality—in poignancy and independence—that is surely partly wish fulfillment. (It also rhymes, curiously, with Jarrell's life; he was devoted to his stepdaughters, and dedicated his *Selected Poems* to them, as well as to Mary, but he had no children of his own.)

The connection of the mermaid to the "oceanic" memory of the original mother is, however, made clear in the book. The hunter has a dream of his dead mother singing, from which there emerges, as he wakes, first the wave-sound, then the mermaid's voice from the reefs. And she has just enough of the Dark Mother about her to make her a sister of the women in Jarrell's poems and to make loving her a significant moral accomplishment. She has the indifference of Mother Nature, which, Dorothy Dinnerstein suggests, is a projection of the infant's feelings about the mother's unpredictable fulfillment of its needs.[20]

29

> Whenever anything reminded the hunter of his father and mother, you could see that he missed them and longed to have them alive again. The mermaid would tell him about her childhood and her family and her sister, the dead one, but she never seemed to want any of it back. The hunter said, puzzled, "Don't you wish your sister were still here?"
>
> The mermaid answered: "She was then. Why do you want her to be now too?" The hunter remembered that he had never seen the mermaid cry; he thought with a little shiver, "Do mermaids cry?"[21]

Yet in other ways the mermaid's pure momentariness is a revivifying force in the hunter's life. And she, in turn, comes to realize that she loves her new family in a different way: "[I]f you died, if he died, my heart would break" (170).

The theme of the lost mother does recur in its full darkness at one point in the book, when the boy is found in the lifeboat and has to be disentangled from the body of his dead mother. There is a dreamlike, slow-motion quality to the passage, in comparison with the rapid conciseness of most of the book. Though the boy reaches out at once to the transitional object ("Nice kitty!"), the lynx, himself frightened, has to run back to the house, wake up the bear, and go through the whole approach all over again, before the boy will go with them, first falling, then taking "two or three uncertain steps" (137). Ambiguities of perception give the whole episode a haunted, nightmarish tinge. "[I]nside the boat something was crying" (132). "The boy looked very small and pale and the bear dark as a mountain, as they went slowly up the beach; the lynx, gray-silver and shining, flowed back and forth ahead of them like the tide" (137). We are momentarily back to the dangerously unsteady, shifting world—the toddler's wavering steps, the ambiguity of good and evil—that runs through the poems, from "A Pilot from the Carrier" to "The House in the Wood." But here, instead of the Witch, the lost child finds the good-enough parents, who have faced the problem of separateness, and cannot be destroyed by it. Things regain their stable, though playful, shapes. The book ends with the boy accepting, and loving, his "parents'" difference ("The difference between the hunter and the mermaid was no greater, to the boy, than the difference between his father's short hair and trousers, his mother's long hair and skirts, is to any child" [157]); and even coming to believe that there is nothing to mourn for, no lack in his own ontological status, because he has "lived with them always" (158).

And so there are two stories: one in which "what was before the world / And will be after" has "black / Breasts," and one in which the only answer to "Do you like your life?" is "Can you not like it?" (162) Both are, in a way, perennial truths about life; and both depend, in another way, on different resolutions to very early psychological conflicts. Which story was truer, for Jarrell, is as unanswerable a question as exactly what led to the events of his last day. The point is, he had the largeness, as an artist, to tell them both.

The issues raised by Jarrell's story, or stories, are, I believe, crucial ones for gender criticism. What some call sentimentality, and others human truth, in his work is his closeness to areas our culture is anxious about: the "unappeasable" yearning, pity, and self-pity that are permissible in women but forbidden in men after the age of five, except in the protected wilderness of Romantic Love. (It may seem ironic to speak of being "permitted" to feel those very emotions that play so large a role in the negative stereotypes of women; but such ironies are not uncommon when basic human traits are strictly polarized by gender.) Jarrell did pioneering work as an artist by refusing those polarities (even in the limited, ambivalent way he did), by continuing, throughout his work, to interrogate the internalized mother and her grieving child. Jarrell's poetry adumbrates the history of forgotten infancy behind these suspect emotions. And it suggests some of the consequences for the human psyche—the male psyche in particular—when that history stays unresolved: the dread of female powers; the horror both of helplessly merged states and of isolation. When these dynamics are better understood, gender criticism may look with a more sympathetic eye on the difficulties both of male writers who embrace female identification (like Jarrell's hero Rilke) and of those who fight it with all their might, like the later D. H. Lawrence.

Rilke's Solitude

RILKE SEEMS almost to have existed to be a thorn in the side of feminist criticism. On the one hand, he was the most female-identified of all male modernists. He was close to very few men, but he chose extraordinarily talented women as his friends and lovers (Lou Andreas-Salome, Paula Modersohn-Becker, Clara Westhoff, Marina Tsvetayeva, the pianist Magda von Hattingberg), and he forwarded their ambitions without a trace of competitiveness or condescension. He frequently voiced the belief, which many feminists now share, that creativity was naturally more feminine than masculine, because gestation—a slow, unconscious, nonlinear coming together—was a better model for it than will, control, logic-chopping obtuseness. "The deepest experience of the creator is feminine—; for it is experience of receiving and bearing. The poet Obstfelder once wrote, when describing the face of a strange man: 'it was' (when he began to speak) 'as if there were a woman in him—'; it seems to me that would fit every poet who begins to speak."[1]

But in his life, Rilke seems the prototype of the man incapable of lasting commitments or familial responsibilities. He left his wife only a few weeks after their child was born, claiming it was better for both of their artistic careers; none of his later relationships lasted more than a few months, or a year, without dwindling into friendships. He can even be accused—perhaps accused himself—of carrying out quite a successful career as a Don Juan, under the guise of empathy and concern. More-over, his very adulation of women always threatens to carry over into the age-old male myth that, in Sartrean terms, women exist *en soi* rather than *pour soi:* their intuitive perfection entails a lack of self-division, doubt, active power, resistance, or anger.[2]

> Are you really the same
> as those children who
> on the way to school were rudely

shoved by an older brother?
Unharmed by it.

> While we, even as children,
> disfigured ourselves forever,
> you were like bread on the altar
> before it is changed.[3]

So Adrienne Rich quotes, with approval, a sentence about the "work of love" women have done through the centuries, but goes on to say: "Nowhere in his musings does Rilke acknowledge even faintly what the cost of doing this 'work of love' for men—in a word, mothering—has been for women. Depending for encouragement and protectiveness on a series of women, soulmates and patronesses, he remained essentially a son."

Yet Rich also writes: "We read Rilke in part because he often seems on the verge of saying—or seeing—further than other male writers, in the sense of knowing, at least, that the relationship of man to woman is more dubious, more obscure, than literature has assumed."[4] My intention here is to explore just what Rilke did understand about that "dubious[ness]," and how his female identification both aided and impeded his efforts to imagine a wider, more generous kind of love.

Rilke's deepest originality, it seems to me, is that he saw the problem of love as a problem of identity. (Surely the gender wars of our time have shown the prescience of this insight, for women as well as for men.) He saw that people wanted love to give them a self; but that the need for, and the terror of, merging, and the problems of living with another person, could be endured only by an already formed self—one that could also tolerate loneliness. His notorious saying "To love means to be alone" is best understood in its less well-known context, the seventh letter of the *Letters to a Young Poet*:

> For one human being to love another human being: that is perhaps the most difficult task that has been entrusted to us, the ultimate task, the final test and proof, the work for which all other work is merely preparation. That is why young people, who are beginners in everything, are not yet *capable* of love: it is something they must learn. . . . But learning-time is always a long, secluded time, and therefore loving, for a long time ahead and far on into life, is—solitude, a heightened and deepened kind of aloneness for the

person who loves. Loving does not at first mean merging, surrendering, and uniting with another person (for what would a union be of two people who are unclarified, unfinished, and still incoherent—?), it is a high inducement for the individual to ripen, to become something in himself, to become world in himself for the sake of another person. . . .

But how can they, who have already flung themselves together and can no longer tell whose outlines are whose, who thus no longer possess anything of their own, how can they find a way out of themselves, out of the depths of their already buried solitude?[5]

Rilke reminds one of Rimbaud's *il faut réinventer l'amour,* or of Tolstoy, in his scorn for the attempt to fit individual encounters to social scenarios —"the many conventions that have been put up in great numbers like public shelters on this most dangerous road." And the "immoral" conventions ("cheap, safe, and sure, as public amusements are") come in for as much of this scorn as the conventions of marriage do.

Too much has been written, I think, about Rilke's renunciation of love for the sake of art, and not enough about the urgency with which he tried, year after year, "to get a more natural and human footing in life," as he put it in a letter to Lou Andreas-Salome.[6] Rilke's problem, indeed, may have been that he was too prone to the illness he diagnosed so clearly in others—the belief that ideal love could solve problems of identity, could correspond to, and confirm, what he most deeply *was.* So he writes, to his "You who never arrived,"

> All the immense
> images in me—the far-off, deeply felt landscape,
> cities, towers, and bridges, and un-
> suspected turns in the path,
> and those powerful lands that were once
> pulsing with the life of the gods—
> all rise within me to mean
> you, who forever elude me.

Of course, Rilke—in his writing, at least—saw very clearly how a merged relationship could be a threat to individuality: how the guilt, the beholdenness, the need to account to the other could interfere with those very experiences of inward fusion with the world it was supposed to echo and confirm. In "Requiem," he savagely berates Otto

Modersohn for having once refused to let Paula Becker walk out on a narrow breakwater by herself. In the letters to Benvenuta, he speaks of his fear that love would interfere with those experiences of Hopkins-like inscape (feeling, for instance, what it would be like to be a dog) that have been, he says, "the bliss of my earthly existence":

> You see, and when one loved, this was the first thing that fell away—the dog would come along: an inexpressible pain would arise, one no longer had the prodigal freedom to merge with him.
> There was someone in the background who called you "mine" (that irresponsible word) and the dog would have to introduce himself first to that person and ask permission to let you enter him for one imperceptible, secret moment, exactly the way one asks permission to take a little girl out for a drink of hot chocolate. No dog would think of doing such a thing, and if he did, it would ultimately not be the same, indeed it would not be anything at all.[7]

Of course, these issues open out onto Kleinian, preoedipal ones, of the kind we discussed in relation to Jarrell. The strange-seeming desire that the world seen in a deeply, aesthetically fused way should actually *be* the beloved with whom one sees it is utterly comprehensible once one remembers that the world is initially given to the child in the fused relationship with the mother. And the counterside—that one would have to ask permission from the beloved to have such experiences without her, and that this would, in and of itself, invalidate the experience—this, too, is most comprehensible in terms of the fear of the all-powerful mother who might retaliate, and spoil even the child's inner experience, if the child asserts too much independence.

It is in the relationship with "Benvenuta" (Magda von Hattingberg) that we see most clearly the strength—and the self-defeatingness—of Rilke's attempts to confirm his own identity through an ideal love. Benvenuta's memoir—though effusive in some ways, reticent in others —has a ring of intimacy we do not get in the later *Letters to Merline*, in which an older, more jaded poet uses his philosophizing as a distancing device, almost from the very beginning. With Benvenuta he wanted marriage, or at least some form of permanent companionship. Their relationship began as a relationship by correspondence. She wrote him a fan letter about the *Stories of God*. It survives, and is a quite striking letter—whimsical, bold, and vulnerable in its presumption of immediate intimacy. One can see how it would have affected the poet who had just recently written "You who never arrived." Within days he was writing to her voluminously, retelling his entire life story and describing his present moods with "a trust as deep as it was difficult to comprehend."[8] She became his perfect witness—a witness, moreover, who transformed the quality of what was witnessed: "It is because my thoughts acquire purity in you, and no impure thought can exist since it cannot exist in you. The life of the mind for which I have been struggling all these unbearable years (do you understand, the mind that is so mightily mind that it can sweep all things into itself, excluding nothing), that infinite life of the mind comes true for me in you."[9] She was, he wrote—in a metaphor that wonderfully combines protective enclosure with the permission to expand and grow—"you greater circle around the infinite circle of my heart."[10] Perhaps, as Elizabeth Tallent has noted, this is an image of pregnancy—the beloved, gestating, perhaps eventually giving birth to, the true self.[11] But even more clearly, it recalls the holding environment that the good-enough mother, in Winnicott's terms—the mother Rilke perhaps never had—provides for her child, as he ventures out into the world.

In his letters to Lou Andreas-Salome, Rilke again stressed the almost ontological quality of his relationship with Benvenuta:

> If ever a deeply troubled person can become pure, I became so in those letters. The everyday and my relationship to it became to me in an indescribable fashion sacred and responsible,—and thence a strong confidence seized me, as if now at last the way out of the lazy being-dragged-along in the always fateful had been found. How much, from then on, I was in the process of changing I could also note from the fact that even what was past, when I happened to tell about it, surprised me by the manner in which it emerged . . . so that for the first time I seemed to become the owner of my life, not by interpretive appropriation, exploitation and understanding of what had been, but simply by that new truthfulness itself which flowed through even my memories.[12]

But what did Rilke mean by "pure" in these descriptions? Judging by all the rest of his writings, it is extremely unlikely that he meant "nonsexual." He seems, rather, to mean something almost existential—that through Benvenuta his relation to the "everyday," to moment-to-moment existence, becomes active, "responsible," no longer de-realized by his neuroses. It is, probably, a common enough feeling in introverted adolescents; what is astonishing is the force with which it seized on an already great poet, in his thirty-ninth year. Yet a tension is set up: he has to be his ideal (or at least, his clarified) self all the time, because only that self is worthy of being told to her; and he tells her everything.

I suspect Benvenuta was available to this kind of idealization because she was an idealizing personality herself. One senses in her—for all the independence and richness of feeling—a certain turn-of-the-century type: the flowers, the music, the good causes, the "simple and comfortable" —but always wealthy—friends; and a potential hardness toward anything that might break the decorum of that world. We get a first hint of this hardness when the question of psychoanalysis comes up: "He had been advised to submit to the treatment of the psycho-analyst, Professor Freud, but rejected the idea with great vehemence. I understood him only too well. I had met Professor Freud only twice, but his personality, his way of speaking, above all his theories had impressed me unfavourably; indeed I felt disgusted by them."[13] But—as Rilke's reply to Benvenuta makes firmly clear—she did not understand him "only too well": "These men were important and significant for me, their whole orientation and method certainly represents one of the most essential movements of medical science, indeed of that *human* science that does not yet properly exist."[14] It was only for himself—and only, as we shall see, after prolonged hesitation—that he found psychoanalysis an unsuitable remedy.

Perhaps it is just as well that Rilke did not go through a Freudian analysis. It would be more than half a century before object-relations theory would have terms for the "narcissistic deprivation"—and its attempted remedies—that his relationship with Benvenuta so clearly suggests. Alice Miller, Winnicott, and Jessica Benjamin all tell us that we will not be able to know our experiences as our own, as constituting a self—to "become the owner[s] of [our] lives"—if a parent has not, in very early childhood, acknowledged and accepted that experience, just as it is. But some parents are too fragile in their own sense of identity to do this; such a parent can recognize the child only insofar as the child assumes a role in the parent's own inner scenario. Rilke's mother, as is well known, did not want a boy; so she dressed him in girl's clothing and called him by female names. In 1914, according to

Benvenuta, she was still exhorting him to be a "zealous Catholic" and reminding him that "it was her exclusive privilege to wash his gloves."[15] A stark poem of 1915 describes the relationship very much as an object-relations theorist might see it (I quote Michael Hamburger's translation):

> Oh, misery, my mother tears me down.
> Stone upon stone I'd laid, towards a self
> and stood like a small house, with day's expanse around it,
> even alone.
> Now comes my mother, comes and tears me down.
>
> She tears me down by coming and by looking.
> That someone builds she does not see.
> Right through my wall of stones she walks for me.
> Oh, misery, my mother tears me down.[16]

His mother's unseeing gaze tore down his effort to build his experiences into a self; the gaze of the perfectly understanding woman would build it up again. Except, of course, that only a "pure" self could be shown to her.

But there may be a further level to an object-relations view of Rilke's difficulties with love. In his brilliant introduction to Stephen Mitchell's translations, Robert Hass suggests that Rilke's internal femininity—the fictitious identity imposed on him by his mother—may have itself become the object of love and excluded any real beloved:

> It would be wrong to conclude . . . that Rilke was simply narcissistic, if we mean by that a person who looks lovingly into the shallow pool of himself. He was, if anything, androgynous. . . . Androgyny is the pull inward, the erotic pull of the other we sense buried in the self. . . . Rilke—partly because of that girl his mother had located at the center of his psychic life—was always drawn, first of all and finally, to the mysterious fact of his own existence. His own being was otherness to him.[17]

My first impulse was to reject this hypothesis—as too fancy, on the one hand, and as too dismissive of Rilke's real struggles to love and to be loved, on the other. Yet Lou Andreas-Salome, who knew Rilke intimately, said something congruent in her psychoanalytic notes on him: "Rainer's bisexuality is sufficiently developed for the feminine element to impair his full enjoyment of normal sexual intercourse; such appears to be the case at present. On the other hand, neither can his masculinity attain full satisfaction, since its most complete expression lies in [literary] production and takes a rather contemptuous view of this [sexual] enjoyment."[18] Moreover, D. W. Winnicott describes an uncannily parallel case of a man who experienced himself as androgynous because his mother "saw a girl baby when she saw him as a baby" and "held him and dealt with him in all sorts of physical ways as if she failed to see him as a male." Such a man, Winnicott argues, is likely—exactly as Rilke was—to have a series of intense attachments to women, without full physical satisfaction, rather than to become homosexual:

> The man who initiates girls into sexual experience may well be one who is more identified with the girl than with himself. This gives him the capacity to go all out to wake up the girl's sex and to satisfy her. He pays for this by getting but little male satisfaction himself, and he pays also in terms of his need to seek always a new girl, this being the opposite of object-constancy. . . .
>
> It is interesting that the existence of this split-off female element actually prevents homosexual practice. In the case of my patient . . . putting homosexuality into practice would establish his maleness which (from the split-off female element self) he never wanted to know for certain.[19]

It is not clear exactly what went wrong between Rilke and Benvenuta. He was terrified of actually meeting her—terrified, in part, of his own capacity for coolness and withdrawal. Yet it was not a simple case of the reality deflating the expectation. A few weeks after they met, he was talking of "stay[ing] together all our lives"; she was the one holding back.[20] Though herself divorced, she was conventional enough to be bothered by his having a wife and child. Moreover, the dark, suffering side of his personality troubled her deeply. She had had two frightening encounters with his sudden psychosomatic illnesses; and an early letter about the "evil" and "sickness" he found in himself "almost finished everything."[21] Was Benvenuta incapable of going beyond a prettified ideal of love? Or did Rilke, as his friend the Princess Marie von Thurn und Taxis apparently believed, demand a perfect, even a subservient, mirroring and withdraw into ambivalence when he could not get it? A little of both, I would suspect. Their climactic quarrel seems to have come when Rilke forced her to listen to a reading of his essay on dolls.

As a child, Benvenuta had had an uncomplicated, confiding relation to her doll, and she found the peculiar bitterness of the essay "horrifying," to the point that she had to play a Bach fugue to clear the air.[22]

But the dolls essay is itself a very interesting text, from the object-relations point of view. In it, Rilke seems almost to anticipate Winnicott's concept of the transitional object, by which the child negotiates "the transition from a state of being merged with the mother to a state of being in relation to the mother as something outside and separate."[23] "It made no response whatever, so that we were put in the position of having to take over the part it should have played, of having to split our gradually enlarging personality into part and counterpart. . . . The things which were happening to us incomprehensibly we mixed in the doll, as in a test tube, and saw them there change color and boil up."[24] But Rilke persists in asking the question Winnicott says one must never ask: *"Did you conceive of this or was it presented to you from without?"*[25] Once he becomes self-conscious about the doll's lack of initiative, the doll is a "frightful obese forgetfulness," an "externally painted watery corpse."[26]

Perhaps Rilke is really describing the "decathect[ing]" of the transitional object, the "threat of its becoming meaningless," which, Winnicott says, often reflects a disturbance in the relation to the mother.[27] It is noteworthy that the doll is unique among childhood possessions in seeming thus inert and soulless. The "[g]reat, courageous soul of the rocking-horse," by contrast, is praised for its power to carry the child off over "famous battlefields"; there is no doubt that its soul is "proud, credible, almost visible." Under its heels the boy, become "St. George," can even break "the beast of [the doll's] stupidity."[28]

Is it too simple-minded to think that the real difference here is that the rocking horse belongs to Rilke's "natural," little-boy identity; whereas the doll reflects his mother's failures of recognition, by way of the little-girl identity she forced on him? Certainly, some of Rilke's rhetoric, extravagant in relation to the doll, has an all-too-simple logic in relation to the mother: "Are we not strange creatures to . . . be induced to place our earliest affections where they remain hopeless? So that everywhere there was imparted to that spontaneous tenderness the bitterness of knowing that it was in vain? Who knows if such memories have not caused many a man afterwards, out there in life, to suspect that he is not lovable? If the influence of their doll does not continue to work disastrously in this or that person, so that they pursue vague satisfactions, simply in opposition to the state of unsatisfied desire by which it ruined their lives?"[29]

One wonders whether Benvenuta understood all too much about Rilke from hearing this essay: his unadmitted suspicion of women, his despair when his feelings were not mirrored perfectly, the likelihood that he would move on from one "vague satisfaction" to another. On the surface, she merely felt (as with Professor Freud?) that she could not "bear to hear the simplest, most innocent feelings and pleasures destroyed and picked to pieces."[30] But Rilke, in the aftermath of their relationship, was certainly ready to take the entire blame on himself; he felt his "difficult[y]" would defeat "the most warranted, most spontaneous heart."[31]

THE *Duino Elegies* represent Rilke's fullest articulation both of his philosophical pessimism about love and, in a subtler way, of the psychic pressures undergirding that pessimism. They can even be seen as a kind of auto-analysis, replacing the analysis with Freud's disciple von Gebsattel that Rilke famously refused to undertake, fearing it would take away his "angels" along with his devils. In fact, there seems to be a very close relation between the refusal of the analysis and the genesis of the *Elegies*. It was during his stay at Duino, on January 14, 1912, that Rilke, tormented by his romantic failures as well as psychosomatic symptoms, a massive writer's block, and a vaguer feeling of being "shut . . . off" from the world, as if by a "wall," actually broached the question of analysis.[32] But when von Gebsattel pressed him for a quick decision, he abruptly reversed himself; on January 24, he wrote Lou Andreas-Salome (who had actually advised him against analysis) the famous letter about the angels and the devils.[33]

The chronology of these letters is important because—as Donald Prater was apparently the first to note—they overlap with another event that has become far more famous: the voice out of the storm that gave him the first lines of the first Duino elegy, which he then completed within a day. Stephen Mitchell places this event between January 12 and 16; but Prater believes it occurred on January 20, the day Rilke received von Gebsattel's reply and had to make up his mind.[34] (It can hardly have been before January 14, unless Rilke is guarding his secret with the most superstitious kind of duplicity, since he says to von Gebsattel, "I long for work . . . but we do not meet.")[35] We know he sent the First Elegy to Princess Marie on January 21 and that he had decided against analysis by January 24. Is it not likely that the voice out of the sky *caused* his change of heart? Or, indeed, that the hallucination was itself a product of Rilke's desire not to be analyzed; to work out the problems of love, the unconscious, neurotic suffering and its relief, within his own stubbornly aesthetic or existential terms? Having broken his writer's block on his own—or with such an indication of supernatural help— he could feel that, however unhappy, he was once again in control of his life, in all its essential dimensions.

The *Elegies* define the problem of love, once again, as a problem of innerness. What they see, with peculiar clarity, is that although, or be- cause, love is an intense encounter with the outside, the feelings it stirs up—the longing, the terror of losing oneself, the strangeness—go far beyond the individual beloved or even the conscious self, back into the prehistory of the psyche. Yet, in the moment, we can never draw those distinctions clearly:

> we never know
> the actual, vital contour of our own
> emotions—just what forms them from outside.

And if we want to feel secure in love, we cannot help dreading that other dimension a little, both in ourselves and in the other person:

> Where can you find a place
> to keep her, with all the huge strange thoughts inside you
> going and coming and often staying all night.

But what, more precisely, lies behind the romantic rhetoric of "huge strange thoughts" *(grossen fremden Gedanken)*? Surely they are in part the independent experiences of empathy or receptivity—the experience with the dog, in the letter to Benvenuta—that Rilke feared the beloved would be jealous of. (That is why they are figured as brief sexual en- counters—"often staying all night.") But I suspect that they are also the alienated, confused feelings that simply being in love brought with it for Rilke—the fear of merging, the estrangement from the normal self, the activation, as in the dolls essay, of conflicted identity feelings from earliest childhood. These, too, would be incommunicable to the beloved without the fear of inflicting psychic damage.

In the Fourth Elegy, Rilke will put the basic insight more harshly, though very hauntingly:

> Aren't lovers
> always arriving at each other's boundaries?—
> although they promised vastness, hunting, home.

When we fall in love we expect infinite adventure, expansion, newness, and at the same time to be infinitely accepted and familiar—at "home." Impossible, and contradictory, expectations—and when they come up against the quirks and limits of any particular beloved, we are likely to feel as if we had bumped into a solid oak door when we thought we were walking into a grassy field. It is in this mood, I think, that Rilke comes to the notorious remarks about the unrequited lovers, who "could love so much more purely than those who were gratified." The unrequited lover, presumably, does not have to be disappointed in those "boundaries"; her love—because, like the mystic's, it no longer wants anything—can become what the mystic's is, a pure assent to the other person's existence.

But Lou Andreas-Salome was surely right to wonder why the unrequited lover was always a "she," and why Rilke seemed so obsessed with, almost personally connected to, her. Andreas-Salome suggests that, in identifying with these women, Rilke is, in effect, seduced by his own feminine side. By splitting himself, he both experiences the infinite, the merged love that part of him desires, and continues to run away from it. Thus, he avoids the fear of engulfment that might follow from seeking such love outwardly: "The 'desire for unrequited love' found as early as in Malte Brigge, acts contrary to his glorification of woman's capacity for love, like a temptation 'to be loved like that.' But the woman in Rainer feels corrupted by it, identifies with it, and so lives its life fully. By this circuitous route the man in him is seduced by the woman in him—not by the external woman—whence the conflicts arise."[36]

It is easy to take the *Elegies*—as Hass very nearly does—as an escape from, or a devaluation of, physical love. That this is an oversimple reading, the Second Elegy, I think, makes clear:

> You, though, who in the other's passion
> grow until, overwhelmed, he begs you:
> "No *more* . . . "; you who beneath his hands
> swell with abundance, like autumn grapes;

> you who may disappear because the other has wholly
> emerged: I am asking *you* about us. I know,
> you touch so blissfully because the caress preserves,
> because the place you so tenderly cover
> does not vanish; because underneath it
> you feel pure duration. So you promise eternity, almost,
> from the embrace.

Rilke knew, very vividly, how the caress, the being "tenderly covered," makes the body, and the self in the body, exist as it has never existed before. It creates *Dauern*, "duration," the Bergsonian moment that is like "eternity" because it is experienced without division, without clock-measurement. The loved self becomes a complete self, an inexhaustible "abundance, like autumn grapes"—so complete, indeed, that it can even afford to take pleasure in its own disappearance "because the other has wholly / emerged" into the same utter, self-sufficient goodness.

It hardly needs to be said, perhaps, that these descriptions refer to infantile states, prior to conscious memory. Rilke's genius, perhaps, was to recognize that it is the reliving of these states that makes sexual love the culminating experience it is. But the difficulties of infancy, too, are bound to make themselves felt. Sooner or later, as Klein observes, the timing will not be perfect; the breast will be offered too soon, or too late.[37] Selves will cease to be wholly satisfied and, therefore, inter-changeable; and the resulting rage or guilt will be in proportion to the enormity of the expectation. Rilke's imagery returns to precisely such issues when, toward the end of the Second Elegy, he again argues for the riskiness, the imperfection, of love:

> When you lift yourselves up
> to each other's mouth and your lips join, drink against drink:
> oh how strangely each drinker seeps away from his action.

How does a drink drink from a drink? How can one be active and passive at once? How can one take the "part" of the "drinker" (as Spender and Leishman render "action") without becoming the separate self who may be punished for his wilfulness by losing the power to taste—the self that is, for Rilke, unloving, adult, and male?

The Third Elegy, I think, is the core of Rilke's auto-analytic work. It comes from late 1913, the year Lou took Rilke to a psychoanalytic congress, introduced him to Freud, and actually conducted a brief dream-analysis with him, during their trip to the Riesengebirge.[38] Perhaps it was the influence of Lou, and of Freud, that made Rilke for once focus on the masculine side of his own impulses. Lou represents Rilke as discussing, with approval, Freud's remark that "our ancestors celebrated the instinct but we legitimize it by means of the object." And the opening lines of the Third Elegy do attempt to conjure up a "profound, almost religious conception of the instinct itself,"[39] the "lord of desire":

Oh the Neptune inside our blood, with his appalling trident.
Oh the dark wind from his breast out of that spiraled conch.
Listen to the night as it makes itself hollow.

Yet the "religious" emotion here seems less reverence than outright terror. And Lou intimates, in her psychoanalytic notes, that Rilke had an early experience of his own sexuality as something almost outside himself, and threatening: "a feeling since his early erections as of a living thing, part of himself, but also as a power outside him: something too great, too gigantic, only with an effort maintained as a part of him and experienced painfully. . . . Anxieties associated with old prohibitions of masturbation by his father seem to play a part."[40] This, too, then, is part of what makes "the night . . . hollow": what fills erotic experience with alienated and superhuman feeling-states, projected beyond the self.

Rilke's first response, ironically, is to flee back to precisely that romanticization of the "object," rather than of the impulse, which he and Lou had agreed was "embarrassing." The lover is "shock[ed]," filled with a sense of "ancient terrors," "dark companions," as he begins to fall in love; and he turns to the beloved to protect him from himself, as well as to repair (as in the Second Elegy) the precious and threatened possibility of mutual recognition. Wistfully, he asks if the lover's "secret insight" into the beloved's "pure features" "[d]oesn't . . . come from the pure constellations?"

The implied answer, however, is no. And the rest of the elegy is really a meditation on the conflicting roles, in the making of the male psyche, of the "guilty river-god of the blood," whom Freud, and Lou, had forced Rilke to acknowledge, and the preoedipal mother, the source of the possibility of recognition and "secret insight," about whom Rilke, in his intuitive way, really knew more than Freud himself. For the desire for "home," the desire to be completely understood in love—and the stranger desire that, as in "You who never arrived," love will make the world itself understandable and expressive—have their own prehistory in the psyche. The mother of the Third Elegy is not so much Freud's oedipal mother as (again, years ahead of her time) Winnicott's "good-enough mother," whose mediation creates the very possibility of a "self" in a mutually constructive relation to a "world," a "human space."

> Ah, where are the years when you shielded him just by placing
> your slender form between him and the surging abyss?
> How much you hid from him then. The room that filled with suspicion
> at night: you made it harmless; and out of the refuge of your heart
> you mixed a more human space in with his night-space.

Rilke's evocation of this stage is, surely, one of the most poignantly nostalgic in literature. Yet, we paid a price for its security. "Mother, *you* made him small," Rilke says, as if the mother were to blame both for the child's size and for the enormous importance her power to comfort gives her. And if there is one element the elegy does not explore with full honesty, it is the anger, and the shame at dependence, that makes the boy later fear the very thing he wishes to recover, a symbiosis with a woman. (What the elegy represses even more deeply is the fact that Rilke's particular mother ceased to comfort, ceased to mirror, as soon as her son manifested a will of his own.)

But, the elegy would like to argue, this rift was inevitable in any case. What interferes is, in Freudian terms, infantile sexuality—the contrast, as the boy falls asleep, between the "gentle world" the mother has created and "the floods of origin inside him." These "floods" are clearly sexual ("that hidden guilty river-god of the blood")—both the flood from which the child has so recently taken his origin and the flood of his desire to originate. Guilty desire is, in this myth, the beginning of innerness. The world of dreams, a world that cannot be spoken of, separates off and becomes itself an object of desire.

> How he submitted—. Loved.
> Loved his interior world, his interior wilderness,
> that primal forest inside him, where among decayed treetrunks
> his heart stood, light-green. Loved. Left it, went through
> his own roots and out, into the powerful source
> where his little birth had already been outlived.

Strangely, the inner world seems already to have been there, waiting to be discovered, like a rain forest of dead trees on which the new growth rises. Here Rilke begins to sound more like Jung than like Freud, describing a collective unconscious, waiting in everyone, that the newly created individual unconscious reawakens. But we must remember that 1913 was the year Freud published *Totem and Taboo,* the book in which he most resembles Jung; in which he argued that the Oedipus complex was so compelling because a primal father had actually been murdered by his sons, at the beginning of human consciousness.[41] That is why the child, in Rilke, discovers the "ravines / where Horror lay, still glutted with his fathers." That explains—to Rilke's satisfaction, at least—why "Terror" is bound up with male sexuality, from the beginning.

It is, then, an immensely populated psyche that we bring to adult love. How can that not cause a great deal of trouble? We will confuse the new beloved with all of its characters:

> Dear girl,
> this: that we loved, inside us, not One who would someday appear, but
> seething multitudes; not just a single child,
> but also the fathers lying in our depths
> like fallen mountains; also the dried-up riverbeds
> of ancient mothers.

Furthermore, these characters, in the unconscious, remain very much active agents, with a will of their own. Won't the never-forgotten mother be jealous of the girl who supplants her? Isn't male desire bound to seem brutal, even to the man himself? After all, it descends from the primal father and his murderous sons. And what, too, of the child-self, with its never quite fulfilled longing?

> What passions
> welled up inside him from departed beings. What
> women hated you there. How many dark
> sinister men you aroused in his young veins. Dead
> children reached out to touch you.

Love for a particular beloved will always be, in part, an attempt to "escape" from these "dark companions"—a wish that, by beginning anew, the lover may finally "begin himself."

Rilke attempts, in the Third Elegy, to affirm the possibility of this victory by stressing the particularity of the beloved, her ability to inhabit the outside world so vividly that it becomes as real as the inner world:

> Oh gently, gently,
> let him see you performing, with love, some confident daily task,—
> lead him close to the garden, give him what outweighs
> the heaviest night.

Of course, this way of affirming the beloved's individuality—so entirely within the maternal, protective role—has offended feminists more than Rilke's most pessimistic utterances. (It is true, though, that Rilke assigns a rather similar healing function to artists in general.) Rilke's wish, moreover, seems defeated in advance by its need to freeze love at the idyllic moments. What of the moments that are not the "garden"— that are the push-and-pull of adjusting personalities and discovering disharmonies? that are the discovery, for instance, that one's beloved cannot endure to hear dolls spoken of unlovingly? Can these moments, too, add to the weight, the confidence-inspiring solidity, of the real? And can the beloved's function ever cease to be partly maternal, in a disciplinary sense: to "restrain him" from his still unresolved darkness?

Still, Rilke's wish might almost have given birth to Benvenuta, whose daylight world, her "radiant being,"[42] correspond so perfectly to *der Nachte/Ubergewicht*, "night's counterweight" in the most literal rendering. The relationship, begun only weeks after the Third Elegy was finished, speaks equally to its concluding moment of hope and to its abiding blind spots.

It is easy to see only self-flattery in Benvenuta's conviction that she was the crucial loss, the end of possibility, in Rilke's life. But surely she was at least a turning point. Look at the poems Rilke wrote after their breakup, when he returned to Paris "so dull and benumbed that I cannot do much more than sleep."[43]. There is "Lament," in which "the whole tree of my jubilation / is breaking." There is "'We Must Die Because We Have Known Them,'" whose title, borrowed from an ancient Egyptian text, speaks to the depth of the fear both of women and of the emotions they call forth in the man—"pathless" feelings that "play inside him as though in quivering cages."

Finally, "Turning-Point" itself, from the same month, presents, for the only time ever, a "confessionally" literal portrait of Rilke's uprootedness and loneliness, in its characteristic setting—"the hotel's distracted unnoticing bedroom," "the avoided mirror." Here, ghostly female voices "debate . . . his heart," and "pas[s] their judgment: / that it did not have love."

Yet the turning point Rilke calls for, even here, is ambiguous. It appears at first to be a turning away from the aesthetic, toward the love of actual people. But at the last minute, Rilke slides away from this demand, suggesting that the object of love is really still "your inner woman," the imaginary composite beloved, as in "You who never arrived," indwelling in the world, "attained from a thousand / natures."

A much greater world weariness and fear haunts Rilke's next strong attachment, which was to Lulu Albert-Lazard. His first poem to her begins forebodingly, "Again and again, though we know the landscape of love."[44] And the stepped-up Don Juanism of the war years in Munich can be read as despair, as well as fame and susceptibility.[45] The Fourth Elegy seems to me the record of that profound giving up on himself (or, perhaps, resolution in a different direction). Here he seems to recognize how strong the negative component of his feeling is, how labile and transferable the enthusiasm:

> But we, while we are intent upon one object,
> already feel the pull of another. Conflict
> is second nature to us.

(Spender and Leishman render this: "Hostility's our first response.") Rilke recognizes, too, that his yearning for "cosmic space" has not melded, but interfered with his power to love an individual. And finally he seems to throw over the entire enterprise, going back, ironically, to the hated doll:

> I won't endure these half-filled human masks;
> better, the puppet. It at least is full.

It was seven years before Rilke returned to, and completed, the elegies (a gap it is tempting, but probably too facile, to explain by the failure of his auto-analytic work to resolve his erotic difficulties). By this point, Rilke had reached the mystic's solution to the problem of love, which Princess Marie von Thurn und Taxis had been recommending to him as early as 1914. The object of love becomes existence itself, and joy arrives simply, in the setting aside of the ego with its hopes and fears. Rilke's version of this solution is far more Buddhist than Christian: there is no asceticism and no assurance of an afterlife; transcendence itself is rejected, in a turning toward the world of things—"being here" as the true realm of enlightenment. When love is mentioned, it is accepted without bitterness or anguish, but always directed toward a goal beyond itself—as in the climactic passage of the Ninth Elegy:

> Isn't the secret intent
> of this taciturn earth, when it forces lovers together,
> that inside their boundless emotion all things may shudder with joy?

And among the objects we are "here" to name, Rilke lists tenderly, but with an implied acceptance of transience,

> Threshold: what it means for two lovers
> to be wearing down, imperceptibly, the ancient threshold of their door—
> they too, after the many who came before them
> and before those to come . . . , lightly.

But perhaps what really happens to Rilke's love difficulties, in his mysticism, is an astonishing internalization (but one that, if Hass and Lou Andreas-Salome are right, was there in potential all along). By the second "Sonnet to Orpheus," the "inner woman" has become completely and unambiguously inner. Like a female Endymion, she sleeps eternally in his unconscious, having "no desire / ever to wake." And his love affair with her *is* his own passivity and receptivity, his oneness with the universe, as realized in his art.

> [H]er sleep was everything:
> the awesome trees, the distances I had felt
> so deeply that I could touch them, meadows in spring;
> all wonders that had ever seized my heart.
>
> She slept the world.

So, in the end, Rilke becomes "world in himself," in the words of the early letter, only when he ceases to locate the gestating, "sleep[ing]" woman anywhere except in the "bed" she has "made herself . . . inside my ear." The last of the "Sonnets" puts the paradoxes of this situation even more trenchantly. How can one not remember the language of the Second Elegy, "drink against drink"—the protest against separateness itself, the contradictory wishes to take both the active and the passive role—when one comes to this remarkable prescription?

> If drinking is bitter, change yourself to wine.

Lawrence and the "Oedipal Riddle"

D. H. LAWRENCE's critical reception, as a writer dealing with gender, has been astonishingly skewed, in two contradictory directions. From the 1930s through the 1950s he was read as a prophet, calling for the affirmation not only of the value of sex but of a blood-knowledge of a better way of living than any industrial-rationalist civilization had to offer. *The Priest of Love,* Harry T. Moore titled an influential biography. Then, with—actually a little before—the advent of feminism, certain obvious facts were pointed out: that Lawrence's heroes were almost always in a white-hot rage against women, in particular and in general; that he was obsessed, for a while, with all-male, quasi-fascist authoritarian movements; that his belief in male domination reached the point, in *The Plumed Serpent,* of suggesting that women should not have orgasms—or, at least, only vaginal orgasms. When evidence also accumulated that Lawrence was bisexual, in life as well as in his writings, his homophobic vision of decadent men as "sewer rats," and his restless need to perfect heterosexual love, could be reimagined as defense mechanisms. Lawrence passed from being a prophet to being a case history; while a third possibility—that he was first and foremost an artist, whose work embodied more about the origins of sexual conflict, as well as sexual happiness, than his opinionated self ever knew—was scarcely even considered. Even though it was Lawrence himself who said, of his beloved American writers, "Never trust the teller, trust the tale."

Our first key to understanding Lawrence in this third way comes from one of his least orthodox critics. Norman Mailer, replying, in *The Prisoner of Sex,* to Kate Millett's feminist attack, suggests that the most salient fact about Lawrence is his female identification, and that his obsession with power and maleness must be understood in terms of the all-encompassing early link to his mother.[1] Lawrence, Mailer writes, "reminds us of the beauty of desiring to be a man, for he was not much of a man himself, a son despised by his father, beloved of his mother."[2]

He was, Mailer expands, "a man who had the soul of a beautiful, im-
perious, and passionate woman, yet he was locked into the body of a
middling male physique. . . . What a nightmare to balance that soul! to
take the man in himself, locked from youth into every need for profound female companionship, a man almost wholly oriented toward the
company of women, and attempt to go out into the world of men, indeed even dominate the world of men, so that he might find balance."[3]
Allowing for Mailer's own romanticization of masculinity, this seems
to me almost entirely right. (A later study, Carol Siegel's *Lawrence
among the Women,* confirms that Lawrence's female identification, and
the difficulties it gave him with men, were keenly visible to the women
around him.)[4] Lawrence's passage from mother-identified son to angry
masculinist is one of the clearest and most fascinating instances in literary
biography of what Jessica Benjamin has called "the Oedipal riddle"—
fascinating precisely because that "riddle" was suffered through, with
tortured ambivalence, over many years, not solved quickly and brutally,
as it is in so many male lives.

No book has ever recorded the identificatory, as well as the oedipal,
love of mother and son more passionately than *Sons and Lovers.* Mrs.
Morel, Lawrence suggests, can never quite separate from Paul, because
of her guilt at not having wanted him to begin with. "She no longer
loved her husband; she had not wanted this child to come, and there it
lay in her arms and pulled at her heart. She felt as if the navel string that
had connected its frail little body with hers had not been broken."[5] She
believes, and Lawrence apparently wants us to believe, that Paul has
been endowed with a sorrowful temperament, and a vocation to understand sorrow, from a prenatal understanding of her state of mind: "Did
it know all about her? When it lay under her heart, had it been listening
then? Was there a reproach in the look?" (41). It is under the spell of this
conviction that she gives him his name, holding him up to the setting
sun and saying, "I will call him 'Paul.'" It is a strangely ambivalent
gesture. Mrs. Morel fears that it still expresses her hostility, "her impulse
to give him back again whence he came" (41). But it is also clearly the
Transfiguration, the Election scene of a future great man; "Paul" is the
Apostle, the "only . . . man" whom Mrs. Morel's father "drew near in
sympathy . . . to" (15). To us as readers, who know D. H. Lawrence the
prophet of solarity, the ceaseless seeker after the primal energy that
will enable him to go on living, the scene has a triple poignancy.

As Paul grows older, his mother's fantasy of unbreakable connection is fulfilled in the kind of symbiotic attunement, the inability to conceive his own selfhood separately, that we are familiar with from Alice Miller: "As a rule, he seemed old for his years. He was so conscious of what other people felt, particularly his mother. When she fretted, he understood, and could have no peace. His soul seemed always attentive to her" (61). His oedipal championing of her seems an overlay on this earlier understanding: "When she was quiet, so, she looked brave and rich with life, but as if she had been done out of her rights. It hurt the boy keenly, this feeling about her, that she had never had her life's fulfilment: and his own incapability to make up to her hurt him with a sense of impotence, yet made him patiently dogged inside. It was his childish aim" (69). His sense of his own being remains inextricably bound up with hers. He falls ill, and nearly dies, when she withdraws her interest after his brother William's death; when her love returns, and he "realize[s] her" (141), he is able to recover.

Because of Paul's hatred of his father, he does not experience the need to disidentify with the feminine at the age Benjamin tells us is culturally normal. His first school prize is for an essay on "famous women"; and "he would almost rather have forfeited the prize than have to tell his father"—not because he expects, or gets, any kind of macho disapproval, but because the father "was shut out from all family affairs" (66). Well into adolescence, Paul's investment in his mother's appearance, her clothes, remains erotically charged; yet its aesthetic keenness seems, at times, as much another woman's as an admiring man's.

> Suddenly she appeared in the inner doorway, rather shyly. She had got a new cotton blouse on. Paul jumped up and went forward.
> "Oh my stars!" he exclaimed, "what a bobby-dazzler!"
> She sniffed in a little, haughty way, and put her head up.
> "It's not a bobby-dazzler at all!" she replied. "It's very quiet." . . .
> He went and surveyed her from the back.
> "Well!" he said, "if I was walking down the street behind you, I should say: 'Doesn't *that* little person fancy herself.'" (123)

Most of all, Mrs. Morel remains the repository, the sounding board, for Paul's inner life as a burgeoning artist. He seems to feel absolutely no need for distance, no fear of intrusion. "He directed his mother, what she must see, and what not. And she was quite content" (125). "'I can do my best things when you sit there in your rocking-chair, mother'" (157). He even sketches the colliery, while she sits and watches, and it becomes an object of aesthetic perception, shared and disputed between them, not an activity in which he, as his father's son, might participate (124). Far into the book, when Paul is already locked in conflict with his mother over Miriam, Lawrence still observes: "All his work was hers" (182).

And yet, on some level, Paul is aware of something he needs from his father. Ease in handling the physical world is the one quality Paul values that his mother does not possess. (Stiles are an index of this, throughout the book. Mrs. Morel, a "duffer of a little woman," climbs them "cautiously" (125); Miriam is paralyzed with terror; Clara leaps down from them, "laughing" [299].) Lawrence wants us to connect this physical inhibition to Mrs. Morel's middle-class, Dissenting puritanism. She will not dance; and though she once admired her husband's dancing, she hates the fact that he has been a dancing teacher almost as much as she hates his drinking. But this "sensuous flame of life" (16) remains the one area in which Walter Morel can come into his own, and claim his children's love, as in the famous fuse-making scene, in which the children "unit[e] with him in the work, in the actual doing of something, when he was his real self again," and he calls Paul "my beauty," being "peculiarly lavish of endearments to his second son." (67)

Paul will have to incorporate this physically easy side of his father to come into his sexual birthright: as many critics have noted, he lapses into his father's dialect both in his flirtation with Beatrice Wyld and in his first passionate encounter with Clara. To this degree, at least, his "Oedipal riddle" is no different from the ordinary young man's.

But Paul also learns a darker lesson from his father, a lesson about how to deal with guilt toward women—that guilt which, as Klein and Dinnerstein inform us, has a peculiarly implacable intrapsychic authority, from the residues of the preoedipal phase.[6] The father's way of dealing with such guilt is to deny it; indeed, to go on the attack again, as if punishing the woman who had reproached him would refute the reproach. In Walter Morel, Lawrence gets the unbounded quality of male guilt toward women: how it affects the very integrity of the self; how humiliating it is to admit to, for that very reason, as if it reduced one to childhood impotence; how the sense of excessive punishment, even though largely self-imposed, builds the spiral toward violence again. When Walter injures his wife by, in a drunken fit, flinging a drawer at her, he feels the "violent pains in the head" himself (45). But even this cannot bring him to apologize; he "trie[s] to wriggle out of it," persuading himself that "It was her own fault." "Nothing, however, could prevent his inner consciousness inflicting on him the punishment which ate into his spirit like rust, and which he could only alleviate by drinking" (44).

If Paul is exempt from such rudimentary forms of denial, this may not be in all ways a good thing. Because his feeling of symbiosis makes the guilt even more unendurable, he may have to go to the more drastic extreme of inwardly annihilating the object. We get our first inkling of this—and of rage as a dimension of Paul's character—in the strange episode of the doll Arabella, of which Paul's sister Annie is "fearfully proud, though not so fond." One day, Paul accidentally damages the doll. His guilt, like his father's, is invasive: "'You couldn't tell it was there, mother; you couldn't tell it was there,' he repeated over and over. So long as Annie wept for the doll he sat helpless with misery" (61). But Paul's solution is disturbing, to Annie and to the reader: "'Let's make a sacrifice of Arabella,' he said. 'Let's burn her.'" And he proceeds to do exactly that, on an "altar of bricks," with "wicked satisfaction." At the end, he even smashes all the still recognizable parts of the doll with stones. "Which disturbed Annie inwardly," the narrator tells us; "He seemed to hate the doll so intensely, because he had broken it" (61).

The theme of unbreakable attachment leading, through guilt, to annihilating rage runs through all the important relationships with women in the second generation. Before it begins to work itself out in Paul's life, we see a smaller but emblematic instance in William's tortured relationship with his fiancée, Gypsy. This tends to be one of the most underread episodes in the book, critics having taken at face value Lawrence's Freudian summary: "William gives his sex to a fribble, and his mother holds his soul. But the split kills him."[7] Not that "a fribble" is an altogether unfair description of Gypsy; but William's mixed feelings of bondage and resentment establish one of the crucial patterns for the entire book.

William's sense that the bond is unbreakable is attributed, implicitly, to turn-of-the-century ethics: a decent young man must marry a girl he has slept with, if she is of decent social background herself. "I can't give her up, now, it's gone too far," he simply repeats, to all of his mother's objections (132). But this ethic itself derives much of its intrapsychic force from the sense of the vulnerability, and the unanswerable claims, of mothers—as Paul will reflect later in the book: "A good many of the nicest men he knew were like himself, bound in by their own virginity, which they could not break out of. . . . Being the sons of mothers whose husbands had blundered rather brutally through their feminine sanctities, they were themselves too diffident and shy. They could easier deny themselves than incur any reproach from a woman. For a woman was like their mother, and they were full of the sense of their mother" (272). Moreover, in William's affair, the theme of rescue sounds insistently, as it will in Paul's relationships. Gypsy's self-centeredness is put down to her being "an orphan" (122), and having "had no love" (119). Because he finds her shivering on the station platform one morning, William buys her warm underclothes. (132).

The other side of the coin, however, is the rage with which William attacks Gypsy for her deficiencies, over and over, until even his mother says, "I am ashamed of you" (133). Mrs. Morel is always a third party to these outbursts, so it is tempting to feel that Gypsy is being offered up as a sacrifice to her supremacy, as when, earlier, William burns his love letters in his mother's presence. But Gypsy is an audience of these tirades, as well as their object. It is as if, at some level, William has folded her and his mother into one omnipotent presence, who can change Gypsy into his ideal, if only he protests loudly enough—as a baby can bring its mother back by crying. Mrs. Morel herself seems to sense the infantile quality of William's dissatisfaction: "Why don't you be more manly?" (133).

And so the "split" that "kills" William may be not only between "sex" and "soul," but between the need to be symbiotic with, and the need to repudiate, one and the same object. Something of the kind is suggested by the strange phrase, from a business letter, that William keeps repeating on his deathbed: "'Owing to a leakage in the hold of the vessel, the sugar had set, and become converted into rock. It needed hacking—'" (136). To allegorize bluntly: through an intrapsychic "leakage," the sweetness of the earliest bond freezes like "rock" to its later, possibly unworthy, objects. Distance can only be attained by the "hacking" William "need[s]" but ultimately cannot bring himself to perform. The grim lesson of William's fate stands always in the background as Paul begins to engage his own turbulent inner life with women of his own generation.

Paul initially retains his female identification as he ventures out into the world. At the factory, "Paul liked the girls best. The men seemed common and rather dull. He liked them all, but they were uninteresting" (111). Even when, later, he will take the masculinist position that "work *can* be nearly everything to a man. . . . But a woman only works with a part of herself," he effectively groups himself on the feminine side: the first sentence ends, "though it isn't to me" (402).

Moreover, all of the women in Paul's life come to be, in one way or another, fulfillments of his "childish aim" of protection or rescue. He teaches Miriam French; he gets Clara her job back. With the beleaguered working girls at Thomas Jordan's, his attitude is not only profoundly protective; like his attitude toward his mother, it is erotic enough to be flattering without ever being purposeful or predatory. We see this in the scene in which, sensing that "she wanted to" be admired for it, he "carefully" unpins the hunchback Fanny's hair, so "the rush of . . . uniform dark brown slid over the humped back," all the while exclaiming, "What a lovely lot!" (113) (He does *not* say, "You look just like anybody else," as one flat-footed co-worker does at this juncture.)

But, as Paul moves out into the world, he also begins to understand psychodynamics and ethics in a more hostile, masculinist way—displacing onto safer objects a fear of engulfment, of loss of male autonomy, whose earliest object has to be the mother herself. As soon as Paul moves away from his mother onto the transferential stage of the Leivers household, he understands, only too clearly, the manipulative aspect of female long-suffering, of the claim to judge issues by a higher, more "religious" criterion. Where he would never dream of suggesting that his mother caused his father's violence, he now sees Mrs. Leivers's masochism as inviting her sons' sadism, thus making it less reprehensible. He sees the sadism, indeed, as a kind of ontological self-defense: "The over gentleness and apologetic tone of the mother brought out all the brutality of manners in the sons. . . . It puzzled Paul. He wondered vaguely why all this intense feeling went running because of a few burnt potatoes. The mother exalted everything, even a bit of housework, to the plane of a religious trust. The sons resented this; they felt themselves cut away underneath, and they answered with brutality, and also with a sneering superciliousness" (146). Paul, of course, is careful always to emphasize how "different" this "atmosphere" seems from his own mother's "logical" ways (146–47). But Walter Morel could surely offer the same excuse—he has been "cut away underneath," often enough, by Gertrude's middle-class proprieties.

The relationship with Miriam Leivers is—to reapply one of Paul's own metaphors—the threshing floor on which his tremendously conflicted feelings about masculinity and femininity are to be sorted out. Their relationship is, in certain crucial ways, an extension of the symbiotic relationship with his mother. Paul and Miriam, too, meet particularly in the feelings that are the matrix of his art: "Anthropomorphic as she was, she stimulated him into appreciating things thus, and then they lived for her. . . . It was in . . . this meeting in their common feeling for something in nature, that their love started" (148). Lawrence applies maternal metaphors to this communion, in which Paul is at once the impregnating father and, in his imaginative self, the gestating child: "All his passion, all his wild blood, went into this intercourse with her, when he talked and conceived his work. She brought forth to him his imaginations. She did not understand, any more than a woman understands when she conceives a child in her womb" (199). As he paints best in his mother's presence, so he needs Miriam, even if he "trample[s] . . . upon her soul," to become sure of himself in the realm of opinions. "She alone was his threshing floor. She alone helped him towards realisation. Almost impassive, she submitted to his argument and expounding. And somehow, because of her, he gradually realized where he was wrong" (223).

And yet Paul—who has never shown the least ambivalence about depending on his mother in this way—becomes hypersensitive to whatever seems to him possessive or devouring in Miriam's character. As Marguerite Beede Howe remarks in *The Art of Self in D. H. Lawrence* —so far, the best psychological account of *Sons and Lovers* I have come across: "The worst traits of the oedipal mother are displaced from Mrs. Morel onto Miriam. . . . The anxiety a domineering mother causes in her son is considerable, yet none is ever mentioned in Paul; instead it is Miriam who makes him feel anxious and trapped, Miriam whom he inexplicably hates. His horror of the girl's 'possessiveness' and 'willfulness' . . . are absent from his feelings about his mother."[8]

Whether Miriam is embracing her little brother, or caressing a flower, Paul feels she "want[s] to pull the heart out of [things]" (214).

When they are discussing Michelangelo, "he felt that she wanted the soul out of his body, and not him. All his strength and energy she drew into herself through some channel which united them" (191). And her influence, he feels, diminishes his own sense of ontological substance, at the same time as it makes him more permeable to the world. In the same Michelangelo conversation, he feels he enters a different area of his imaginative life, that fascinates but terrifies him, "as drug taking might." In a passage Edward Garnett excised from the manuscript, now available in the Cambridge edition, Paul goes on to describe this "ghostish, disembodied" state of mind: "'Even now, I look at my hands, and wonder what they are doing there. That water there ripples right through me. I'm sure I am that rippling. It runs right through me, and I through it. There are no barriers between us.'"⁹ In reaction against Miriam, and perhaps against this area of his imaginative self, Paul develops, for the first time, a "jolly," emotionally unexpressive, conventionally masculine way of being, which Miriam always considers his "lesser self." (She grasps, quite clearly, the hostility involved in it: "She wondered why he always claimed to be normal when he was disagreeable" [216].) Assuming this persona enables Paul to approach sexuality and be sexually venturesome, as he cannot in his tenderer, more inward mode —as we see in the rather cruel scene in which Paul flirts with Beatrice Wyld in front of Miriam. It also leads him finally to adopt the masculinist values—common sense, aggressiveness, the rejection of empathy as fanciful and unreal—which, Jessica Benjamin says, most boys are converted to at the end of the oedipal period. When Clara tells him it is wrong to pick flowers, and Miriam suggests that it is all right if one does so "with reverence," Paul says, "you get 'em because you want 'em, and that's all" (233). He then goes on to describe the flowers in a way that masculinizes them, removing all threatening associations with the vagina: "'Look at these,' he continued, 'sturdy and lusty like little trees and like boys with fat legs—". (We see the same thing earlier, when Miriam sees her favorite rose bush in clearly female erotic terms— "some incurved and holy, others expanded in an ecstasy"—where Paul must make the flowers implausibly brisk, active, and untrappable: "'They seem as if they walk like butterflies, and shake themselves'" [159].)

To understand Paul's failure with Miriam in terms of his need finally to shake off the preoedipal bond does not necessarily contradict other explanations. Paul does back away from Miriam, more than once, in compliance with his mother's explicit oedipal jealousy. Nor is Dorothy Van Ghent's reading—a reading, conditioned by later Lawrence, that at one time was immensely influential—that Miriam really does represent "a twisted desire to 'possess' other persons," which is connected to a "transgress[ion] against the natural life-directed condition of the human animal," entirely off the mark.[10] (That is why the Paul/Miriam chapters represent one of the great portraits of a failed relationship in literature: the answer to questions of blame is always both/and, not either/or.) Lawrence's portrait of a kind of schizoid withdrawal from the body, a dissociation from impulse, in Miriam, is vivid and convincing: "Her body was not flexible and living. She walked with a swing, rather heavily, her head bowed forward, pondering. She was not clumsy, and yet none of her movements was quite *the* movement. Often, when wiping the dishes, she would stand in bewilderment and chagrin, because she had pulled in two halves a cup or a tumbler. It was as if, in her fear and self mistrust, she put too much strength into the effort" (153).

Lawrence also catches, decades before R. D. Laing, the need to maintain a separate, inner world, the fear of being taken by surprise, the fear of becoming an object of another person's perceptions, that can accompany this lack of ease with the body. Paul notices how Miriam "start[s] . . . as if something had come breaking in on her world," at a sudden noise from outside; and how, when she notices him watching her, "Instantly her broken boots and her frayed old frock hurt her. She resented his seeing everything. . . . And afterwards her hands trembled slightly at her work. She nearly dropped all she handled" (145). That Lawrence should connect such difficulties about embodiment with a difficulty about physical sexuality (particularly in someone whose mother has told her that "'there is one thing in marriage that is always dreadful, but you have to bear it'" [283]), seems fair enough. And yet, it is clear to us as readers that Miriam's feeling for Paul *is* sexual—when she can feel sufficiently at ease, in control—and that Paul has his own difficulties with being taken by surprise, with becoming an object to someone else. "She loved to see his hands doing things," we are told; and once, when he is repairing his bicycle, his back turned to her,

> she put her two hands on his sides, and ran them quickly down.
> "You are so *fine*!" she said.

He laughed, hating her voice, but his blood roused to a wave of
flame by her hands. She did not seem to realise *him* in all this. He
might have been an object. She never realised the male he was. (187)

Lawrence's distance from Paul is very problematic here. We do not know
whose judgments we are hearing; for to us, as readers, it is precisely as
a "male" that Miriam does "realise" Paul, in the skill of his work, in
his bodily ease and self-forgetfulness. It is in a far more Laingian, ontological sense that Paul dislikes becoming an "object," feeling his subjectivity is thereby denied. (Here the Miriam-haters among Lawrence's
critics might still respond that the real problem is that Miriam could
not accept the vehemence of desire her act provokes in Paul: "She always
wanted to embrace him, as long as he did not want her," Lawrence tells
us, again with very ambiguous point-of-view [187]. But, as we shall see,
becoming an "object" to women remains a very touchy area, throughout Lawrence's later work.)

The upshot of all this confusion is, once again, rage. As William tries
to hector Gypsy into providing more than a sexual connection, so Paul
tries to hector Miriam into providing the psychic distance, or playful-
ness, that would allow him to feel sexual at all. His analyses of her
"communions," her way of fondling flowers, her "eternal and abnormal craving . . . to be loved" (215), are so brutal they remind one of the
annihilation of the doll Arabella. Yet, Lawrence tells us, they are largely
unconscious on Paul's part: "He had not the faintest notion of what he
was saying" (215).

One reason that Paul's rage may be out of his conscious understanding and control is that it is overdetermined. Sometimes, as in the
Arabella story, rage is the only way of abolishing the woman from his
consciousness and thereby escaping guilt: "Those short sleeves, and
Miriam's brown-skinned arms beneath them, such pitiful, resigned arms,
gave him so much pain that they helped to make him cruel" (286–87).
Sometimes, Paul seems to be enraged at Miriam's fear of the world, her
lack of self-confidence, in and of itself—as in the scene where he teaches
her algebra. (Jessica Benjamin reminds us that boys reject the weakness
and incompetence of their own early childhoods when they reject the
mother, so that the two are forever after confused.)

Of course, anger can also be a conversion of repressed sexual feeling:
"It was as if his fretted, tortured soul, run hot by thwarted passion,

jetted off these sayings like sparks from electricity" (215). But this in itself raises the problem, especially for Walter Morel's son, of the relation between male sexual assertiveness and male violence. In several of the quarrel scenes—especially when Miriam seems afraid of Paul—phrases like "it made his blood rouse" (155) are used in an ambiguously sexual and aggressive sense. When Paul wishes to avoid saying something hurtful to Miriam, he instead digs a sharp stick into the ground (216, 287). In the algebra quarrel, he actually flings a pencil in her face, as his father had flung a table drawer at his mother, years before. And this sadistic side of his personality may be, ironically enough, something he wants to protect Miriam from, by leaving her.

With Paul's second crucial relationship, with Clara Dawes, the Lawrence we all know steps out into the open for the first time: the prophet of unashamed sexuality, of the human, ethical, and religious value of contacts based on the "blood" rather than on spiritual communions and mutual analysis. The rhetoric announcing this discovery remains immensely seductive, even after eighty years in which we have seen far greater sexual liberties and many feminist doubts, in its promise of reconciling the principle of separation with the principle of a now cosmic, not personal, mergedness: "What was she? A strong, strange, wild life, that breathed with his in the darkness through this hour. It was all so much bigger than themselves that he was hushed. They had met, and included in their meeting the thrust of the manifold grass-stems, the cry of the peewit, the wheel of the stars" (342). This rhetoric is so powerful, in fact, that it has been easy for critics of the Van Ghent stripe to recast the novel at this point as a simple morality play: Miriam represents bad spirituality, Clara good passion. In fact, it is greatly to Lawrence's credit that Clara is not simply a passionate body but a complex character who offers Paul a different model for negotiations between the sexes. Their relationship may start out on a healthier basis than Paul's with Miriam simply because there is a firmer sense of separateness. Clara is experienced, and a married woman; by approaching her sexually, Paul will neither damage her as much nor entrap himself. He is both intrigued and hurt by her feminism. When he shows her his painting, she reacts one way or the other—"Sometimes she praised his work, sometimes she was critical and cold" (258) —but she shows no wish to alter her judgment by entering into his intentions, as Miriam might. Finally, it is true that, precisely because

Paul's response to Clara is so intensely sexual, he must acknowledge her as something outside himself, a mystery to him, though more a "what" than a "who."

Perhaps Clara remains a "what" to Paul for a more primordial reason, not often noted in Lawrence criticism. (Again, Marguerite Beede Howe is an exception here: she writes of the "infant eroticism" of the scene at the theater.)[11] The intense physicality of their relationship gives Paul a way of reliving the experiences of infancy, inaccessible to conscious memory, that lie at the root of the whole problem of individuation and merging. When Paul is powerfully attracted to Clara, he feels "he was not himself, he was some attribute of hers, like the sunshine that fell on her" (298). "He was Clara's white, heavy arms, her throat, her moving bosom" (321). And this oneness, this feeling that "there was no himself," gives her an overwhelming scale and power, like the preoedipal mother's. "Then he felt himself small and helpless, her towering in her force above him" (321).

In a later scene, on the beach at Theddlethorpe, we see an opposite distortion of scale. Here Paul experiences what Jessica Benjamin, following on Winnicott, calls the child's need to "destroy" the mother, to experience the panic and freedom of his own autonomous will:[12] "'Look how little she is!' he said to himself. 'She's lost like a grain of sand in the beach—just a concentrated speck blown along—a tiny white foam-bubble. . . . Why does she absorb me?'" (346). In Winnicott's framework, the desirable outcome would be for the child to realize that the parent has survived the internal "destruction," and thereby gain the sense of separateness, equilibrium, and freedom from guilt that comes with a fundamental ontological equality. But for Paul, when Clara comes close again, she again becomes overwhelming, both positively and negatively: "When they were drying themselves, panting heavily, he watched her laughing, breathless face, her bright shoulders, her breasts that swayed and made him frightened as she rubbed them, and he thought again: 'But she is magnificent, and even bigger than the morning and the sea.—Is she?—is she?'" (347). And so Paul's reliving is not, ultimately, purgative. Equilibrium is never reached; and the adult woman remains an Other, frightening or sustaining, but not a fellow human being with whom life can be shared companionably.

For the real sadness of the Clara relationship is how far, in spite of passion, it follows the patterns established with Miriam. Paul's quickness to anger, his inability to tolerate sexual frustration, his very limited ability to anticipate the woman's feelings when he has put her in a painful or embarrassing situation—all are signs of the mother-raised son who cannot help refiguring all his relations to women in infantile terms. Nor do Paul's difficulties about fullness of intimacy, which might draw him back into the preoedipal black hole, vanish with a more sexually realized relationship. Whatever mystical insights Lawrence may derive from Paul's way of "just go[ing] like a leaf down the wind" when he makes love, Clara is surely right to diagnose it as a way of reserving himself—"as if all of you weren't there"—just as his exclusive spirituality with Miriam had been. Her relation with Baxter was "more whole," she says, because he was capable of being passionate and focusing on her as an individual at the same time (351).

The relation with Clara comes to essentially the same end as the relation with Miriam, when Clara, perhaps predictably, moves from her initial, wary, critical stance to being the more dependent partner, and Paul again feels "imprisoned," and—in a more directly preoedipal metaphor—suffocated, "as if he could not get a free deep breath, as if there were something on top of him" (347). As with Miriam, he starts to "figh[t] away," telling Clara brutally that love must be kept "out of work hours" (344).

Then there is the curious matter of Baxter Dawes. Some have seen here a foreshadowing of the homoerotic plot of middle period Lawrence, Paul's deeper interest moving toward the man through the woman they share. But the curiously flirtatious quality of Paul's connection with Baxter is perhaps better understood, at this stage, as another transference, through which Paul works his way toward his mixed feelings about his father—another working-class man who has sunk into "cowed defiance" and "disapprov[al] of himself" (224) as he has mistreated the crucial woman in his life.[13] From the beginning, Paul's curiosity about Dawes obtrudes—often quite disruptively—onto his own developing intimacy with Clara. "Weren't you horrid with him? Didn't you do something that knocked him to pieces?" (269). Before Garnett made his cuts, there were actually more of these scenes, and they were more prolonged; and there Paul treats Clara's shock at his breach of boundaries as further evidence that she feels "superior" and thereby makes men "ashamed."[14]

This theme of superiority seems particularly to nag at Paul: "You made up your mind he was a lily of the valley, and it was no good his being a cow-parsnip, you wouldn't have it" (348). Clara is understandably astonished at this diagnosis: she is working-class herself, and snobbery does not seem to play much role in her anger at Baxter. But, of course, the diagnosis fits perfectly in another context: Gertrude and Walter's early married life, as we have seen it in the opening chapter. We remember Gertrude's unforgiving middle-class horror when she learns that Walter has bought their furniture on credit; her ambivalence, even, about his skill at dancing, which first attracted her to him. It is as if—without ever consciously breaking his loyalty to his mother —Paul is using Clara and Baxter, more pointedly than he used the Leiverses earlier, to see his parents' marriage from his father's point of view. In doing so, he moves into the "mature" Lawrence's masculinist understanding, in which his father's physical vitality becomes the uniquely desirable trait, and middle-class woman's refinement and covert power politics are the root of all evil.

All this gives a poignant logic to the ending of the book, in which Paul rescues Baxter from the hospital, after the fight that nearly kills both of them, and gives Clara back to him. It is a rite of exorcism for the tragedy of his own family romance. As Daniel A. Weiss puts it, "With his mother dead, and his father reduced to ineffectuality, Paul's feelings of guilt and 'responsibility' are transferred to Clara and Dawes. In giving her back to Dawes, he says in effect, 'I took you from my father with disastrous results. Now I give you back to avoid making the same mistake.'"[15] But the act of reparation has its price. Paul must take into himself the bad father, seeing himself as a man who always "wronged [his] women" (340). Clara despises him for giving her back, giving up on the possibility of a less "humble," more self-affirming relationship they offered each other. Many critics have noted Paul's use of his father's dialect in the sex scenes; few have noted that Clara sees him, in the end, exactly as Gertrude saw Walter, two hundred pages earlier. "Clara thought she had never seen him look so small and mean. He was as if trying to get himself into the smallest possible compass" (393) (cf. Gertrude on 194: "'If he didn't hurtle himself up as if he was trying to get in the smallest space he could'"). The tragedy of *Sons and Lovers*— if the book is ultimately tragic, which of course is open to question—

lies not just in Paul's inability to let go of his mother, even in death, or to find in either of his two later loves a reason for living. It lies, also, in the terms on which he has begun to accept his father's world.

IT SEEMS CLEAR that the balance of Lawrence's sympathies shifted to the male side sometime between the completion of *Sons and Lovers* and the publication, in 1920, of *Women in Love*. It is less clear just when, and why, this change occurred. Cornelia Nixon, in the most interesting book so far on this phase of Lawrence's life, *Lawrence's Leadership Politics and the Turn against Women,* argues persuasively that *The Rainbow,* written in the first flush of Lawrence's union with Frieda, still speaks from his female identification. It emphasizes strong women and procreative sexuality, gives a measured approval to its heroines' increasing need for professional and sexual autonomy, and, on the whole, echoes Lawrence's belief, in a letter written around the same time, "that men should go to women to get their 'souls fertilized by the female . . . (not necessarily woman but most obviously woman),' in order to get a vision, one that 'contains awe and dread and submission' on the part of the man, 'not pride or sensuous egotism and assertion.'"[16]

Nixon attributes the change in Lawrence not, as is often said, to his general embitterment toward humanity, the result of the war and of his own first experience of being stigmatized as an obscene writer. Rather, she contends, drawing on Lawrence's letters after his meeting with John Maynard Keynes, and his unfinished tract *The Crown,* it was his discovery of, and reaction formations against, his own homosexuality that led both to his increased hostility to women (and to humanity in general) and to his idealization of special instances of male bonding.

It is an important insight. But it risks reifying "homosexuality" into the ultimate, irreducible truth about a man's life (as homophobes, indeed, fear that it is), and thereby understating the complexities of Lawrence's needs and anxieties toward women. Oddly, another of the least orthodox Lawrence books, John Middleton Murry's *Son of Woman,* can help us fill out the story, even though it is a defensive book by a hurt friend, and in fact the first book to insist on the importance of "sexual failure" and anal eroticism as Lawrencean themes. For Murry's early chapters, taking us back to poems written after Lawrence's mother died, and in the early years with Frieda, actually make a powerful case for the intertwining of sexual with identity difficulties.

Love—the kind of unhedged, unqualified love that is not experienced in *Sons and Lovers*—brought upon Lawrence, Murry suggests, an extremity of implicitly preoedipal need, the kind of need in which the very existence of the self depends on acceptance by the beloved. The feeling, in "The Song of a Man Who Is Not Loved," that "the space of the world is immense, before me and around me," is, Murry shrewdly remarks, "the same feeling which swept over Paul Morel at the death of his mother."[17] In one poem that Murry quotes, Lawrence openly draws the maternal analogy:

> How quaveringly I depend on you, to keep me alive,
> Like flame on a wick!
>
> . . . .
>
> Suppose you didn't want me! I should sink down
> Like a light that has no sustenance
> And sinks low.
>
> . . . .
>
> Nourish me, and endue me, I am only of you,
> I am your issue.[18]

In a poem called "Humiliation," he asks,

> What should I do if you were gone again
> So soon?
> What should I look for?
> Where should I go?
> What should I be, I myself,
> "I"?
> What would it mean, this
> "I"?[19]

Murry believes that the anxiety over being abandoned suggests that there was already a sexual difficulty between the couple: he reads the phrase "The charge of fulfillment" as suggesting that "she gives him fulfillment; he does not give it her." Though this is not self-evident, Murry is surely right to argue that "need so naked as that must inevitably pass into hate"; that "it is an extremity of dependence against which he must rebel. He can surrender himself to it for the moment, but he will hate himself and her for the humiliation of his own surrender."[20]

Lawrence uses metaphors of invasion, usurpation, even for the initial impact of love, in "Snapdragon"[21]:

> She moved her hand, and again
> I felt the brown bird cover
> My heart; and then
> The bird came down on my heart,
> As on a nest the rover
> Cuckoo comes, and shoves over
> The brim each careful part
> Of love, takes possession, and settles her down
> With her wings and her feathers to drown
> The nest in a heat of love.

And it is as a counterphobic response to these feelings that the idea enters Lawrence's work that women should "serve" men "Implicitly"; that it is woman, not man, who is nothing by herself, or in her procreative role, with "The mere fruit of your womb."[22]

An interesting wrinkle in this complex of feelings has to do with women appreciating men—an issue we have already encountered in *Sons and Lovers,* in the scene with Miriam and the bicycle. Murry quotes at length from the poem "'She Said as Well to Me.'" And I shall, too, for it is a classic statement of this problem:

> She said as well to me: "Why are you ashamed?
> That little bit of your chest that shows between
> the gap of your shirt, why cover it up?
> Why shouldn't your legs and your good strong thighs
> be rough and hairy?—I'm glad they are like that. . . .
> And I love you so! Straight and clean and all of a piece is the body of a man,
> such an instrument, a spade, like a spear, or an oar,
> such a joy to me—"
> So she laid her hands and pressed them down my sides,
> so that I began to wonder over myself, and what I was. . . .
>
> So she said, and I wondered,
> feeling trammeled and hurt.
> It did not make me free.
>
> Now I say to her: "No tool, no instrument, no God!
> Don't touch me and appreciate me.
> It is an infamy.

You would think twice before you touched a weasel on a fence
as it lifts its straight white throat.
Your hand would not be so flig and easy.
Nor the adder we saw asleep with her head on her shoulder,
curled up in the sunshine like a princess;
you did not reach forward to caress her. . . .

"Is there nothing in me to make you hesitate?
I tell you there is all these,
And why should you overlook them in me?—"[23]

Murry comments: "The wild and untamed masculinity which is here affronted . . . is . . . something which Lawrence desires to possess, and does not possess. He is a child to the woman, and resents the humiliation. In his dream he is a wild, untamed, dominant male. Yet he wants to be child: that is happiness and oblivion. And he wants to forget that he has been a child; above all he wants the woman to forget it. She must forget it instantly their naked flesh is parted."[24] I would put it a little differently: that because his dependence is childlike, he cannot see the woman's appreciation as other than infantilizing. He cannot, at some level, believe that he *is* the man she praises, and, therefore, that her praise is an acknowledgment. He must have her fear him, before he can be sure enough that she—and, more important, he—recognizes him as unquestionably, inviolably male. Love cannot confer this recognition, *because* it restores the union that existed before "maleness" was achieved; hence, the terrible myth that will come to dominate in *Women in Love* and the leadership novels, the myth of absolute male separateness.

But this separateness is also, as Murry understands, a separating off of part of the self—the preoedipal, mother- identified self of "emotional attunement . . . and imaginatively perceiving the others' needs and feelings," to quote Benjamin again. Lawrence was "afraid" of "his own wonderful tenderness," Murry says, "as though he said to himself, this is my weakness which must not be exposed." Murry's testimony that "in his life it was radiant" is all the more moving and credible because their own friendship ended so badly. But in his work, Murry says, Lawrence did not believe he could experience "tenderness" and "detachment" together; there he directed tenderness only across a "gulf," to people at a distance, animals, his dead mother. Intimate relationships he needed to see as primarily conflictual: "With the woman near and living, it is always the heat of struggle, the anguish of humiliation, or the desperate quiet of inviolable otherness."[25]

Perhaps this explains why, in *Fantasia of the Unconscious* (completed in 1921), we find Lawrence inveighing against mutuality or likeness between men and women; inveighing against "emotional attunement" in men; and attributing both errors to exactly the kind of upbringing he records affectionately, if ambivalently, in *Sons and Lovers*. "We should keep boys and girls apart," he says, because "on mixing with one another, in becoming familiar, in being 'pals,' they lose their own male and female integrity. And they lose the treasure of the future, the vital sex polarity, the dynamic magic of life."[26]

Lawrence repudiates the Freudian notion that there is natural bisexuality. Instead, he argues, men, while remaining "purely male," have come to "pla[y] woman's part," because the modern age has come to overvalue the "ideal": "Our ideal has taught us to be gentle and wistful: rather girlish and yielding, and *very* yielding in our sympathies. In fact, many young men feel so very like what they imagine a girl must feel, that hence they draw the conclusion that they must have a large share of female sex inside them. False conclusion" (132). Lawrence is very clear in singling out exactly the preoedipal qualities Benjamin mentions as "feminine" in men. By nature, he contends, men are "assertive and rather insentient"; they live from the "volitional centres," in which, in Lawrence's neuropsychological schema, we experience ourselves as distinct from, and in opposition to, the rest of the world. "Girlish men," by contrast, live from the "sympathetic" side: "He begins to have as many feelings—nay, more than a woman. . . . He worships pity and tenderness and weakness, even in himself" (134). (On the same page, we find Lawrence using this theory, as Nixon notes, to explain away homosexual impulses: having become "the emotional party," "man begins to show strong signs of the peculiarly strong passive sex desire, the desire to be taken." But later in the book, Lawrence will insist that heroic male bonding, by contrast, has no sexual component.)

Lawrence's theory of role reversal underwrites his need, as Murry observes, to see heterosexual relations, at least in the contemporary world, as inherently combative. Our ideal, Lawrence says, has forced men to become effeminate by preferring the archetype of "woman, the great Mother, who bore us from the womb of love," to that of "man, the doer, the knower," and insisting therefore that man's "highest moment

is now the emotional moment when he gives himself up to the woman"
(133)—a position, of course, that Lawrence himself held at the time of
The Rainbow. But once the matter is conceived this way, woman's
emotional union with man becomes a form of power politics. If "man
has assumed the gentle, all-sympathetic role," then "woman has become
the energetic party, with the authority in her hands" (132). "She is now
a queen of the earth, and inwardly a fearsome tyrant. She keeps pity and
tenderness emblazoned on her banner. But God help the man whom
she pities. Ultimately she tears him to bits" (134). With this sense of
the inherent combativeness of relations between men and women, and
of preoedipal emotionalism as a danger for men, we are fully on into
the world of *Women in Love.*

Women in Love is a strange book, a strange masterpiece. It has disturbed readers from its first appearance, for a number of reasons. There
is the homoerotic plot, and its problematic relation to Birkin's project
of making heterosexual love at once male-dominated and free of passion. There is the prominence of rage, in the temperaments of almost
all the characters. Within the first two chapters, at least three of them
wish the people in front of them would simply vanish—a wish that later
expands, famously, into the desire for a depopulated world, with just "a
hare sitting up."[27] And both attempted murders in the book are experiences of ecstasy.

There is, finally, the sense that, as Robert Langbaum has observed,
most of the characters are "static"; they do not "slowly change," but
"unfold a potentiality totally given at the outset, usually through symbols emerging from the realistic portrayal."[28] They are, in effect, divided
into the saved and the damned.

But I think what most disturbed me—from early in my repeated
experiences of the book—was the symbolic typology that seemed to
divide the saved from the damned, and its implications about selfhood,
being, and gender. Let me illustrate with an emblematic episode:

> One morning the sisters were sketching by the side of Willey Water,
> at the remote end of the lake. Gudrun had waded out to a gravelly
> shoal, and was seated like a Buddhist, staring fixedly at the water-
> plants that rose succulent from the mud of the low shores. What
> she could see was mud, soft, oozy, watery mud, and from its fes-
> tering chill, water-plants rose up, thick and cool and fleshy, very
> straight and turgid, thrusting out their leaves at right angles, and

having dark, lurid colors, dark green and blotches of black-purple and bronze. But she could feel their turgid, fleshy structure as in a sensuous vision, she *knew* how they rose out of the mud, she *knew* how they thrust out from themselves, how they stood stiff and succulent against the air.

Ursula was watching the butterflies, of which there were dozens near the water, little blue ones suddenly snapping out of nothingness into a jewel-life, a large black-and-red one standing upon a flower and breathing with his soft wings, intoxicatingly, breathing pure, ethereal sunshine; two white ones wrestling in the low air; there was a halo round them; ah, when they came tumbling nearer they were orange-tips, and it was the orange that had made the halo. Ursula rose and drifted away, unconscious like the butterflies. (178)

We see the "static," damned character sitting "like a Buddhist" (Lawrence disliked Buddhism, of which he knew little, because it seemed to him to make passivity a positive value), and looking into a world of "soft, oozy, watery mud," a world in which things decay and lose their form ("festering"), and in which new form as it arises, "succulent," keeps its connection to the "chill" matrix. The saved character, by contrast, prefers an air-world, in which boundaries are firm, or else demarcated by an aura, a "halo," of individuality, and the moment of origination is, as in the book of Genesis, an impenetrable mystery: "suddenly snapping out of nothingness into a jewel-life." It is hard not to connect the first vision with men's ambivalent feelings about the female body: its fluidity of shape that can be seen as shapelessness; its swampy recesses in which we once were almost nothing and could become almost nothing again; the "succulent" nourishment it gives the barely differentiated newborn. (That the water plants are also obviously phallic, as a number of readers have pointed out to me—and as their reuse in the emblematic characterization of Gerald emphasizes—is not necessarily a contradiction. Rather, it is evidence of Lawrence's deep distrust, at this stage of his career, of mutual enmeshment between men and women.)

Moreover, the swamp-world suggests not just the female body but the fluidity of preoedipal consciousness itself, in which the lines of demarcation between self and other are never clear, flow back and forth with the tidal forces of projection and identification, "envy" and "gratitude." It is, in very truth, that interdependence that Buddhism, if Lawrence had understood it, does assert to be a fundamental fact of existence.

Ursula's world, by contrast, is the ideal of the *Fantasia,* in which boys are boys, girls are girls, there are no corrupt intermixtures, and the independent will is the human characteristic most to be prized. (Butterflies, we remember, were the metaphor of masculine independence Paul Morel set against Miriam's "incurved" roses.) Reading this passage, one understands very well why the patriarchal religions have linked their "jewel"-like unique souls to the idea of a "sudden" creation "out of nothingness."

Moreover, the two landscapes also imply two modes of consciousness. Ursula's is natural, spontaneous, and analogical. She "drifted away, unconscious like the butterflies": because her independence of spirit is "like" theirs, she does not need to focus on them consciously in order to get the message, the beauty, of their being. Gudrun, by contrast, "*knew*" the water plants (Lawrence's italics) with her conscious mind; more important, perhaps, she almost becomes them, with the same empathic fusion Paul Morel felt—and dreaded feeling—when he was under Miriam's influence.

All this might seem an absurd overreading of a single descriptive passage, if its metaphors were not so obsessively repeated through the entire book. When Gerald, Gudrun's doomed companion, approaches, he is compared to "a stem" and a "marsh-fire" (179). When Birkin is still under Hermione's spell, he copies a Chinese drawing of geese in a marsh and feels the empathic quality of Chinese art as "an inoculation of corruptive fire—fire of the cold-burning mud—the lotus mystery" (145). In the "Water Party" chapter, Birkin finds the smell of a little marsh "alarming," associates it with female sexuality and the cult of romantic love ("our sea-born Aphrodite, all our white phosphorescent flowers of sensuous perfection"), and finally draws from it the metaphor for the decadence of Western civilization, the "dark river of dissolution," that he will return to, over and over, throughout the book (238–39). It is no accident that this tirade shortly precedes one of the book's most terrifying emblematic scenes, in which a wilful young girl falls into the water and embraces and drowns her rescuer, while her equally wilful sister screams her deathly nickname in a kind of demonic antiphon: "'Di - Oh Di - Oh Di - Di -!'" (247).

The moral seems all too evident: women are lethal to men because of their natural affinity for the watery underworld, the world where things decay and lose their boundaries. Yet—perhaps obviously—Lawrence would not evoke this world with such a brilliance of hostile rhetoric if it did not have a certain appeal to him. As Daniel Albright points out in *Personality and Impersonality*—still a green isle in the deep wide sea of Lawrence criticism for the way it reframes all the old, too-familiar issues —when Lawrence fails to catch himself out, the Edenic "first world" of his nature poems is suspiciously like the interconnected world he loathes in *Women in Love*. In the poem "Grapes," "the universe of the unfolded rose" is contrasted with a preworld, "a dusky, flowerless, tendrilled world / And creatures webbed and marshy. . . . Before petals spread, before colour made its disturbance, before eyes saw too much." Albright comments: "But if we look more deeply at the language of this poem we see that there are no distinct creatures, no distinct race of men, that all such attribution of subject is verbal convention: the whole world consists of tendriled creatures and tendriled men in tendriled marshes, in short, the world is a sphere, each point of which is linked to every other point . . . an egg groping with delicate gravity toward its own hatching. The fact that the creatures are webbed, soft, suggests that they are fetal, their limbs still not fully articulated."

Albright is absolutely on target in characterizing this vision as "fetal," and in connecting it to the myth, in *Fantasia of the Unconscious,* that "there must exist a single finite being at the core of the universe, prior to the articulation of either time or space."[29] This myth has been attacked as a male preemption of the female power to give birth.[30] But it more probably refers to the early stages of infancy, in which the child does, experientially, create a world as he/she emerges from the original timelessness and undifferentiation. D. W. Winnicott calls this the stage of the "transitional object," and finds in it the source of all creative activity.[31] If Lawrence valued the images of this preworld in one mood, but was horrified by them in another, surely the explanation lies in his troubled, incomplete separation from maternal symbiosis.[32]

In *Women in Love,* Birkin agrees with Herakleitos that "'a dry soul is best'" (239). His way of pursuing dryness leads to the two most controversial aspects of the book, new sexuality and the insistence on male bonding. As the imagery of the "Sketch-Book" chapter suggests, Gerald's intensely phallic quality does not differentiate him from the marshworld, but entangles him more deeply into it: "his body, stretching and surging like the marsh-fire . . . his hand coming straight forward like a stem" (179). And so Birkin, in his first approaches to Ursula, is wary not only of saying he "loves" her, but of making any sexual advances. As Nixon suggests, Birkin and Ursula do appear to make love in the traditional way after the water-party (the language is cloudy here, but at this point in his career Lawrence was writing in extreme fear of the censor). But even while they are doing so, Birkin protests, "Not this," and feels that "far away, there seemed to be a small lament in the darkness" (255–56). And the results are disastrous: the next day, they have a ferocious quarrel, Birkin falls seriously ill, and Ursula drifts into a "white flame of essential hate" toward him (268).

In his illness, Birkin "meditate[s]" along lines that foreshadow the *Fantasia*. He "hate[s] sex," because "he wanted to be single in himself, the woman single in herself. . . . The merging, the clutching, the mingling of love was become madly abhorrent to him" (269–70). He even rewrites Aristophanes' myth from the *Symposium*, so that love will not reveal us to be "broken fragments of one whole" but will make men more purely men, women more purely women: "Rather we are the singling away into purity and clear being, of things that were mixed. Rather the sex is that which remains in us of the mixed, the unresolved. And passion is the further separating of this mixture, that which is manly being taken into the being of the man, that which is womanly passing to the woman, till the two are clear and whole as angels, the admixture of sex in the highest sense surpassed" (271). And, as in *Fantasia*, he blames woman's "greed of self-importance" for the "horrible and clutching" aspects of love: "Everything must be referred back to her, to Woman, the Great Mother of everything, out of whom proceeded everything and to whom everything must finally be rendered up" (270).

At the deepest level, as on the surface, this seems to me to refer primarily to a psychological fear of maternal engulfment. Yet Nixon is surely right that the rhetoric of a "horrible . . . clutching," a "hot narrow intimacy," also suggests genital intercourse, and particularly any female pleasure in it. Before Birkin and Ursula can safely return to a genital relationship, they must discover a different, a "still" and "gentle"—and a more separate—mode of contact. And this, Nixon argues, through a closer reading of the "Excurse" chapter than any other critic has given, culminates in an "anal caress"—in Nixon's view, an acceptably heterosexual sublimation of Birkin's, or Lawrence's, passive homosexual desires.[33]

Whether Nixon is right—whether homosexuality is the cause, or merely one effect, of Birkin's fear of merging with women—would be easier to decide if Lawrence had written the more courageous book his "Prologue" points to.[34] Then we would have been able to judge how far Birkin's physical attraction to Ursula (which is powerfully rendered, even if not genitally focused) is in competition with his physical attraction to Gerald. But in Lawrence's revisions, as Charles Ross explains, "Lawrence's basic shift of strategy . . . was to keep the knowledge of a need for *Blutbruderschaft* submerged or unconscious in both Gerald and Birkin—until it surfaces midway through the novel. . . . Whereas the early versions present a conscious but hopeless desire for men which is merely the obverse of a failure with and hatred for women, the novel suggests that male friendship can complement a revitalized relationship with women. Thus Lawrence transformed a repressed desire, breeding misanthropy and despair, into an admitted and conceivably sustaining *Blutbruderschaft*."[35] Though this is not Ross's emphasis, it could be argued that Lawrence's changes made male love even more an "obverse" of heterosexual difficulties. The two major homoerotic scenes now seem fairly direct reactions to setbacks in Birkin's relationship with Ursula. The *Blutbruderschaft* conversation occurs after their first sexual encounter, and subsequent quarrel, have made Birkin feel "he hated sex"; the famous "Gladiatorial" takes place immediately after "the fiasco of the proposal." When Gerald learns of this emotional context, he understandably "stare[s] in amazement and amusement," and then says, "'And so you came here to wrestle with your good angel, did you?'" (353–54). Birkin professes not to understand this remark (perhaps the only time in the book he is thus at a loss). But I think the reader understands it pretty well. "Angels," in the earlier passage, stand for the "clear and whole" being of those who have "surpassed" "the admixture of sex" (271). Birkin has turned to his homoerotic side, after a heterosexual defeat, to be confirmed in his male separateness and strength—just as Jacob, in the Bible, is given a new name, and an assurance of triumph, when he wrestles with his angel.

None of this is to deny Nixon's ultimate point, that the emphasis on male bonding in *Women in Love* is the beginning of a politics—one that will ultimately serve Lawrence all too well, to deny weakness and effeminacy while acting out homosexuality. But within this book, it seems almost more of an insurance policy; it allows Birkin finally to let down his defenses with Ursula, without feeling he will be (in more than one sense) swamped.

Why, one might ask, do readers continue to be fascinated with a book whose underpinnings are in some ways so obviously neurotic? One answer is offered by Sandra M. Gilbert and Susan Gubar: that they are *not* simply neurotic, but reflect a sense of bitter combat between men and women general in the culture in the years of the suffrage movement and World War I.[36] Another answer might be Lawrence's acute understanding of the conflictual relationships that, as Murry observes, he considered the norm, and of how they tap back into the earliest experiences of life. Even in the "healthy" relationship between Birkin and Ursula, the mood-swings have a preoedipally categorical quality closer to Rilke's *grossen fremden Gedanken* than to what we expect from most love stories. When Ursula reacts against her incipient attachment to Birkin, "her whole nature seemed sharpened and intensified into a pure dart of hate. . . . It seemed to throw her out of the world into some terrible region where nothing of her old life held good" (267). And when they are finally happy with each other, "This was no actual world, it was the dream-world of one's childhood—a great circumscribed reminiscence" (394).

But it is the relationship between Gerald and Gudrun that gives Lawrence his great opportunity to examine blockages, sadomasochistic conversions, the failure, with the best will in the world, to transform the wish to love into the capacity. While Langbaum may be right that Gerald and Gudrun are in some way static characters, doomed from the start, this should not prevent us from seeing that there are many dimensions, or at least many possible formulations, of their failure with each other.

One problem with the relationship—a problem not often mentioned, perhaps because it is too obvious—is that it is so conventional. Gudrun is drawn to Gerald partly because he is rich. In her very first conversation with Ursula about marriage, she speaks of finding "a highly attractive individual of sufficient means" (54). And repeatedly thereafter, she thinks of Gerald as "the most important man she knew" (229), "her escape from the heavy slough of the pale, underworld, automatic colliers" (179), "the master of them all" (414). And Gerald, like many hard-driving, successful businessmen, falls in love with an artistic woman rather than cultivating his own artistic side. (To do the latter, one suspects, might make him too feminine, as he perceives Birkin to be.) A "conquer[or] of outer space" par excellence, in Benjamin's terms, he is convinced Gudrun "has the good things inside." From the beginning, "he wanted to come up to her standards, fulfill her expectations. He knew that her criterion was the only one that mattered" (159). She also represents to him the side of feeling, the possibility of nurturance. When his father is dying, she is the only person he "can talk to sympathetically" about his inner state, without being "dictate[d]" to, as with Birkin; and, soon, she is the only person who might alter it: "If he could put his arm round her, and draw her against him as they walked, he would equilibrate himself" (412).

One of Lawrence's great insights—which feminism ought to applaud —is that so extreme a division of psychic powers, and dependencies, is bound to lead to envy and resentment. Early in the book, in the "Diver" episode, Gerald's male freedom and activity makes Gudrun feel "as if damned." She bursts out, "You're a man, you want to do a thing, you do it. You haven't the *thousand* obstacles a woman has in front of her" (98). Moreover, Gudrun is not altogether wrong to see Gerald as an "unutterable enemy" (416); his conventional maleness involves a strong sadistic streak, that likes to mirror his "strength" in women by "destroy[ing]" them (117). Yet in his need of Gudrun there is a regression to childhood, and even prenatal, dependence: "He felt himself dissolving and sinking to rest in the bath of her living strength. . . . He was a man again, strong and rounded. And he was a child, so soothed and restored and full of gratitude" (430). And Gudrun, in her turn, feels a poignant resentment, because she is denied the opportunity to regress: "Ah, she could shriek with torment, he was so far off, and perfected, in another world. . . . And here was she, left with all the anguish of consciousness" (432).

Whatever uses Lawrence's ideology may make of Gudrun, she is one of his very great character creations. In her grief at never being able to achieve either oneness or separateness, she passes utterly beyond the femme fatale or New Woman stereotype, becoming as subtle an artist-portrait as Paul Morel (and perhaps as revelatory of an aspect of Lawrence himself). Her character, like Miriam's, is a study in ontological insecurity. "For always, except in her moments of excitement, she felt a want within herself" (466). Whenever another character seems whole or spontaneous to her, she is stricken, and needs to call attention to herself to compensate: "Ursula seemed so peaceful and sufficient unto herself, sitting there unconsciously crooning her song, strong and unquestioned at the centre of her own universe. And Gudrun felt herself outside. Always this desolating, agonised feeling, that she was outside of life, an onlooker, whilst Ursula was a partaker, caused Gudrun to suffer from a sense of her own negation, and made her, that she must always demand the other to be aware of her, to be in connection with her" (231).

Like Miriam, too, Gudrun is afraid of the pressure, the uncontrollableness, of reality. When she must walk through the "amorphous ugliness" of Beldover, "exposed to every stare" of the hostile, working-class people, she feels she "submit[s] herself" to "insufferable torture" (57). "And she felt as if she were treading in the air, quite unstable, her heart was contracted, as if at any minute she might be precipitated to the ground" (58). Irony is her way of protecting herself: "'Ursula, it's marvellous, it's really marvellous—it's really wonderful, another world. The people are all ghouls, and everything is ghostly'" (58). This stance of self-protection through half-appreciative mockery is perfectly epitomized in her slightly grotesque miniature sculptures: "'She likes to look through the wrong end of the opera glasses'" (88). Yet even her artistic ambition, Birkin feels, is hedged by a fear of "giv[ing] herself away" if she is "too serious" about anything (151). Later in the book, confronted with Gudrun's obsessive concern with how she is perceived by others, what is known about her, Ursula reflects: "She was never quite sure how many defenses Gudrun was having round herself" (468).

But Gudrun's need for distance has an interior dimension as well. Like many very self-conscious people, she handles moments when her boundaries are in fact broken by turning them into stories. When she feels "she would swoon, die" in the intensity of Gerald's first embrace, she remembers how in that same place, under the viaduct, "the young colliers stood in the darkness with their sweethearts. . . . So the colliers' lovers would stand with their backs to the walls, holding their sweethearts and kissing them as she was being kissed" (414–15). Or she sees what is happening through the eyes of an onlooker: "Through the man in the closed wagon Gudrun could see the whole scene spectacularly, isolated and momentary, like a vision isolated in eternity" (170). Alternatively, she may focus on some object at the periphery, to preserve the experience for her while removing her from it: the "close patch of yellow lights on the unseen hill" (431) in the viaduct scene, the song outside the window in the Alps.

Perhaps for the same reasons, the things that do break through to Gudrun's inner sense of reality have at once an aestheticized quality and a peculiar, infantile timelessness, "vision[s] isolated in eternity." They also have a violent, "fatal" quality, if only because the experience of being reached is itself violent to her. At the moment when she realizes she is in love with Gerald, she wishes "to die, to die," because it is "too final a vision" (249). Perhaps such moments seem "fatal," too, because their ultimate goal is the abolition of the distancing, ironic self, the return to unattainable, infantile, even prenatal oneness—as at this later moment in the Alps: "This was the centre, the knot, the navel of the world, where the earth belonged to the skies, pure, unapproachable, impassable. . . . At last she had arrived, she had reached her place. Here at last she folded her venture and settled down like a crystal in the navel of snow, and was gone" (492). And this, beyond all Lawrence's ideology, makes credible Gudrun's attraction to a "destructive" image of sexuality—the masochist in her that will match the sadist in Gerald, and then, given her envy and resentment, become a sadist in turn.

Lawrence the teller uses this side of Gudrun, there is no question, to make his case against a "nervous gratification" and a "knowledge in sensuous understanding" (513, 547) that have come to include not only aestheticism but perhaps female sexuality itself. But his more truthful tale shows us the violent seesaw between the polarities of infantile experience—the fear of oneness, the fear of being cast out. Gudrun needs to draw "isolation . . . round herself" (538), yet accuses Gerald of not loving her. Gerald, like many a mother-raised son, is rendered speechlessly guilty by this accusation, which his ambivalence rises to confirm. And it may, indeed, seem that he simply imposes "his own will blindly." Yet in his inner experience his vulnerability to her, "this strange, infinitely-sensitive opening of his soul," is at once "an open flower" and a "wound"—the female imagery of course suggesting the dimension of early childhood that is recovered. "His cruelest joy," this new sensitivity has become the only alternative to "sheer nothingness" (543). Benjamin remarks, with a terrible shrewdness, that one consequence of the dissociation of inwardness is to make male "desire" seem "the property of the object," and therefore beyond the man's power to control or escape on his own.[37] Small wonder, then, that the only way Gerald can imagine being free of his dependence on Gudrun is to kill her.

Gudrun herself, as the crisis approaches, has a horror-vision of her distancing, ironic self and the meaninglessness it imposes on life: "She knew she was not *really* reading. She was not *really* working. She was watching the fingers twitch across the eternal, mechanical, monotonous clock-face of time. She never really lived, she only watched. Indeed, she was like a little, twelve-hour clock, vis-a-vis with the enormous clock of eternity—there she was, like Dignity and Impudence, or Impudence and Dignity" (565).[38] She still wishes there were "somebody" to offer her merging and unconsciousness, "somebody who would take her in their arms, and hold her to their breast, and give her rest, pure, deep, healing rest." And then, once again, she turns on Gerald, with homicidal fury, because "he needed putting to sleep himself": "What then! Was she his mother? Had she asked for a child, whom she must nurse through the nights, for her lover. . . . Ooh, but how she hated the infant crying in the night. She would murder it gladly" (565–66).

The murderousness in *Women in Love,* then, *pace* Gilbert and Gubar, cannot just be put down to new tensions between the sexes in the culture at the time; or, *pace* Nixon, to a counterphobic response to Lawrence's homoerotic impulses. It is also an aspect of frustrated infantile need, infantile rage, exacerbated in the gulfs created by the "Oedipal riddle." And if the book has taught any pernicious lesson to its three generations of readers, it may be that it is better to hedge one's lovemaking in with theories and programs, as Birkin does. For the emotions involved in love are just too dangerous, left to themselves.

Yet Lawrence, I believe, was never completely satisfied with the solutions he came to in this book, especially around the issue of male dominance. Nixon is right, of course, that the book is less dialogic than some of its critics have argued: Ursula later quietly adopts many of those positions of Birkin's that she at first loudly opposed.[39] But one of the few arguments in the book that nobody wins is the one about the horse and the train. If we had only the scene itself, I think it would be fairly clear how Lawrence intended us to react to it. Gerald's forcing his mare to stand still at the crossing while the train passes, his "mechanical relentlessness" (170), are a kind of ritual sacrifice of the organic to the industrial, of living impulse to will.[40] It is a precise parallel to what Gerald has done to the living humanity of his miners ("reduc[ing them] to mechanical instruments") in his industrial reforms, which Lawrence calls "the first great phase of chaos, the substitution of the mechanical principle for the organic" (304–5).

Moreover, we have the reactions of the two onlookers. Ursula, the saved character, is utterly unambivalent in her wish to stop the outrage: "'No -! No -! Let her go! Let her go, you fool, you *fool* -!'" (169) Gudrun's response is much more conflicted. She "hate[s]" Ursula for making herself vulnerable, "naked," by "being outside herself." Yet beneath her self-protectiveness, she is experiencing one of her violent epiphanies—a masochistic identification with the cruelty of the scene: "It made Gudrun faint with poignant dizziness, which seemed to penetrate to her heart. . . . And then on the very wound the bright spurs came down, pressing relentlessly. The world reeled and passed into nothingness for Gudrun, she could not know any more" (169–70). The masochism, as elsewhere in the book, is capable of a sadistic conversion. When Gudrun does turn on Gerald, it is with an undermining personal attack, "like a witch screaming out from the side of the road" —"'I should think you're proud'"—and not with Ursula's "pure opposition" to Gerald's actions (170–71). The moral seems clear: male sadism begets female masochism, which in turn can generate a subtler, more corrosive form of hostility. Truly healthy characters, like Ursula, distance themselves from both.

Yet as soon as male characters start to react to the incident, this clarity fades. The gatekeeper at the crossing draws a clear distinction between Gerald's behavior and his father's, but refuses to join in Ursula's wholehearted condemnation, "as if he would say nothing, but would think the more" (171). When Birkin hears of the episode, it appeals far too strongly to his sense of the hierarchical for him to protest; and his understanding of the metaphor, like Gudrun's, is immediately sexual. "'And woman is the same as horses: two wills act in opposition inside her. With one will, she wants to subject herself utterly. With the other she wants to bolt, and pitch her rider to perdition'" (202).

Birkin may be Lawrence's spokesman in the book as a whole; but there are a number of reasons to think his views do not prevail here. One is the immediate approval they get from "damned" characters. Gerald takes Birkin's remarks as underwriting his own sadomasochistic approach to love: "'There's more fun'" (203). Moreover, Hermione has initially approved of Gerald's action, feeling "it is false to project our own feelings on every animate creature." Birkin agrees: "Quite. . . . Nothing is so detestable as the maudlin attributing of human feelings and consciousness to animals" (200–201). It is only when Hermione draws a parallel to her own principle of self-control, her belief that "the will can cure anything," that Birkin inconsistently bursts out, "'Such a will is an obscenity'" (201). The text never emphasizes the analogy between real animals and the "animal"—the spontaneous, control-resisting element—within the self, but it is there for the reader.

A final indication that something is out of whack in this scene is the bond it creates between the best and the worst female characters, Ursula and Hermione. Hermione, herself inconsistent, has withdrawn from the whole argument after Birkin's attack on her. Now, after her own hostile interchange with him, Ursula too withdraws, into a purely feminine, appreciative world that for once draws no negative rhetoric from Lawrence, and, indeed, reminds us of the world Paul Morel once shared with his mother. She and Hermione walk "along the bank of the pond, talking of beautiful, soothing things," and Ursula wishes for a dress the color of the cowslips (203). Within this world, they articulate an objection to "all this criticism and analysis of life" that would, in other contexts, be Lawrence's own; and articulate, too, the one criticism of Birkin that the novel never completely refutes—that he lives too much trapped "in the head," that he will have to approach life less as a philosophical question, if he is to achieve the spontaneity he desires (204).

There is one final piece of evidence in the horse-and-train debate, a plot irony the narrative never explicitly points up. When we next see Gerald, he has his hand bandaged from an industrial accident. This time, it is his own flesh he has sacrificed to the machine-god—one of many foreshadowings of his suicidal end.

The whole episode is a telling one and, in a way, rather courageous; it encodes an impasse Lawrence could not get beyond in his own thinking. On the one hand, he knows that a "will" that discounts the otherness of obstacles—whether within the self or outside—is an "obscenity," and is at the root of the whole industrial-rational culture he despises. He knows, even, that his characters cannot commit themselves to such a "will" without ultimately destroying their own human wholeness. On the other hand, a side of Lawrence participates in his male characters' conviction that empathic feelings are a threat to male dignity. (Birkin finds such feelings "maudlin"; to Gerald, the only alternative to "us[ing the horse] as he likes" is "to go down on his knees to it" [201, 200].) Like Birkin, Lawrence believes too strongly, in Benjamin's terms, in "freedom against nurturance," entirely to oppose the principle of domination.[41] *Women in Love* does not resolve this problem—but, in dramatizing it, it remains a work of art, compelling in its tensions, not a thesis-machine.

ONE REASON to read *Fantasia of the Unconscious,* for all its perversities, is to see *Sons and Lovers* rewritten from the point of view of someone who now believes most of the things Rupert Birkin believes; to see how profoundly Lawrence's increasingly antimaternal bias has changed his account of his own history. As is famous, Lawrence parts from Freud in asserting that there is no natural incest-motive. Rather, Lawrence blames "the idealism of yearning, outgoing love, of pure sympathetic communion and 'understanding'"—enforced by mothers—for "abnormally, inflamedly excit[ing]" the "centre of upper sympathy," and thereby creating "a painfully false relation . . . a relation as of two adults, either of two pure lovers, or of two love-appearing people who are really trying to bully one another" (150–51). It is this appeal—motivated, often, as in *Sons and Lovers,* by the mother's loss of interest in, and respect for, her spouse—that "willy-nilly arouses the lower centres" (154) and so creates an artificial infantile sexuality that can find no natural outlet. (It is one of the many ironies in the history of psychoanalysis that current feminist writers on incest, and the Alice Miller of *Thou Shalt Not Be Aware,* would completely agree.) The result of this blocked, premature sexuality is "introversion," and the "sex-in-the-head" Lawrence so often castigates: "The child does not so much want to *act* as to *know.* The thought of actual sex connection is usually repulsive. . . . But the craving to feel, to see, to taste, to *know,* mentally in the head, this is insatiable. Anything, so that the sensation and experience shall come through the *upper* channels" (155). (Of course, the very fact that Lawrence analyzes these problems in an implicitly male "child," but portrays them most powerfully in a female character, Gudrun, suggests how little the problem of "sympathetic understanding" has been resolved.)

And so Lawrence manages to lay all of his bêtes noires—the "ideal," the preference for love and understanding over individuality, even "sex-in-the-head"—at the door of mothers. Just how bitter this accusation has become, and how pointed its application to Lawrence's own life, may be gauged from the following quotations:

> Any excess in the sympathetic mode from the upper centres tends to burn the lungs with oxygen, weaken them with stress, and cause consumption. So it is just criminal to make a child too loving. (97)

> It is despicable for any one parent to accept a child's sympathy against the other parent. And the one who *received* the sympathy is always more contemptible than the one who is hated. (131)

And, perhaps most tellingly, this:

> The son gets on swimmingly for a time, till he is faced with the actual fact of sex necessity. He gleefully inherits his adolescence and the world at large, without an obstacle in his way, mother-supported, mother-loved. Everything comes to him in glamour, he feels he sees wondrous much, understands a whole heaven, mother-stimulated. Think of the power which a mature woman thus infuses into her boy. He flares up like a flame in oxygen. No wonder they say geniuses mostly have great mothers. They mostly have sad fates. (159)

Yet Lawrence is not, even at this point, able to maintain his mother-hatred without a certain degree of Kleinian splitting. Consider this passage, from one of his endless tirades against the "ideal": "Never for one moment, poor baby, the deep warm stream of love from the mother's bowels to his bowels. . . . Our miserable infants never know this joy and richness and pang of real maternal warmth" (173). The reader of *Sons and Lovers,* I think, will immediately protest, and on the basis of some of its most flagrantly oedipal passages: "Paul loved to sleep with his mother. Sleep is still most perfect, in spite of hygienists, when it is shared with a beloved. The warmth, the security and peace of soul, the utter comfort from the touch of the other, knits the sleep, so that it takes the body and soul completely into its healing. Paul lay against her and slept, and got better" (70–71). Mrs. Morel does give Paul "the deep warm stream of love," as well as the power to "flar[e] up like a flame in oxygen"; and his attachment to her is guiltily Oedipal as well as preo-edipally symbiotic. It is this very inclusiveness that makes later life so difficult. And so Lawrence tries to deny the inclusiveness, by splitting off one part of his mother, and castigating it as the "ideal"; by praising

85

a more indifferent, even hostile, style of upbringing; by emphasizing male bonding and even, to some degree, validating his father's violence.

But none of these stratagems, I believe, ever entirely worked, if *worked* here means that the stratagems freed Lawrence from the loving side of his bond to his mother. We can see this from a passage in *Kangaroo,* that honest, and considerably underrated, later novel. It is one of the few passages in Lawrence's later fiction that even acknowledge the mother as an important presence in his life. The hero, Richard Lovat Somers—a much fuller, less idealized Lawrence-surrogate than Birkin—has just put his belief that "the pure male activity should be womanless, beyond woman" to the test.[42] He has refused to tell his wife Harriet what Jack Callcott has told him about the quasi-fascist paramilitary movement Somers is thinking of joining. Harriet's reaction is hurt and hostile: "Either her marriage with him was not very important, or else this Jack Callcott stuff wasn't very important" (93). But when Somers finds her in tears, "at once his heart became very troubled: because after all she was all he had in the world, and he couldn't bear her to be really disappointed or wounded." He says nothing, believing the conflict unsolvable, "like a navel string" that "can only . . . be broken or cut" (94). But his dreams then present him with a monstrously aggrandized version of "what she was feeling":

> Bitter the woman was grieved beyond words, grieved till her face was swollen and puffy and almost mad or imbecile, because she had loved him so much, and now she must see him betray her love. That was how the dream woman put it: he had betrayed her great love, and she must go down desolate into an everlasting hell, denied, and denying him absolutely, in return, a sullen, awful soul. The face reminded him of Harriet, and of his mother, and of his sister, and of girls he had known when he was younger—strange glimpses of all of them, each glimpse excluding the last. And at the same time in the terrible face some of the look of that bloated face of a madwoman which hung over Jane Eyre in the night in Mr. Rochester's house.
>
> The Somers of the dream was terribly upset. He cried tears from his very bowels, and laid his hand on the woman's arm saying:
>
> "But I love you. Don't you *believe* in me? Don't you believe in me?" But the woman, she seemed almost old now—only shed a few bitter tears, bitter as vitriol, from her distorted face, and bitterly, hideously turned away. (94)

The dream tells us how enormously powerful women are to Somers; and this is not, as Lawrence's theory would have it, in their sexual pride, but in their grieving and bitterness—all that Paul Morel was so sensitive to, in his mother. (In the light of contemporary feminist criticism, the choice of the madwoman in *Jane Eyre* as the emblem of this is positively uncanny.) But the dream also tells us that Somers feels responsible for this grieving. It is as if, by asserting any autonomy, he were making the women grow old and die. (When he wakes up, he thinks of Harriet "in the past tense, though [she] lay sleeping in the next bed.") And beyond this, the dream tells Somers how much, for all his brave words, he still needs maternal sustenance and recognition, in order to recognize himself. "Don't you *believe* in me?' is his bitterest question within the dream, and on waking he realizes that he "feel[s] that he could never take the move into activity unless Harriet and his dead mother believed in him" (95).

"In his full consciousness," Lawrence tells us, Somers "was a great enemy of dreams." *Fantasia* confirms that this was true of Lawrence himself, and it is no wonder. Somers' dreams tell him how alive all the preoedipal issues are, how deep and ambivalent his inter-identity with women is, how much he fears hurting them by separation. The dreams reveal how much of his ideology is defense and denial—a discovery he can handle only by consigning it to the dead past. "When he was asleep and off his guard, then his own weaknesses, especially his old weaknesses that he had overcome in his full, day-waking consciousness, rose up again maliciously" (95). In fact, Somers's "weaknesses" have not been left behind in the past. He is truly relieved only when he finds that the dream is wrong in one respect: Harriet's dissatisfaction, unlike the Bad Mother's, is not infinite. "Harriet, however, said nothing for two days. She was happy in her new house, delighted with the sea and the being alone" (95).

Lawrence's outward solutions to his "Oedipal riddle," in sum, are not unconventional, only delayed. Yet, because he was, when all is said, a genius, the uneasiness, the contradictory knowledge, straining underneath is always registered. And what Murry called his "wonderful tenderness," what Benjamin calls "emotional attunement, sharing states of mind, empathically assuming the other's position," remain alive in his work, as well. Judged simply by their plots, his later novels can be, and have been, represented as caricatures of male supremacism, male anxiety: *The Plumed Serpent*; "The Woman Who Rode Away," who finds fulfillment offering herself as a human sacrifice to help a remote tribe regain its primal potency; even *Lady Chatterley's Lover,* where the "lady" learns the vaginal orgasm in the arms of yet another game-keeper, another redeemed Walter Morel. Yet we go on reading these books, in part for the moments when doctrine and anger are silent and there is a tendril-like connection, a disinterested transparency—often through the eyes of a female character—toward a landscape, an animal, a religious tradition, as in this portrait of New Mexico from *St. Mawr:*

> From her doorway, from her porch, she could watch the vast, eagle-like wheeling of the daylight, that turned as the eagles which lived in the near rocks turned overhead in the blue, turning their lumi-nous, dark-edged-patterned bellies and under-wings upon the pure air, like winged orbs. So the daylight made the vast turn upon the desert, brushing the farthest outwatching mountains.[43]

At such moments, we might be back with the young Paul Morel sketch-ing the colliery, his mother not far away.

Pavese's Despair

WHY IS MALE despair, over lost or unrequited love, so volcanic? Female despair gets more attention, both in theory and in popular culture (e.g., the self-help book *Women Who Love Too Much*); and it is easier to explain, the lost man representing not only worldly security but, often, the split-off venturesome, confident part of the self.[1] But why, then, should the powerful, the supposed masters of the world, stake the whole value of their lives on powerless women?

The subject is downright irritating to some thinkers. After all, male need can be bullying, "murderous, bloody, full of blame," as Shakespeare said of lust. It can certainly "objectify," failing to comprehend, or assigning no importance to, the subjectivity of its victim. Yet its intensity is a psychic fact; and, like all deep psychic facts, demands an explanation that is at least partly compassionate, partly from within.

Once again, Benjamin's concept of the "Oedipal riddle" offers the best way of thinking about this problem that I have encountered. With the repudiation of the identificatory relation with the mother, the sense of having a "good object" within the self—so strongly an attribute of the mother—is also lost. The self can no longer comfort or console itself, make itself feel that life on its own is sufficient or good. So the male self, for all its vaunted "autonomy," is born in a sense of dryness, of lack, as profound as that lack that women supposedly experience from the absence of the penis: "As Dinnerstein has noted, once the mother is no longer identified with, once she is projected outside the self, then, to a large extent, the boy loses the sense of having this vital source of goodness inside. He feels excluded from the feminine world of nurturance. At times he feels the exclusion more, as when he idealizes the lost paradise of infancy; at other times he feels contempt for that world, because it evokes helplessness and dependency. But even when mother is envied, idealized, sentimentalized, and longed for, she is forever outside the masculine self."[2] Dinnerstein, in the passage Benjamin cites, makes the point even more clearly: "the mother-raised boy," she says, has a "sense that the original, most primitive source of life will always be outside himself, that to be sure of reliable access to it he must have exclusive access to a woman."[3]

Furthermore, boys tend to lose, along with the maternal identification, any easy mode of sharing their inner lives, feeling recognition and continuity, with anyone else. "Emotional attunement, sharing states of mind, empathically assuming the other's position . . . these are now associated with cast-off femininity."[4] Male bonding is notoriously more competitive, based on deflections and objectifications—sports, tools, politics, and for the elite, intellectual debate.

And so, an enormous number of human satisfactions come to be deferred, at the oedipal stage—not only the "oceanic" experience of oneness with another person, which both sexes share, but the sense of having an inner "good object," the possibility of "sharing states of mind" as part of ordinary interchange. In the boy's need, in order to have access to these "good things," to "regain and conquer [Mother] in her incarnations in the outside world,"[5] the enormous urgency of male longing, and male idealization of the very femininity that has been rejected, come into being.

But the very intensity of this longing is also—as Benjamin clearly perceives—a source of male fear of women. If the woman contains all psychic "good" within her, and the man none, then his attraction toward her will be as helpless, as independent of his own will, as toward a magnet. He will lose any sense of agency in his own desire:

> His adult encounter with woman as an acutely desirable object may rob him of his own desire—he is thrown back into feeling that desire is the property of the object. A common convention in comedy is the man helpless before the power of the desirable object *(The Blue Angel)*. . . . In the oedipal experience of losing the inner continuity with women and encountering instead the idealized, acutely desirable object outside, the image of woman as the dangerous, regressive siren is born. The counterpart of this image is the wholly idealized, masterful subject who can withstand or conquer her.[6]

And, of course, the woman whose attraction is so overpowering cannot be seen by the man as a merely, or fully, equal subject. If she rejects his desire, it is not the response of one fallible, replaceable human being, but a judgment like God's. Out of this grows the male sense—perfectly sincere, though exasperating to feminists—that women are immensely powerful and cruel; and that a hostile defensiveness is a legitimate part of male erotic feeling. Dorothy Dinnerstein puts it even more bluntly: "Attachment to a woman is emotionally bearable, consistent with the solidarity among men which is part of maleness, only if she, and one's feelings toward her, remain under safe control."[7]

There is, I believe, a further wrinkle to this already intricate predicament, which neither Benjamin nor Dinnerstein brings completely into focus. Perhaps it applies most to young men who have never entirely lost their identification with the feminine, never felt they quite embodied the paternal definition of maleness. Such men may feel longing as acutely as other men do. But as soon as an actual relationship begins to bring back the experience of "emotional attunement," the early experience of likeness to a woman, they will begin to fear that they are, by that very fact, disqualified. They will expect the woman, sooner or later, to prefer a man who is more truly her opposite—the brutally strong, "masterful" father imago of the oedipal phase. Such expectations can, of course, become self-fulfilling prophecies. But beyond that, the boy's anger and sorrow that the woman would reject what was "like" herself, and prefer something opposite, even evil, becomes, ironically, a cause for misogyny—and, particularly, distrust of female sexual agency.

No figure in the history of literature embodies these tensions more hauntingly than the Italian novelist and poet Cesare Pavese, who committed suicide in 1950, at the age of forty-one, after the failure of two love affairs in quick succession.

Pavese's relations with women appear to have been both overcharged and almost masochistically unlucky, from the very beginning. In high school, he could not bring himself to approach a girl named Olga, but fainted dead away when he saw that name on the side of a boat.[8] In the 1930s, he had an affair with an anti-Fascist activist, "the woman with the hoarse voice." He seems never to have been very confident either of her fidelity or her good opinion of him. Nevertheless, he allowed her to use his address as a *poste restante* for subversive letters; when the police raided, he took the blame, and was sentenced to village exile in Calabria. The day before he returned, she married someone else.[9]

Pavese appears to have taken this disaster as setting a fatal pattern for all his later serious relationships, including the climactic one, in 1950, with the American actress Constance Dowling—particularly in terms of the fear that the woman would always prefer a stronger man. His biographer, Davide Lajolo, testifies: "I have never forgotten what he told me late one night in Milan: 'She [Constance Dowling] fled at night from my bed and she went to bed with another, with that actor you know. Like the other woman, even worse. Do you remember the one from Turin [the 'woman with the hoarse voice']? She is the one who ended it between me and women.'"[10]

Pavese's romantic failures, also from the beginning, brought with them ferocious self-hatred and temptations to suicide. He appears to have suffered from some kind of sexual dysfunction, which he sometimes blamed for his bad luck. Probably it was premature ejaculation ("a man who ejaculates too soon had better never have been born. It is a failing that makes suicide worth while.")[11] Some diary entries speak of "impotence," but, given the frequency and intensity of his involvements, this sounds like a characteristically self-hating exaggeration.[12] Whatever his difficulty, he seems to have regarded it as part of his fate; neither a Freudian explanation, nor an explanation involving male fear and awe of women, figures in his writings.

Pavese's poems to Constance Dowling record, as clearly perhaps as has ever been recorded, the sense of woman as containing the inner "good object," the access to the lost world of early childhood in which things were alive, and the self had an inherent, unanxious capacity:

> Where you are, as where light is, it is morning.
> You were the things and their life.
> Awake in you we could breathe
> under the lost sky that remains within us,
> not pain, not fever, not
> the burdened shadow of the crowded, scattered
> day.[13]

And Pavese's diaries abundantly confirm that it was the loss of this feeling of value—or its utter dependence on something outside himself—that spurred him on to suicide. "One does not kill oneself for love of a woman, but because love—any love—reveals us in our nakedness, our misery, our vulnerability, our nothingness."[14]

Yet, side by side with Pavese's idealization of women, the conversion—to contempt, distrust, and fear—that Benjamin and Dinnerstein predict is constantly evident. The diaries are insistently bitter, worldly, misogynist in their assessment of sexual motives and probabilities. A few quotations will give the flavor:

> Not only does she make a fool of him in the eyes of the world, but, and this is important to a woman, the most rational animal in existence, she convinces herself that it suits him to be a fool, and so her conscience is clear.

> The women who are most careful to choose a rich lover are those who protest that money means nothing to them. Because, to despise money, one must have plenty of it.

> Think the worst. You will not be wrong. Women are an enemy race, like the Germans.[15]

Pavese is particularly preoccupied with the idea that to fall in love wholly and unguardedly is bound to drive the other person away.

> Why has almost everyone been deluded by love? Simply because they fell in love so eagerly that it was bound to play them false, by the law that lets us have only what we ask for with indifference.[16]

Yet, on some level, Pavese seems to have felt that he needed, or sought, such rejection; that he could not accept being loved. He told Lajolo: "I abandon women, those whom you call maternal, as soon as I deceive myself into thinking they love me. I am always desperately seeking the woman who has never loved me and never will."[17]

Hence Pavese is never entirely able to "idealize" Benjamin's image of the "masterful," unemotional man who can control the "regressive siren," though that image haunts him. He freely admits that when he is cut off in this way from the early fusion, he becomes bored. "I ought to be the master and take my pleasure calmly, as though by right. I shall be loved more. Only so shall I be truly loved. But shall I enjoy it more? Whenever I have been the possessor, I have had no pleasure at all. The old story."[18]

But perhaps this refusal of "normal" masculine defenses is the beginning of Pavese's greatness. For where we might expect a macho, objectifying writer, who sees women entirely in terms of their effect on men, in fact Pavese is intensely female-identified. His anxiety about women seems to lead to curiosity, which leads, in turn, to compassion. Even in the diaries, one comes on such suddenly wry, sympathetic comments as the following: "To understand why a woman seems thoughtful, embarrassed and apologetic when she is with several young men, think how you feel yourself among five or six prostitutes, all watching you and waiting for you to make your choice."[19] Much of his best work is taken from the point of view of women, often hard-bitten, worldly women who have to struggle and face disapproval—in short, precisely the unnurturing women whom, judging by his diaries, we would expect him to fear. There is the tough manager of a boutique who is the narrator of *Among Women Only;* there are the many prostitutes in *Hard Labor.* In his extraordinary letters to Fernanda Pivano, he not only tries to analyze her sexual difficulties from her point of view, he even imagines her as a boy, so that his own love for her will have no threatening, aggressive aspect. (Even in this fantasy, however, unbridgeable distance remains, since Pavese's "narrator" cannot quite acknowledge his own implied homosexuality.)[20]

Perhaps Pavese's problem, on some level, was that sympathetic or nurturing women were precisely *not* "maternal" for him, in Lajolo's phrase. Pavese's background sheds considerable light on his otherwise almost unbelievably contradictory complex of attitudes. He had almost no opportunity for paternal identification: his father was ill with a brain tumor from the time he was born, and died when he was six. His mother was both vulnerable—she had lost three children before Cesare was born, and was "long tried by grief"—and forbidding:

> All the family responsibilities fell on his mother's shoulders. Cesare's mother was courageous, austere, and strong: a Piedmontese who had learned not to waste words but to work hard, be thrifty, and keep a tight rein on her children. . . . Behaving more like a harsh father than a gentle mother, she made her children feel the weight of authority rather than the warmth of tenderness. . . . When his mother placed the food on the table, she would not tolerate discussions; it was necessary to force oneself to eat everything, above all the squash soup that made Cesare nauseous. . . . It was difficult for him to confide in her. As the years passed, their relationship became increasingly cold.[21]

Easy to see how someone with such a background would need women tremendously; but also identify with their grief; and also expect that the ones he cared for the most were the least likely to be accepting of him.

The eyes that follow him so often in his poems are, tragically, both the eyes of the judge, for whom he can never be manly or stoical enough, and the eyes through which he has had his first experience of a mutually shared world. "The Mother," in *Dialogues with Leuco,* very nearly says as much: "You have to have seen those eyes. Seen them from childhood on, to know them, live with them, to feel them fixed on your every step, your every action, for days, for years, and to know that they're getting old, that they're dying, and to suffer what they suffer, to hurt yourself by hurting them, to go in terror of offending them."[22] And another of the *Dialogues*—the wonderful and terrible one on Endymion—sums up that sense of the mother's, the beloved's, vulnerability that demands that the poet accept her indifference and *see* what she has seen, even if it includes her destruction of him: "She stands there before me, a slight, unsmiling girl, looking at me. And those great transparent eyes have seen other things. They still do see them. They *are* those things. Wild berry and wild beast are in her eyes, and the howling, the death, the cruelty of flesh turned stone. . . . Her caresses are like the caresses you give to a dog or a tree. But she *looks* at me, stranger, she *looks* at me—a slight girl standing there in a tunic, like a girl from your own village."[23]

Joanne Feit Diehl has argued that a work of art inevitably reproduces the holding environment, the "idiom of care," of the author's early childhood.[24] Surely Pavese's is such an art—not only in its deep identification with the woman who is at once victim, watcher, and judge or its inability to admit the possibility of mutual satisfaction, but also in its feeling-tone of stony, irreparable despair.

In Pavese's first book of poems, *Hard Labor,* much of this is still in the future. Yet the book's seeming impersonality allows it to dissect some of the conflicts Benjamin and Dinnerstein describe, and to do so with an unparalleled clarity and objectivity. "The Goat God"—Pavese's first great poem about sexuality—is a poem of male discovery, its wonder and horror:

> To the boy who comes in summer the country
> is a land of green mysteries. Certain plants
> are bad for the she-goat; her paunch begins to swell
> and she has to run it off. When a man's had fun with a girl—
> girls are hairy down there—her paunch swells with a baby.[25]

It's also a poem about crossing the boundary between civilization and nature, between what can be controlled by knowledge and what cannot.

> The boys snigger and brag when they're herding the nannies,
> but once the sun goes down, they start looking nervous and scared.
> The boys can tell if a snake's been around, they know
> by the wiggling trail he leaves behind him in the dust.
> But nobody knows when a snake is sliding through the grass.

But when that boundary is crossed by female sexual agency—by definition, out of male control—a feeling of bewilderment, disgust, sorrow, and fear enters in:

> There are nannies who like to lie in the grass, they lie
> right down on top of the snake, they like to be suckled.
> Girls like it too, they like being touched.

The fear is that female sexuality, uncontrolled, will prefer an archetypally brutal, prehuman form of male energy—a snake, perhaps, or the "wild goat":

> Sometimes girls in heat
> come down to the woods, at night, alone;
> they lie in the grass and bleat, and the wild billy comes running.

There are a number of psychic mechanisms at work here. Since the boys "snigger" about, and devalue, their own sexuality, they cannot quite accept a woman's valuing or wanting it either (hence the tone of disbelief about "Girls . . . like being touched"). All these motives—self-distrust, anger at women, oedipal aggrandizement of the bad and all-powerful father—find a kind of expression in the crowning sadistic fantasy: that when "the moon is high," the wild goat "goes berserk" and "gores" his animal and human lovers. Male sexuality, in its pure, unrestrained form, is murderous.

The poem therefore resolves in favor of controlling both male and female sexual energy. Female energy is controlled by traditional patriarchal repression:

> If a boy comes home at dark, with one of the nannies missing,
> or a girl goes roaming at night, they're punished, beaten.

Male sexuality is controlled by making it mechanical, blunting its emotional, yearning aspects.

They make their women pregnant, the peasants, and go on working
just the same. Day or night they wander where they like.

It is because the men treat their own emotional lives *senza rispetto* (the
words Arrowsmith renders, oversimply, "just the same") that they are
immune to the dark forces lurking in external nature; they can wander
"[d]ay or night," and "[t]hey aren't afraid of hoeing by moonlight, or
making a bonfire / of weeds and brush in the dark." And out of their
immunity springs the traditional pastoral victory, tamed nature, landscape given a human face:

> And that's why the ground
> is so beautifully green, and the plowed fields at dawn
> are the color of sunburned faces.

But this victory rests on a rock-bottom conviction that pure sexuality is
monstrous; that "work," sublimation, is good because it distracts our
attention and blunts our energies:

> if you don't make an animal work,
> if you keep him only for stud, he likes to hurt, he kills.

Ending with these lines—rather than, say, with the fields like sunburned
faces—gives the poem the grim honesty so characteristic of Pavese. He
admits the darkness of his, or his culture's, view; admits the cost of the
choices he cannot help approving. (But, as I have suggested above, this
coming to rest on grimness also reflects the "idiom of care" of Pavese's
childhood.)

The more complex masculine economy whereby denigrating women
is a defense against the sense of lack, of suicidal despair, is also in evidence in these poems. Feminist readers—who, for good reason, value the
female-identified Pavese—are often shocked and saddened when they
come on "Ancestors." The misogynist statements in this poem seem as
beyond qualification or excuse as the anti-Semitic ones in Pound:

> The outsider was stuffy,
> tightfisted, cruel, and mean: a woman. . . .

> Oh, we've got our faults, and whims, and skeletons—
> we, the men, the fathers—and one of us killed himself.
> But there's one disgrace we've never known:
> we've never been women, we've never been nobodies.

And yet, so many savagely negative points about these "ancestors" are simply conceded that it is impossible to take the masculinism at face value, either. How can one read the following lines out loud without admitting a tone of appalled irony?

> In our family women don't matter.
> What I mean is, our women stay home
> and make children like me, and keep their mouths shut.
> They just don't matter, and we don't remember them.
> Every woman adds something new to our blood,
> but they kill themselves off with work.

Rightly understood, I think, the poem is both a straight and an ironic —and therefore a tragic—account of the narrow kind of strength Pavese has wanted to hew to, to postpone the fate of the "one" who "killed himself." The poem begins with an utter sense of powerlessness, of inability to connect with the world, as a young man:

> Bewildered by the world, I reached that age
> when I punched the air with my fists and cried to myself.

The male ancestors help him out of his powerlessness partly simply by ratifying it, calling it autonomy. The stories about their lack of obligation to others often verge on masochistic passivity. One of them

> used to read novels in the store—
> people talked about *that*—and when customers came in,
> they'd hear him answer gruffly, no,
> there wasn't any sugar, he was out of Epsom salts,
> he was all out of everything.

Even if this man did "later on . . . hel[p] his partner, who went broke," his edgy behavior throws light on the family misogyny. To "wander . . . with no women" and to be "good at doing nothing" are both forms of self-reserve—avoidance of vulnerability—so deep they fall into the self-destructiveness they are meant to avoid. The Italian phrase that William Arrowsmith translates "we've never been nobodies" in fact emphasizes this self-reserve. It reads *"mai ombre a nessuno* (never anyone's shadow)," bringing us back to Benjamin's theme, the association of preoedipal dependence with being a "woman."

But the vulnerability to women that lies behind such defenses is also vividly recorded in these poems. Benjamin's sense that "desire is the property of the object" is in evidence in "Revelation," where the woman's "deep, probing look . . . imposes / on the boy" his own feelings.

> All the womb's
> sweetness, throbbing with desire, blazed
> from those eyes. The secret blossomed out like pain,
> like blood. Everything went huge and scary, terror seized
> the boy. Sky and trees were shining, a quiet light.

Arrowsmith, as translator, comments on these "eyes"—their maternal implication of inescapable witness and judge, as well as temptress: "Pavese's possessive but unpossessable *she,* whose *eyes*—combining mother, wife, and fury—follow him everywhere, relentless, demanding."[26]

Woman's potential unconcern for the man on whom she has such an effect is a constant danger—a token of inhumanity and superhumanity, of how assuredly she has the "good things" within herself:

> No man yet has left a mark on her.
> Every trace of him disappears, dissolving like a dream,
> like a dream in the light. Nothing else is left. Only she.
>
> .   .   .   .
>
> Nothing changes the smile that hovers on her face,
> shining in things. Decisive, poised, in everything she does;
> but each time seems the first, fresh always, alive,
> in all of every moment.
>
> ("A Memory")

Even the man who has seen such a woman "humbled by passion" will only "pay" more, knowing that her desire is independent of him, and could be enjoyed with someone else.

"Sultry Lands" is a greater, more complex poem about the danger, and the allure, of encountering female sexual agency. As Arrowsmith observes, the title refers to two landscapes, the urban landscape of sexual adventure and the landscape of frustrated male desire, the parched seacoast village where the local youths listen to the "skinny young stranger" talk about Torino.[27] Of the actual local landscape, we get two details: the "pounding and throbbing" of the "huge sea," suggesting the limitless, oceanic nature of longing, and the "desperate row of figs . . . dying of boredom on the reddish rocks." (Figs—in Mediterranean, and other, cultures—are a sexual plant.)

What the "skinny young stranger" sees in Torino is a paradise of liberated, unentangling sexuality—light-years away from the restrictions of Catholic village life. He emphasizes particularly the freedom, the self-reliance of the women. "Every woman works for the dress she wears, / but she suits it to every light."

> Those women are so free they even smoke alone.
> You pick them up at night and leave them in the morning,
> like friends, at the cafe. They're always young.

Because claims on each other are so limited, even "friend"-ship between men and women becomes possible. Yet the idea of female sexual autonomy brings a tone of bemusement, awe, even fear, into the poem. The women are envied, almost, for their capacity to remain the pampered darlings of early childhood: "Nothing is ever refused them," though "they crumple like little girls if it starts to rain." Yet they are also the true adults, the masters of situations men are always overwhelmed and confused by: "they know how to love. They know more than the men." Most dauntingly, they can pass from the terrain of everyday selfhood to the terrain of intimacy, scarcely acknowledging a difference: "Even when they're naked, they talk / as vivaciously as ever."

Is this a vision of paradise, then, or a vision of terror? Of the inadequacy imposed on men by their excessive longing, their distance from the easy intimacy of their prehistoric pasts? The poem ends:

> My eyes are riveted on this skinny young stranger.
> I saw that green country once. I saw it with my own eyes.
> I'll stay up late and smoke, I won't notice the sea.

With these lines, we see that the paradisal vision of unencumbered sexuality ("that green country") is one the speaker has had to give up on, through unspecified bitter experience. Only masculine isolation—"smok[ing]" and perhaps writing—insulates him against the "pounding and throbbing" of a longing now, and perhaps forever, unresolved.

There are a few poems in *Hard Labor* in which a bridge is built across the gap between men and women—but in so tentative and fragile a way as to make the gap all the more salient. In "Two Cigarettes," the speaker is picked up by a prostitute, who asks him for a light. The title refers to an earlier cigarette butt he notices "already lying there on the worn pavement," indicating he is not her first conquest of the evening.

Nonetheless, the woman manages to conjure up a sense of human contact between them, precisely by emphasizing her sharedness, creating a homoerotic bond between him and one of her former lovers, the "sailor" who gave her a "scarf . . . from Rio":

> No, she doesn't see him now. If I come up to her room,
> the woman whispers to me, she'll show me a snapshot of him—
> tanned and curly-headed. He shipped on dirty tramps
> and kept the engines clean. But I'm better-looking.

The other lover's profession becomes—as in the "ships in the night" cliché—a metaphor both for the adventure and the futility of setting sail for another human being.

> That window at the top—the woman points—is ours. But
> it isn't heated. At night, in the wake of the passing liners,
> a few lights shine or only the stars.

(In the Italian, the sense of lack of illumination—implying both domestic warmth and guidance—is more explicit: "*[I] vapori sperduti / hanno pochi fanali* (the lost steamships / have few lights)." The poem is moving or pathetic, depending on one's mood, because both characters are in fact "warm[ed]" by such utterly contingent contact.

The oedipal issues this poem raises—the inevitable sharedness of women, what kind of man they really prefer—become central in "Portrait of the Author." At first glance, the title seems odd indeed. The poem records a dream or a fantasy in which the speaker and a "friend," who "smells" and "has hair from his legs to his face," start to undress in the street. A woman appears in a window; the friend jumps through, and apparently they begin to have sex immediately. Left alone, the speaker reflects:

> I don't smell, I'm not hairy. The cobbles make me cold,
> and women like the feel of my naked back
> because it's so smooth: is there anything women don't like?

It is a marvelous portrait of the predicament of the oedipal son. The qualities that make him less adult—and less animal—leave him more vulnerable to the coldness of the world. But, confusingly, they are not unattractive to women, who also miss the element of likeness in the preoedipal bond. The speaker tries to reduce his friend's success to the story of a "bitch in heat" and a "male dog . . . so wet / he stinks." But the reduction does not quite work; in fact, the strength of the poem may be its inability to keep the dualism, animal father/spiritual son, firmly in place. Is a dog that is "soaked to the skin" the proper object of contempt? or of compassion? Is animal recognition-by-smell a metaphor for more "serious" forms of human rapport? What does it mean to be male? The poem ends, it seems to me, with all the antinomies confused, the speaker sure only of his immature incomprehension:

> At last,
> a kid comes walking around the corner, he's smoking.
> He has legs like me, legs like an eel, curly hair,
> and rough skin. Someday the women will want to undress him,
> they'll sniff him to see if he has a serious smell.
> He walks by, and I stick out my foot. He trips and falls,
> and I ask for a butt. We sit there smoking, not a word.

ONE OF DINNERSTEIN'S most provocative insights—derived, in part, from Simone de Beauvoir—is that because woman provides the earliest holding environment, she is never clearly distinguished from nature, or even the nature of things. Superhuman healing powers are attributed to her, but so is monstrous capriciousness and indifference:

> She is the source of food, warmth, comfort, and entertainment; but the baby, no matter how well it is cared for, suffers some hunger or cold, some belly-aches or alarming sudden movements or unpleasant bursts of noise, some loneliness or boredom; and how is it to know that she is not the source of these things too? . . . Her body is the first important piece of the physical world that we encounter, and the events for which she seems responsible the first instances of fate. Hence Mother Nature, with her hurricane daughters Alice, Betty, Clara, Debbie, Edna. Hence that fickle female Lady Luck.[28]

Hence, too, we—women as well as men—will never get the quality of female subjectivity quite right, making it at once too great and too small. "Female sentience, for this reason, carries permanently for most of us the atmosphere of that unbounded, shadowy presence toward which all our needs were originally directed."[29] Hence man will use woman, in his imagination, as "intermediary between his conscious self and the natural surround." "A ship, a city, any entity that we half-seriously personify, is called 'she.' 'She' designates the borderline between the inanimate and the conscious."[30] In poetry, of course, this "she" is called the Muse: men imagine female consciousness as a way of slipping past their own rational boundaries, being on more intimate terms with the universe.

No reader immersed in Pavese will fail to notice how deeply his love of his early landscapes is interfused with the love of woman.[31] How often woman appears as the vehicle for a more intimate relation to landscape; or conversely, is lovable because she seems to embody a particular locality. The goddess in the Endymion dialogue is divine precisely *because* she is "like a girl from your own village."[32] The poem "Encounter" describes the genesis of this Muse figure, this intermediary:

> These hard hills which made my body
> and whose many memories still shake it so, have revealed the miracle—
> this *she* who does not know I live her and cannot understand her.
>
> I encountered her one evening, a brighter patch of scrub
> under the flickering starlight, in the summer haze.
> The smell of these hills was all around me, everywhere,
> a smell deeper than shadow, and suddenly I heard a sound.
> as though it came from these hills, a voice at once purer
> and harsher, the voice of things past.

Her function as a dissociated part of the poet's imagination seems unexpectedly clear, in his conscious understanding: "I live her." But perhaps that very fact, combined with the distance of landscape itself, accounts for her elusiveness: "always her reality / slips through my fingers and carries her far away." Pavese also seems clear—as clear as Dinnerstein herself—on the relation of this experience to early childhood, its immediacy and its disappointments. The voice is "at once purer / and harsher"; "a voice of things past," being a projection of the young self, as well as of the mother.

Pavese understands, finally, that he has invented this woman as a means of access to the totality, the "ground," of his subject matter; and that, in spite of this fact, she retains the otherness of that ground.

> I created her from the ground of everything
> I love the most, and I cannot understand her.

And yet, nevertheless, she is an embodiment of "firm purpose." Like Dinnerstein's mother, that "being so peculiarly needed to confirm other people's worth, power, significance," it is she, the creation, who permits his confidence as creator.[33]

That the "shadowy" quality of "female sentience" is, in fact, the creative state is made clear by the Endymion dialogue's extraordinary reinterpretation of the perpetual sleep into which the goddess casts him:

> Your sleep is infinite with the cries and the voices of things, it is full of earth and sky and day following day. . . . The loneliness, the wild places of the earth are yours. Love them as she loves them.[34]

This "sleep," this middle ground between consciousness and unconsciousness, becomes "infinite"—has the quality of inner space—because it does not merely describe but "is full of" the objects of nature. Pavese will reuse essentially the same words to describe the inarticulate sentience of the heroine of "Death and the Earth": "you're full of the voices of earth."

But the association of woman with nature also has, as Dinnerstein observes, a much darker side. "People under the most diverse cultural conditions have felt an opposition, an antagonism, between what is humanly noble, durable, strenuous, and the insistent rule of flesh, flesh which is going to die and which even when death is remote makes humbling demands: we must feed it, we must let it sleep, we must get rid of its smelly wastes." Woman, the "carnal scapegoat-idol" in whose presence "the child first discovers the mystical joys and the humiliating constraints" of the flesh, comes to represent that principle exclusively; while man represents the individualistic impulse to transcend, to become the pure consciousness that is considered fully human.[35]

We have already witnessed this process in our reading of "The Goat God." From the discovery of the "green mysteries" of nature, that poem slides immediately to nature's worse implications—illness, vulnerability, the possibility of bodily distortion:

> Certain plants
> are bad for the she-goat: her paunch begins to swell
> and she has to run it off.

Pregnancy is then associated with all of these bad things; and the discovery, or rediscovery, of female physicality ("girls are hairy down there") becomes not only loathsome in itself, but a vehicle for disowning the boys' unease with their own emergent sexuality—leading, thus, to the sadistic fantasy of the "wild goat."

But the final dark implication of Dinnerstein's insight is the association of woman with death. The figure who presided over our first helplessness before materiality—hunger, sleepiness, excrement—will triumph in our last. The not-yet-selfhood we emerged from will become the nonselfhood we dissolve back into: "womb" and "tomb."[36]

All of these implications are, I think, consciously acknowledged and confronted in Pavese's late masterpieces, the mythological *Dialogues with Leuco*—the book Pavese had at his bedside when he killed himself—and the late love poems collected under the title *Verra la morte e avra i tuoi occhi*, which I have rendered "Death Will Come and Look at Me with Your Eyes."

The *Dialogues* concern themselves, on the surface, with the coming of the Olympian gods and the overthrow of earlier nature-religions; but this can easily be read as the coming of the patriarchal order and the end of the preoedipal bond. In the first dialogue, "The Cloud," the past is envisioned as a lost paradise, a fluid oneness between man and a feminized nature. "You can no longer mate with us, the nymphs of the springs and the mountains, with the daughters of the wind, the goddesses of the earth," the Cloud tells Ixion. Now "a law" has arrived, announcing that those who continue to desire such matings will end up doing "something terrible." With this "law" comes the distance of self-consciousness. Things lose their simple existence, in taking on a moral meaning: "You're one of us, Ixion. What you are is what you do, and that is all. But for them, the immortals, everything you do has a meaning that lingers. . . . What you achieve or don't achieve, what you say, what you search for—all these things gladden or displease them."[37] And with the gods' displeasure, a new realm is created, that of "monsters" —chiefly the children of the old, now incestuous, matings.

It is a complex fable, with many dimensions—anthropological, epistemological, as well as psychoanalytic. But in "The Guest," it is retold from the point of view of the arrived patriarchal order. Heracles comes to a remote country, where human sacrifice is still practiced—scattering the victim's dismembered body over the fields, to ensure fertility. He learns that he himself is the intended victim. Here, the old unity becomes the devouring mother, who reminds us of our tie to the earth, and—as in Dinnerstein—because she gives life, must also be the source of death. The king, Lityerses, explains: "Above this field there are no gods. There is only the earth, the Mother, the Cave. She's always waiting, and she comes to life when the blood streams down to her. . . . The blood the Mother has given us we give back to her in our sweat and death and dung." Heracles, in reply, urges the vision of the (male) self transcending nature. The Olympian gods are not one with things; they "rule" them, "as a shepherd keeps his flock or a master governs his servants." Their distance is again associated with the distance of self-consciousness: "They live apart . . . like the thoughts you see in a man's eye when he speaks to you." For them, "the cave," the womb-grave, has become the underworld, Hell, the repressed unconscious, down to which they drive "the monsters" and "men like you who feed the earth with blood." To this, Lityerses rather shrewdly replies that the gods are practicing their own form of human sacrifice—in Freudian terms, that the superego is releasing against the id the aggressions that themselves come from the id. But Heracles ignores this and challenges the king to a mowing contest. "No need to say who won," says Pavese's sardonic note.[38]

Perhaps the darkest line in this dark dialogue is "she comes to life when the blood streams down to her." Here, female sexual arousal seems to be equated with—to require—the sacrificial death of the male, as if sperm were, literally, blood. Many of the fears Dinnerstein discusses—fear of the powerfulness of female sexual initiative; fear of the loss of the precariously isolated self in the preoedipal reexperiencing of sexual union—come together under the rubric of myth. These fears, as Dinnerstein in fact notes, make a powerful explanation for exactly the kind of sexual difficulty Pavese apparently suffered from— the difficulty in maintaining an erection after penetration, the impulse to ejaculate prematurely.[39] They also contribute to the fantasy that only a maleness as dark and demonic as the father's could stand up to, and satisfy, the mother's demandingness.

But the association of woman with death is perhaps clearest, and most poignant, in the dialogue "The Mother." Pavese's headnote tells the story: "Meleager's life was linked to a brand which his mother Althaea drew from the fire when he was born. She was a woman of strong mind, and when Meleager killed his maternal uncle in a fight over the boarskin, she flew into a rage, thrust the brand back into the fire, and let it burn."[40] It is a story that might be understood on many levels. One is the fear that the mother—either as the engulfing presence of infancy or as the collaborator of the oedipal father—does not really want the son to grow up. But, beyond that, it seems that the mother, as in Dinnerstein, because she is responsible for, has once completely contained, the man's life, must be responsible also for his death. When Meleager asks, "Has anyone else had my fate?" Hermes, the guide of the dead, answers, "Everyone," the reason being that "Everyone of them had a mother." "Your lives are forever contained in the burning brand, and your mother draws you from the fire, and you live half blazing. The passion of which you die is your mother's passion, smoldering on in you. What are you but her flesh and blood?"[41] The watching "eyes" of the mother (already noted in the passage quoted earlier) compound the sense that the son exists only in and through her presence and therefore is already doomed.

The dialogue particularly emphasize Pavese's conviction that all the women in a man's life are one woman, and, therefore, that all are fatal. The final illusion Hermes must take from Meleager is that "the young she"—the warrior-maiden Atalanta—was an avenue of escape, because she did not "kn[ow] anything about those eyes." "She didn't know, Meleager," Hermes replies, "She was those eyes"; and offers in evidence the following speech: "'Son of Althaea,' she said, 'the boarskin will lie on our marriage-bed. It will be like your blood-price—yours and mine.' And she smiled, as though asking for forgiveness."[42] It is impossible, Atalanta suggests, to separate their "marriage-bed" from the heroic accomplishment, the oedipal defiance, that will kill him. Easy enough to understand, in Freudian terms. But beyond that, there is an implication that she wills his death, as a kind of revenge for his intrusion on her, her loss of virginity: the "price of . . . [her blood]" (of the hymen) must be "the price of [his]." (This is the literal meaning of the last sentence of her speech, in the Italian: *"Sara come il prezzo del tuo sangue—e del mio."*) The woman gives her own life to the man, maternally or sexually, only on condition of taking back his. We are back, in a way, to the terrible devouring or castrating premises of the Heracles dialogue.

The ambiguous and rather terrifying achievement of Pavese's late love poems is to present this whole complex of feelings and unconscious terrors as it is caught up in his relations with a living person—the sense of doom, and yet, as in the Endymion dialogue, the sense of understanding and likeness. These poems differ drastically, even in style, from those of *Hard Labor* a decade earlier. Their short, stark lines, iconographic imagery, and operatic repetitions seem to pare the world down to the insistences of obsessive feeling. The woman in "Death and the Earth" is at first, like the imaginary woman of "An Encounter," a muse-figure, loved as the distillation of her seacoast landscape. In the opening lines, she emerges from the sea (and from the abyss of male longing that, as in "Sultry Lands," it perhaps represents) like Botticelli's Venus:

> Red earth, black earth—
> you come from the sea
> with its parched green.[43]

The paradox of the sea's "parched green"—*riarso*, implying saltiness, but also carrying the sense of "burned"—points to the double nature of all Pavese's women: they are most frustrating where most connected to the primal merging. And so the woman is "recollection," as well as an earth-spirit, the landscape's

> harsh and sweetest
> word, whose ancientness
> shows in the blood
> pressing up in your eyes.

And, inescapably, she also embodies the darker sides of Mother Nature. It is her silence, her moodiness, her unresponsiveness to the speaker's feelings, that make her like the "poor land" she comes from. A diary entry, from the same month as most of these poems, shows how ready Pavese was to archetypalize this particular woman, and how little he expected of her humanly: "Astarte-Aphrodite-Melita is still sleeping. She will wake in a bad humor."[44] In the poems, she seems imprisoned in her own suffering, in a way that arouses both frustration and compassion:

> When you seem to wake up
> you go on being a sadness.

Like Mother Nature, she is incapable of being "reache[d]" by any other creature's "word," and therefore incapable of constancy:

Like the sea you pick up,
examine, then throw away
everything.

"You cannot speak in words," the poems keep insisting, both because of this likeness to the recessiveness of nature, and because of her connection to the unverbalized sufferings of poverty and infancy. One poem says,

It's a poor land—your low
forehead knows all that.
That, too, goes into the wine.

Another poem observes,

Yet you're full of the voices
of earth—the shock of a bucket
far down a well, fire singing,
the thud of an apple falling,
the resigned words that linger
echoing around thresholds,
a child's first cry—the things
that cannot pass away.
As you can't change. Too dark.

"Death and the Earth" was written at more or less the same time as *Dialogues with Leuco,* and its ambiguous triumph is to merge the speaker's frustration at this particular woman's unreachableness, and her obvious helplessness before it, with that book's darkest anthropological meanings. From the first line, her reserve is associated with materiality: "Red earth, black earth." Her face is "sculpted from stone," her blood "hard earth." She is Aphrodite, born from the sea, and the other mother-goddesses of the diary entry, who once presided over the sacrifice of young men. Her one ecstatic moment of self-discovery, when "A burning silence / consumes the plain," is associated with the fires of Midsummer Eve, which, as the dialogue "The Bonfires" tells us, once held a living victim. Her sexuality, one poem seems to suggest, would give "peace" only to the "countryman" strong enough, or brutalized enough, to accept its deathly implication:

> The country is fatigue,
> the country is sadness.
>
> . . . .
>
> You are the great fatigue,
> and the night deep
> enough to give it peace.

She is a revenant, like Atalanta, both of the preoedipal mother and of prehistory,

> some ancient, savage thing
> that the heart long ago
> knew and closed on, trembling.

And so, in the harrowing, climactic poem "Each time, you come from the sea," she becomes his "enemy"—and, simultaneously, all of his true beloveds—because she embodies the resistance of fate to his will, but also (a crucial discovery for Pavese's literary and human growth) because she mirrors his own inner sense of emptiness.

> We will fight again,
> we'll be fighting forever
> because, side by side, we seek
> the sleep of death,
> and have the same hoarse voice,
> the low, savage forehead,
> and the same poor sky.
>
> . . . .
>
> If either of us surrendered,
> the long night that followed
> would not be peace, or truce,
> or a true death.
> You wouldn't be there.

Thus, in its terrible way—addressing a "you" who is now an aspect of the poet's own need, at least as much as she is a real person—the poem earns the anthropologically laden statement with which the last section begins and ends: "You are the earth and death."

And yet, the final drift of the poem is curiously compassionate—as even the passage from "Each time, you come from the sea" will suggest. As with his mother years before, he has to be the rescuer as well as the victim. If some poems seem to complain that "You cannot speak in words," or that her sadness renders her indifferent to the feelings of others, elsewhere it is he who must reassure her that her isolation need not be permanent. She can recover the experiences of her childhood— "the clouds / and the canebrake"—in both their beautiful and their frightening aspects. When this happens, "You will recover words"— though perhaps, the poem cannot help darkly qualifying, only "beyond this brief life."

And this, I think, is Pavese's greatness: that he can never quite forget that women are vulnerable subjectivities, like himself, even as he dramatizes all the male reasons for such forgetting. His despair, finally, is not over what women are, or even what men must imagine them to be, but over how ultimate, and therefore how hopeless, are the longings both sexes bring to focus in love. In psychoanalytic terms, we would call these longings "oceanic" or "preoedipal"; but it may be best to let Pavese's sense that they are metaphysical speak for itself. In either case, the decisive turn away from misogyny seems to me to begin in the dialogue between Oedipus and Tiresias, called "The Blind." Tiresias retells the story of his double sex-change as a story about overcoming "sexual disgust":

> I felt that my spirit, my sanctity as a priest, my character, were degraded by sex. When I saw those two snakes taking their pleasure, making love on the moss, I couldn't suppress my disgust. . . . Shortly afterwards I became a woman. . . . From man to woman, and vice versa (seven years later I saw the two serpents again), what I refused to accept with my spirit was done to me by violence or lust, and I, proud man or humbled woman, let myself go as a woman and was passive as a man.[45]

He concludes, "Nothing is vile, except to the gods."

Like Lityerses, Tiresias believes there is "no god" above "the rock." But what he means by "the rock" is no longer a demonized matriarch, a Nature whose indifference to us as individuals is interpreted as sadistic female lust. Rather it is simply our inability to see beyond the conditions of our being, as the Olympian gods would wish to, through "names." Sex is "the rock" because it "include[s]" more than the gods —"Life and death are in it"—and because it cannot be mastered:

> Sex is ambiguous and always equivocal. It is an end that seems an everything. Man succeeds in incarnating it, in living inside it, like

a good swimmer in the water; but meanwhile he has grown old, he has reached the rock.

From all this, Tiresias draws a terrible but potentially healing lesson:

> In the end one idea, one illusion, remains: that the other sex is satisfied. Well, don't believe it. For all of us it is wasted effort. I know.[46]

Ironically enough, it is Oedipus—the proud Oedipus of the beginning of the play—who refuses to accept this lesson, insisting that a "healthy man" will simply never feel disgust. "For me in my life, there is nothing ambiguous or wasted."

Pavese's own effort to accommodate Tiresias's wisdom comes in his final sequence, "Death Will Come and Look at Me with Your Eyes." These poems record his sudden reawakening to hope, after two years of "Olympian" withdrawal, in the relationship with Constance Dowling, and its equally sudden disintegration. The sequence is agonized in the contradictions it tries to hold together. The courtly love dimension is there—the Muse, the mother bearing the inner good things, the sense that "things / came to life under your eyes." But so is the dimension of almost immediate fear and betrayal. Because Constance embodies so much for him—

> Limpid water and first
> shoot breaking in the earth
> in germinating silence

—her independent subjectivity is at once hard to hold in focus and a constant threat. "[Y]ou are blood and breath and you live / on this earth," he reminds himself; and then, later in the same poem,

> when you were a child you played
> under a different sky,
> and your eyes have kept
> its silence: a cloud
> pouring sudden as water
> from the blank background.[47]

But, of course, the "sudden" "silence" embodies the terror, for him, of admitting her subjectivity, and its unknown history. The diary says, "She is a child, an unspoiled child. Yet she is herself—terrifying."[48]

One aspect of Constance's unmanageable subjectivity is the sexual demand Pavese never believed he could fulfill. Being "earth" in this sense, she is always on the edge of becoming "earth" in the other sense, the terrible mother demanding blood sacrifice:

> You are the root's
> ferocity; you
> are the earth, waiting.

And so the sequence begins and ends with the night Pavese told Lajolo about so bitterly, the night when he believed he had been betrayed: "'She fled at night from my bed at the hotel in Rome and she went to bed with another, with that actor you know. Like the other woman, even worse.'"[49] "In the morning you always come back" is the title of the opening poem. But even these returns cannot be rejected, because, like the mother's in infancy, they bring life itself:

> The houses are submerged
> in the dawn wind and in
> your footfall, your light breath.
> The city shivers, the stones
> grow fragrant.
> You are life, are the awakening.

So the poems move in a circle of masochistic idealization and repressed rage. But beyond this, even, there is the element of helpless and hopeless identification. "The night you slept," one poem is titled, with the definite article, as if her sleeping in his presence, rather than her leaving and betraying him, were a once-only occurrence. Yet his participation in her night-side becomes as painful as his exclusion from it has been. For her grief, whatever motivates her darker behavior, becomes the entire night-landscape of potential nihilism:

> And the night too resembles you,
> the remote night that grieves
> speechlessly, in the unreachable heart,
> and the stars pass, exhausted.

"Shipwrecked" within her, in his identification, he is all the more alone, because he cannot reach or affect her. "One cheek touches another," but "it's a brief shiver." Finally she seems to him dead, as the despairing mother must once have seemed (perhaps that is one more reason her cruelties can never be met with appropriate self-protectiveness). And with her, the world itself dies:

> You are laid out under the whole night
> like a closed, dead horizon.

All of these themes are brought together in the title poem—often read as Pavese's literary suicide note, though in fact his death came several months later, after yet another attempt to recover through love. The "death" the poem is talking about, the opening lines make clear, is not just the final death, but the daily one of self-hatred, self-limitation, "guilt," "habit," lack of the inner good things. But then, in the most amazing movement in the whole sequence, the poem assigns this sense of lack to the woman's own subjectivity, not just to her effect on the speaker:

>   Your eyes
> will be empty words,
> a suppressed cry, a silence—
> the way you see them each morning
> when you lean toward yourself alone
> in the mirror.
>   O dearest hope,
> on that day we too will know
> that you were life, and you were nothingness.

Female narcissism here ceases to be—as it is for so many men, even perhaps for Freud—the sign of self-sufficiency, assured possession of inner value. Rather, as Tiresias might wish, it becomes the indicator of a search, an inability to express pain, a fundamental emptiness exactly akin to the poet's own. The woman is no longer one with her life-giving glamour; rather, as the "you" shifts from her to the *cara speranza,* she and the poet seem to stand aside in bewildered contemplation of this quality that eludes them both, that is "life" but also "nothingness."

This then is the sense—not merely a reproachful, or masochistic, one—in which "Death will come and look at me with your eyes." It is an ultimate, but, as with Tiresias, a partly healing exposure of the vanity of hope. But it is more than this, too, as self-destruction, from the unconscious point of view, strives to restore the lost oneness of infancy.

Then the habit will be given up,
we will see in the mirror
the dead face reemerging,
the sealed lips will have their voice.

In the apocalyptic moment, the "dead face"—the lost, perhaps, as in Jarrell, the murdered mother—emerges from the mirror; that is to say, again becomes one with the self. The "ridiculous habit," the "empty" insufficiency, drop away. Preoedipal need, preoedipal trauma—whatever was "sealed" up inside Pavese and his inarticulate heroines—at last finds a "voice." But the price is the eternal silence of the individuated self:

And we, the silenced, go down into the abyss.

Questions of Autonomy
Two European Novels

IT IS COMMONLY observed that some human beings are preponderantly attached to the security of monogamy, while others fear the constraint on their freedom, even their conception of authentic selfhood. These preferences tend to be gender-typed, even stereotyped. Dorothy Dinnerstein takes one of her chapter titles from the old rhyme,

> Higamous hogamous, woman's monogamous.
> Hogamous higamous, man is polygamous.

Dinnerstein understands this proverb in terms of a constraint on woman's sexual agency: "a certain rule . . . first, that men act more sexually possessive than women, and second, that women act less free than men to seek 'selfish' sexual pleasure."[1] She offers this preoedipal explanation for both sexes' apparent consent to this "asymmetry":

> To possess a woman . . . is under present conditions every child's early wish. What happens to this wish—which survives throughout life in what used to be called the heart—depends on whether its original object is later reincarnated partially inside, or primarily outside, one's own skin. . . . [The man's] bodily presence cannot in itself call up the atmosphere of infancy for [the woman] in these respects, as literally as hers can call it up for him. In the sense and to the extent that this is the case, his physical infidelity cannot revive the grief of infancy for her so graphically as hers can for him.[2]

Moreover, as we have seen, the woman may not lose her sense of an internal "good object" along with the loss of the beloved, as the man is likely to.

But, of course, female jealousy is often no less virulent, female despair no less annihilating, than male. Dinnerstein ignores the other possible interpretation of the proverb: that, in a patriarchal order, women may *prefer* monogamy for strong economic and social reasons, and, for those reasons, fear and try to control the venturesomeness permitted to men.

More recently, family-systems theory has suggested that in every human being there is "an interplay between two counterbalancing life forces —*individuality* and *togetherness.*"[3] Maggie Scarf, in *Intimate Partners,* acknowledges the gender-typing of these polarized forces, but suggests that it is, at some level, illusory:

> Usually, one spouse (often the wife) experiences herself as wanting more warmth, intimacy, closeness—and having few needs for autonomy and independence. The other spouse (most commonly the husband) experiences himself as always needing more personal space and emotional distance—and no vulnerabilities or need for closeness in relation to the partner. Neither mate, in such a situation, has any conscious awareness that the seemingly irreconcilable wishes and needs to be "an independent self" and "be in a close relationship" *exist inside their individual heads.* The worst kind of confusion, which is the confusion of the self and the other, is what results.[4]

What really happens, Scarf suggests, is that, by the Kleinian concept of "projective identification," each partner takes on the role of embodying one of these principles, for both. "Projective identification has to do with one person—say me—seeing my own denied and suppressed wishes, needs, emotions, etc., in my intimate partner and not experiencing those wishes and feelings as . . . coming from within my own self."

Family systems theory goes on to argue that relationships vary widely in the level of "differentiation" both parties agree on, or experience together. Highly differentiated relationships—where both parties have a strong sense of individuality but experience both needs as existing within both people—are more "flexible," Kerr and Bowen say in *Family Evaluation,* because the partners "are not easily threatened by one another." But "as differentiation decreases, individuality is less well developed, togetherness needs are stronger, emotional reactivity is more intense and more easily triggered, and subjectively based attitudes are more influential."[5] This does not mean, it must be emphasized, that both parties consistently behave in a more "togetherness"-oriented way, in less differentiated relationships. Their conflicts may be more acute, because they define themselves in reaction against each other. Simply acting on one's own, without malice but also without guilt, is what is forbidden. "The 'rugged individualist' operates as much in reaction to others as the compliant person. . . . He has trouble being an 'individual' *without permanently disrupting his relationships with others.*"[6]

Family-systems thinking sees neurotic symptoms (and even apparently physical ones, like certain illnesses) as arising not intrapsychically, or even, causally, in terms of the individual's personal history, but in a kind of fluid exchange, or unconscious contract, with other family members. Yet, in a certain sense, there are more and less "differentiated" individuals, as well as families, if only because individuals learn the "right" level of differentiation in their family of origin and will tend unconsciously to seek a partner at more or less the same level. Familial undifferentiation may show itself in many forms: literal difficulty in leaving the parental fold; repetition of familial career choices, opinions, relationship patterns; incapacitating symptoms; or a purely reactive reversal of parental choices—say, becoming a successful entrepreneur because the family has despised money, and valued only cultural activity.

I intend this chapter as a sort of laboratory test case for the application of family-systems categories in literary criticism. This is not a drastic departure from the methods I have used up to this point; with its emphasis on issues of separation and merging and on the Kleinean concept of projective identification, family systems is really more an extension of object relations than either therapeutic community would wholly acknowledge. In applying family-systems categories, my aim is a subtler understanding of the interpersonal, as well as intrapsychic, meaning of the pain surrounding issues of individuation and oneness that has concerned us throughout.

I have chosen, for this test case, two celebrated European novels about troubled couples. Both involve gender issues; but most contemporary criticism would conceive of these very differently than I intend to. Andre Gide's *The Immoralist* is generally read either as a novel about Nietzschean individualism or about the discovery (or the denial) of homosexuality.[7] Milan Kundera's *The Unbearable Lightness of Being* has been seen as overly male, even misogynist, in its perspectives. I shall argue that both books are at their deepest level parables about individuation and togetherness and the extreme difficulty of reconciling the two principles. They are also books about identification—projective or otherwise—across gender lines.

ONE COULD hardly find a clearer case of familial undifferentiation than is set forth in the opening pages of *The Immoralist*. Brought up by his scholar father after his mother's early death, Michel is "so intensively forced" that, before he is twenty, he knows Latin, Greek, Hebrew, Sanskrit, Persian, and Arabic. He publishes his first scholarly work under his father's name, and "nothing [the father] had written ever brought him so much praise."[8] He marries, too, "without being in love, largely in order to please my father, who, as he lay dying, felt anxious at leaving me alone" (8). At his wedding, the few feelings he has are borrowed: "I felt that others were moved, and that in itself was enough to move me" (7).

On his honeymoon, however, Michel develops tuberculosis. Critics emphasizing the sexual impasse have even suggested that "Michel's disease . . . symbolizes his homosexuality," because "it is secret and rather shameful."[9] Family-systems theory would see it very differently, presuming an "interplay"—though not necessarily an exclusive causative link—"between emotional process and physical illness."[10] Kerr and Bowen write, "The lower the level of differentiation of self, the more likely an event . . . would disturb a system to the extent that serious symptoms develop." They give as an example a woman who developed breast cancer after a painful divorce, was free of the disease for nine years, then suffered a metastasis as soon as she ventured on a second marriage. The triggering event may be either "the addition of something new that has to be dealt with or the loss of something old that was relied on."[11] Michel has suffered both, losing his father just before "something new"—the daily presence of Marceline—"ha[d] to be dealt with." Given his "lo[w] level of differentiation," his illness could be taken as a predictable consequence. (Indeed, family-systems thinking would probably understand the fact that either Michel or Marceline is seriously ill through most of the book as a pattern between them, a trading-off of anxiety, rather than as either a purely physical process or, as Michel fears, a guilty contamination of one by the other.)[12]

Michel's convalescence entails the discovery of a "true self," in Winnicott's sense: "that authentic creature, 'the old Adam,' whom . . .

everything about me—books, masters, parents, and I myself—had begun by attempting to suppress" (43). He compares himself to a "palimpsest," "a very ancient and infinitely more precious text" hidden under "recent writing." He loses interest in his scholarly work, which seems to savor too much of the dead past, "to have a mere accidental and conventional connection with myself" (42). He rediscovers his senses, and the capacity to live in them, without thinking or reading, in a kind of meditative stillness. He finds he can enjoy being alone.

The role homosexuality plays in Michel's new-found authenticity is clear to the reader long before it is clear to Michel himself—if, indeed, it ever becomes fully clear to him. It is intimately associated with Michel's search for a perfectly strong, individuated self. The crystallizing moment comes when Michel "fall[s] in love" with Bachir's "health," contrasting the "brilliant flow of blood" from the Arab boy's cut with his own "almost black . . . horrible" tubercular hemorrhage (21–23). (In Freudian terms, Michel's homosexuality would seem to fit what Kaja Silverman calls the "Leonardo model"—falling in love with an ideal image of oneself at the age of puberty, before the self's full potential has been thwarted or lost.)[13]

And yet, it is surely a strength of the book that Marceline is not, in the first half at any rate, the enemy of Michel's new-found vitality. On the boat to Africa, reflecting that he has never had a long holiday in his life, he remembers the "dances . . . laughter . . . songs" of a short vacation in Spain, after his mother died. Immediately, he notices that Marceline is "very pretty" and that she has "a real and individual life of her own" (11–12). His desire for her, and his alertness to her feelings, grow together—though fitfully and spasmodically—all through his recovery, until, on their return journey, at Sorrento, they finally make love, in "a flashing moment that caught and mingled our souls in its laughter" (53).

The initial difficulties between Michel and Marceline seem more centered around separateness than around sexuality. He resents her care, her constant awareness of him, even as he needs it: "if I had got up, she would have followed me; if I had taken off my shawl, she would have wanted to carry it; if I had put it on again, she would have said, 'Are you cold?'" (28–29). (His fear of engulfment also shows itself when, though he accepts all of her physical ministrations, he will not let her pray for him.) At the same time, he is angry with her if the care is insufficient, even when it is plainly not her fault, as when the hotel serves up an "uneatable hash" (24).

Not surprisingly, the Arab boys become a focal point for Michel's counterbalancing guilt over the slightest divergence from Marceline. He doesn't "dare" to talk to them in front of her, because "I saw that she had her favorites; I, in spite of myself, but deliberately, took more interest in the others." He is "afraid" to invite one of his new acquaintances in, "not knowing what Marceline would say" (30); then gets angry when he finds she has invited one of her favorites, without any such qualms, in his absence. These episodes have a clearer and clearer sexual meaning as the book goes on; but they are also precisely the kinds of anxiety and resentment over independent initiative that family-systems theory would predict in overidentified couples.

Also predictably, perhaps, Michel's positive reversions toward Marceline always carry him to the extreme of total oneness. The sentence "I spent almost every minute of the day in her company" (60) recurs several times in the course of the book. When she suffers a phlebitis attack, after her miscarriage, he has a "kind of physical sympathy which . . . made me . . . feel the fearful throbbing of her heart in my own breast" (100). But as soon as he acknowledges her dependence on him at all—acknowledges, even, that she might not be as satisfied as he is with their "wandering life"—he becomes overwhelmingly guilty and "anxious," exaggerating his own misconduct toward her, seeing her as "sad and pale," foredoomed: "Shall I in my turn have to nurse you, fear for you, Marceline?" (54). And then, having identified a dependent Marceline with the "weakness" he fears in himself, Michel has a further reason to impose distance—projected self-disgust, fear of contagion. When Marceline catches his tuberculosis, she is "marked," "stained," "a thing that had been spoiled" (100). Neither in nurturing her, nor in wandering off on his own, can Michel find an emotionally safe position; and so the circle goes round.

The impossibility of choosing between "individuality" and "togetherness" is brilliantly incarnated in the book's oscillation between two symbolic landscapes, North Africa and Normandy. The desert, where Michel recuperates, is the landscape of autonomy. It is a place of scarcity, of wide vistas, where the few things that grow do so in solitude and by great effort. Arab customs serve to associate it with male domination and with homosexuality. (Though the association of deserts with homosexuality also goes back, in Western tradition, to Canto XV of the *Inferno*. Perhaps, if water is a symbol of fertility and the feminine, its scarcity, and the indirect ways of gaining access to it, are a sufficient explanation.) In his preface, Gide applies the paradox of fertile infertility to the book itself, seen as a paean to "immoralism": "a fruit filled with bitter ashes, like those colocinths of the desert that grow in a parched and burning soil. All they can offer to your thirst is a still more cruel fierceness—yet lying on the golden sand they are not without a beauty of their own" (vii).

The landscape of the feminine, and of interdependence, is La Moriniere in Normandy. It is here that Marceline announces that she is pregnant; it is here that Michel, for the only time, recovers vivid memories of his dead mother. Here, too, he briefly believes in civilization as a "harmony" between "the teeming fecundity of nature and the wise effort of man" (61)—in connection to the feminine as a fitting arena for independent male action.

But above all, La Moriniere is a landscape of wetness and enclosure, "the shadiest, wettest country I know," a land with "no horizon," where "in every hollow there is water" (59). Metaphors of liquidity run through the pages describing it. Michel's memories wait "to close over and submerge me"; "each hour passed with a smoother flow"; "everything . . . melted and mingled into a state of changeless ease" (60). There is no Lawrencean rhetoric of ugliness or decay about this womblike enclosure; but Lawrence's Birkin would understand well enough why Michel cannot rest in it, but must begin the long trek back to the opposing principle. And why it is only at Sorrento, the precise midpoint—geographically, botanically, climatically—between Normandy and the desert, that Michel is capable of physical heterosexual love.

As the book progresses, Michel's alienation from Marceline finds its justification in Nietzschean—but, really, traditionally masculinist—ideology: the belief that women are too concerned with security, too much on the side of civilization, and therefore undermining to male venturesomeness. Michel decides that the Arab children Marceline prefers are "weakly, sickly, and too well behaved" (37). He is convinced, on little evidence, that she will disapprove of his "renascent life" and that he must "dissemble" around her (50).

At this point, Gide, in family-systems terms, triangulates.[14] He brings in a new character, Menalque, to fortify the masculinist side of Michel and drive a wedge between him and Marceline. A world-famous explorer and diplomat, but of "a certain reputation" (89)—implicitly homosexual—Menalque is the incarnation of male autonomy. He refuses to be tied down by property, always speaks his mind, and insists that "I don't like looking backwards and I leave my past behind me as the bird leaves his shade to fly away" (96). He and Marceline dislike each other from the start; and he makes a campaign of persuading Michel that his "calm happiness" and his journey of self-discovery are incompatible.

The conundrum of Michel's relationship with Menalque is that whereas Menalque purports to speak for pure individualism, in human terms he manipulates Michel's lack of differentiation far more skillfully than Marceline ever does, or wishes to. From the beginning, he creates situations in which any show of loyalty to Marceline reads as a betrayal both of Menalque himself and of Michel's true freedom. He prevents Michel from disagreeing with him by the simple expedient of refusing to speak with him further, if Michel tries. He places such a solemn insistence on the importance of Michel's joining him for an all-night "vigil" before his departure, that Michel goes, even though Marceline, who is eight months pregnant, has become seriously ill in the meantime. Michel pleads, not, as individualism might suggest, that he simply wants to go, but "the gravity of my promise" (93). The consequences are as punitive as the superego could wish: Marceline goes into premature labor during the night, the child dies, and no one thinks to summon Michel back from Menalque's hotel room.

This brings us to the extreme—but bizarrely split, bizarrely cooperative—punitiveness of the book's conclusion. But first, we need to look back at a curious motif that sums up the ambiguous relation between Michel's brand of self-assertiveness and true personal integrity: the motif of stealing from oneself. It occurs twice, the first time in North Africa, where Michel finds himself watching an Arab boy steal Marceline's scissors and makes no attempt to interfere, and indeed feels "joy" (38). In the second instance, at La Moriniere, Michel joins a band of young poachers setting snares on his own property—and is forced to sell out and leave when his loyal overseer's son discovers the truth.

On one level, I suspect—*pace* Queer Theory—the motif reflects a belief, still powerful though probably unconscious in Gide, that to be homosexual is to destroy one's own masculinity, at the same time that one affirms it. But we need not linger over this interpretation; for, simply in terms of individuation, the episodes perfectly define the quandary Michel is in. What he is stealing from, one might argue, is his patriarchal "false self"—his role of property owner, heir, good son, good husband. Yet this merely rebellious act brings no benefit to his true self—a point that is grimly brought home when he must both pay a reward for the confiscation of the snares and pay the thieves to replace them.

On another level still, Michel is committing a Kleinean, envious aggression against the maternal. Moktir's theft, after all, is not from him; it is from Marceline. And it is committed by the only one of her proteges Michel likes—the one who, like Michel, becomes a bad boy and betrays her trust.[15] In Normandy, the theme is still there, though indirectly, since the land has come to represent the maternal. Michel refuses his proper relation to it, of benevolent master and cultivator, and instead enjoys its bounty in a forbidden and murderous way. (The scene in which Alcide kills a deer particularly horrifies and fascinates him.)

Murder of the mother/wife is, of course, the true outcome of the book. Michel drags the now tubercular Marceline through a long reversal of their earlier journey, until she hemorrhages and dies in the remote Algerian town of Touggourt. Yet Marceline all but cooperates in her own death, putting up only the most token resistance. In Michel's guilty, and symbiotic, perception, she is only willing to go on living if she is assured of his love. "If she had said aloud: 'Do you really care whether I live or not?' I should not have heard the words more clearly. . . . I fanned my love. And Marceline, as I tell you, began forthwith to recover hope" (118, 121).

Moreover, there is an extraordinary amount of splitting and denial in Michel's own behavior. Through much of the journey, he manages to persuade himself that each new climate will cure Marceline. Within the last few pages, he is still asking, "Why does she cough so in this fine weather?" (136). His guilt, though shockingly misdirected, remains compulsive: "When sometimes I left her for an hour to take a solitary walk in the country or streets, a kind of loving anxiety, a fear of her feeling the time long, made me hurry back to her; and sometimes I rebelled against this obsession" (129). At the end, as Jeffrey Meyers points out, the fatal, magical logic of the vigil with Menalque repeats itself: "Just as he had discovered Marceline's miscarriage when he returned from his intellectual debauch with Menalque, so now he finds her hemorrhaging when he returns from his physical debauch with Moktir."[16] Yet even then, he ends up holding her in his arms, thinking, "oh, can she think I want to leave her?" (142). And she, despite her evident despair, must reassure him that "everything is all right."

Since Michel is clearly not acting out a ruthless, unambivalent commitment to Nietzschean individualism, one must wonder whether Gide is not dramatizing a fear of the consequences of individuation. Fables on this subject have a propensity to lethal outcomes—as we shall see, again, in Kundera. To understand this, I think, we have to go beyond the terms of family-systems theory, back to the terms of *Envy and Gratitude*. There, not to want the mother's ministrations may indeed kill her, in the child's fantasy, or at least entail the permanent loss of the "good object" within her. Our guilt, or envy, at being unable to nurture as well as she can, may turn us into the kind of antinurturer, or parody nurturer, Michel becomes. Yet, to accept nurturance and oneness may kill the self, drown it in its preexistence, as Michel is "submerged" in his memories at La Moriniere. There seems no possible outcome that does not wholly negate one or the other party. And so the outcome is death—a death that, probable or not, thrills and convinces us, as if we always knew this would happen, because it recreates the circumstances under which the very idea of guilt and retribution first entered our psyches.

ONE INDICATION of what a minefield gender criticism can be is one's suddenly finding oneself utterly at odds, on specifics, with the writers one agrees with most, on general principles. So Wendy Lesser, who for me is a model of how to write about the whole issue of female identification: "There are certain male artists—Milan Kundera, for instance, and John Updike—who do strike me as being thorough misogynists."[17] Updike?—I ask bemusedly. I know other feminists have made the accusation. But, as I cast my mind back over the Rabbit tetralogy, there is hardly a single major female character—Thelma, Ruth, Pru, even Janice the "poor mutt"—who doesn't finally have more courage to face reality, more sensitivity to the feelings of others, more altruism and more dignity than the hapless protagonist. We understand their exasperation with Rabbit's self-centered world, even as we find that world poetic.

I suspect that Updike's really unpardonable sin, for feminism, is that he is the poet of men noticing women: "The number of trim youngish professionals in lightweight suits and tight linen skirts has ballooned. . . . The women of this race especially fascinate Harry; they wear running shoes instead of high heels but their legs are encased in sheer pantyhose and their faces adorned by big round glasses that give them a comical sexy look, as if their boobs are being echoed above in hard hornrims and coated plastic."[18] Male writers can be forgiven for "objectifying" —poor dears, they don't know any better. But to find imagination, wit, and even insight into female self-presentation where everyone else has agreed to see only "objectification"—that is a graver sin.

With Kundera, the case is plainer: Lesser and I simply seem to be reading different books. For her, the gestures of postmodern knowingness in *The Unbearable Lightness of Being* (the reminders that these characters are Kundera's inventions, the play with the Nietzschean notion of "eternal return") are the novel's essence and limitation. For me, they are like a pair of asbestos gloves, allowing the author to approach his explosive emotional material. For her, "the only character in the novel who seems at all substantial is Tomas. . . . He is a tremendous womanizer . . . and this promiscuity is clearly an object of intense enjoyment and delight for the author."[19] To me, Tomas's Don Juanism, while perhaps entertaining, is something of a stage prop, significant mainly in the light of his relations to the two truly substantial characters, Tereza and Sabina.

In the opening pages of *The Unbearable Lightness of Being* we find many of the themes of *The Immoralist* reconfigured. Tomas is a "rugged individualist," in the sense of reacting destructively against all forms of familial connection. (He is named after Doubting Thomas in the Bible, Kundera slyly informs us on page 270.) His parents no longer speak to him, because of his abandonment (as they see it) of his son by a previous marriage. "He celebrated the event [his divorce] the way others celebrate a marriage."[20] Convinced he "could be fully himself only as a bachelor," he maintains a network of "erotic friendships," with elaborate rules for preserving distance. He never stays overnight with a woman; he sees the women who remain steady presences in his life no oftener than every three weeks.

But when Tomas meets Tereza, he projectively identifies her with all the need and vulnerability he has denied in himself, the other women in his life, his son. "He had come to feel an inexplicable love for this all but complete stranger; she seemed a child to him, a child someone had put in a bulrush basket daubed with pitch and sent downstream for Tomas to fetch at the riverbank of his bed" (6). He finds himself breaking all of his rules. He not only lets Tereza sleep in his bed; he accepts, even comes to enjoy, her habit of holding his hand all night. He feels jealous when she dances with a younger colleague of his. He lets her move in with him; eventually he marries her.

The one thing Tomas cannot do, however, is give up his "erotic friendships" with other women. Fairly clearly, to us if not to him, this is a question of autonomy and not, in Lesser's terms, one of "delight." He comes to find all the other women in his life "distasteful," except perhaps Sabina; indeed, "he constantly had Tereza's image before his eyes, and the only way he could erase it was by quickly getting drunk," which he proceeds to do, whenever he is with another woman (21).

Moreover, the guiltier Tomas feels over his compulsion, the deeper he is drawn into the relationship with Tereza. "To assuage Tereza's sufferings, he married her . . . and gave her a puppy." As this oddly comic sentence in itself suggests, the puppy will become not only a substitute for the child Tomas refuses to have, but a kind of theater for acting out many resonances of the marriage. This theater begins, in fact, when they have to give the dog a name. The passage is worth dwelling on, among other reasons, because it is a place where Lesser's animus against the book leads her into questionable reading. She comments: "An important character in the novel is a female dog named Karenin. As Russian scholars and readers of Tolstoy will know, Karenin is a man's name. But for various reasons Tomas and Tereza do not want to name their dog Karenina, and she therefore becomes Karenin, after which point in the novel she is invariably referred to as 'he.' Somehow this is indicative of Kundera's attitude toward his human characters, but in reverse: his female characters are just outpourings of a masculine imagination."[21]

Such "somehow[s]" are easily come by, if they confirm a conclusion the critic has already reached. But if we look at the text, we see that Tomas and Tereza are not only perfectly aware of the gender error but intend to refer to a different character than Anna. "'It can't be Anna Karenina,' said Tomas. 'No woman could possibly have so funny a face. It's much more like Karenin. Yes, Anna's husband. That's just how I've always pictured him'" (24). Pets in marriages often embody the simpler, more lovable selves both partners wish they had. But they can also embody the sides both partners fear are unlovable and unacceptable—and give them an oblique way of acknowledging and consoling those sides, in themselves and in each other. I believe "Karenin"—named for Anna's ugly, inept, rejected spouse—fulfills the latter function. S/he represents Tereza's fear that Tomas's Don Juanism renders her unlovable, cast out. S/he also represents Tomas's fear that if he were completely domestic he would be thus vulnerable, diminished, old before his time. That is why "Karenin" has to be androgynous; despite Tomas's intention that "the name . . . be a clear indication that the dog was Tereza's," the name conveys the fusion between them, beneath their polarized roles.

There is a further indication of such fusion: like Michel, Tomas seems most identified with his wife at the very moments he feels guiltiest toward her. Early in the book, Tereza dreams that she is forced to watch Tomas and Sabina making love and jabs needles under her own fingernails, "hoping to alleviate the pain in her heart by pains of the flesh" (16). Though this dream reveals, to Tomas, that she has been reading his private correspondence, he not only forgives her, he feels "the pain under her fingernails" himself—indeed feels "that he himself had knelt before the open desk drawer, unable to tear his eyes from Sabina's letter" (20–21).

We have seen such guilty identifications before, not only in Michel but even in so crude a character as Walter Morel, who feels pains in his own head after he flings a drawer at his wife. Perhaps the Kleinean explanation rings truest here: the need to make reparation to the injured mother stems from, and therefore reawakens, the psychic level at which mother and child are truly indistinguishable. In Tomas's case, there seems also to be an element of taking both roles: he suffers with Tereza because she acts out a dependency that is in him as well (witness his jealousy when she dances with the male colleague), though he will not acknowledge it.

From the very beginning, lethal outcomes seem strangely predicated in the issues between Tomas and Tereza. When he first feels merged with her, death comes into his mind. "He fancied she had been with him for many years and was dying. He had a sudden clear feeling that he would not survive her death" (7). For Tereza, on the other hand, death is associated with the inability to merge with Tomas—that is, to get him to give up his Don Juanism. Her recurring dreams are of being thrown in a hearse or, more frequently, of being led to execution, with Tomas as the executioner. Her exposure to actual danger, during the Russian invasion of Czechoslovakia, is in fact a relief to her, since it externalizes the trauma: "The television series of her dreams had been interrupted and she had enjoyed a few happy nights" (26–27).

We learn little about Tomas's family conditioning, but Kundera takes pains to provide a familial context for Tereza's sufferings. She was an unwanted child; her mother blamed her for the loss of the mother's youth and beauty and therefore particularly persecuted her for considering herself in any way special. Even Tereza's wish to escape her stepfather's advances is taken as evidence of overvaluation of herself: "'Who do you think you are, anyway? Do you think he's going to bite off a piece of your beauty?'" (45). Her mother "insisted her daughter remain with her in the world of immodesty, where youth and beauty mean nothing, where the world is nothing but a vast concentration camp of bodies, one like the next, with souls invisible" (47). In her dreams, Tereza is always being killed along with a large, anonymous crowd of women who consent to their fate. Clearly Tomas—the Don Juan as executioner, who takes away her existential singularity—is merely stepping into a preexisting role.

At the end of the book, Tereza will see herself as, despite appearances, the dominant party in the marriage, whose manipulative dependence has caused the disastrous decline in their worldly fortunes. "She had summoned him to follow her as if wishing to test him again and again. . . . We all have a tendency to consider strength the culprit and weakness the innocent victim. But now Tereza realized that in her case the opposite was true! Even her dreams, as if aware of the single weakness in a man otherwise strong, made a display of her suffering to him, thereby forcing him to retreat" (310). Kerr and Bowen, I think, would partly agree with Tereza's assessment: "It is important to keep in mind that appearances can be quite deceiving in regards to dominance. The one who appears to be 'dominant' may be making decisions based on perceptions of what the seemingly 'subordinate' one wants."[22]

But, in fact, the downfall of Tomas and Tereza seems a subtle interaction of the weaknesses in both their characters with external history. True, Tereza leaves Zurich unilaterally, after she discovers Tomas has mistresses there, too. True, "she had taken advantage of a night of stomach cramps to inveigle him into moving to the country!" (310). But it is Tomas who refuses to stay in Zurich by himself—to live, as he apparently wishes, entirely from his principle of autonomy. And it is Tomas who, once back in Czechoslovakia, acts out his rugged individualism in both noble and self-destructive ways. He not only refuses to recant his anti-Communist article from the spring of 1968, he preemptively resigns from medical practice for fear he will be misrepresented as having recanted, "assuming (correctly) that after he had descended voluntarily to the lowest rung of the social ladder . . . the police would have no more hold over him" (192). Ironically, he also refuses to become a vocal dissident; Kundera connects both decisions to his need to isolate himself, not to be swayed by other people. When he refuses to sign the dissidents' petition, he feels "the same black intoxication he had felt when he solemnly announced to his wife that he no longer wished to see her or his son" and "when he sent off the letter that meant the end of his career in medicine"(220).

Yet, as soon as Tomas does decide to move to the country—and, implicitly, to give up his womanizing—the book takes on a doom-ridden tinge. For the first and only time, Tomas's dreams are recorded. They are extremely Kleinian dreams, full of preoedipal horror and longing, and give the lie to Kundera's earlier suggestion that Tomas is an "epic" womanizer, whom "nothing can disappoint" because he "projects no subjective ideal" (201). In the first dream, he is attracted to a woman "at least five times his size" and monstrously covered with hair; she is "floating on her back in a pool," as the executed bodies are in Tereza's dreams (236). (So she subsumes, perhaps, both the rather grotesque women his "epic" self has been attracted to and the Tereza who has now triumphed over him into one image of the monstrous mother.) In the second dream, he does indeed meet the woman "he had always longed for" and feels he has "abandon[ed] his paradise" for Tereza's sake (238–239).

Then, Tereza's dreams change their quality. Suddenly, it is Tomas who is executed. After death, he dwindles in size (as the woman was enlarged in *his* dream) until he becomes a rabbit, and Tereza, at last "happy," and "with the feeling that she was nearly at her goal," takes him home to her childhood room (306).

The implications of the dreams seem all too clear. If Tomas's principle of autonomy wins, Tereza must die, like Marceline in *The Immoralist*;

if her principle of familial togetherness wins, then Tomas will perish. In her last self-accusing monologue, Tereza sees herself as "like the nymphs who lured unsuspecting villagers to the marshes and left them there to drown" (310). The book all too quickly fulfills these premonitions. Karenin—the symbol of Tereza and Tomas's uneasy union—dies of cancer just before Tereza's rabbit dream. And while the book ends with Tomas protesting, during an excursion to a country inn, "Haven't you noticed I've been happy here," the reader knows—has known for almost two hundred pages—that this excursion, or a similar one, will end in both their deaths, in an auto accident that is itself caused by Tomas's suicidal carelessness in failing properly to repair the truck he drives for his demeaning new job.

It is as if neither this book nor *The Immoralist* will allow any truce in the war between the principles of individuality and togetherness. Some critics might put Kundera's ending down to fear of the engulfing woman—or to a *parti pris* for Tomas's Don Juanism—as Gide's ending can be put down to male guilt. But I hear an even darker, if less reprehensible, message in the tone of Kundera's concluding section, "Karenin's Smile": that it is because it is an "idyll" (295), because both partners are "happy," that it must end fatally. It is as if the elimination of tension, as in Freud's *Beyond the Pleasure Principle,* has to be the victory of Thanatos.

In any case, lest the book seem weighted against the togetherness principle, we have the opposing cautionary tale of Tomas's long-standing mistress, the painter Sabina. Sabina is the type of the woman who refuses the association of the feminine with nurturance, feelingfulness, vulnerability—who lives by irony. Though she attracts many men by her comradeliness and her capacity for intellectual friendship, as well as her frank sexuality, she has far more ironclad defenses against lasting intimacy than Tomas himself. At the turning point of her plot, she resolves her relationship with the "best man" she has ever been with— Franz, a man who has just left his wife for her—simply by running away, allowing him no way of following, seeing, or even writing to her. The cruelty of this seems only partially intended, mainly a reflex of her way of being; the man himself eventually forgives her.

As with Tereza, Kundera provides a personal history that makes the extreme choice plausible. Sabina's father, a traditional landscape painter, is both repressive and sentimental. The rigors of summer camp and art school in the Socialist Realist years reenforce the lesson that the two go together. Sabina paints what is required of her, but begins to add, as her personal signature, a flaw that turns it all into a stage prop: a "trickle" that "looked like a crack" and thereby turned a "building site into a battered old backdrop"; a "landscape showing an old-fashioned table lamp shining through it" (63–64).

Sabina's paintings capture her unresolvable dilemma, as surely as Michel's twin landscapes do. The world other people feel at home in, are comforted by, strikes her as a fraud; yet it continues to block out, to prevent the full imagining of, any other world that might replace it.[23] So, betrayal of any world that begins to take on solidity becomes an endlessly necessary, endlessly repeated act. "Betrayal means breaking ranks and going off into the unknown. Sabina knew of nothing more magnificent than going off into the unknown" (91). Franz's great mistake, with Sabina, is to suppose that his "fidelity"—his leaving his wife for her—will endear him to her. Probably it is because he *has* a wife that she achieves as much continuity in her relationship with him as she does.

I have found, in talking with women friends, that Sabina—as a character imagined by a male writer—often troubles them at least as much as Tomas does. I am not completely sure why this is, but I suspect the element of sexual masochism in her personality plays as large a part as the coldness and libertinism. As Jessica Benjamin notes, "This fact, that women participate in their own submission, has often embarrassed [feminist] critics of psychoanalytic theory."[24] Yet Benjamin stands up for its being a "fact," which can be understood, without denigrating women, in terms of "the ability to play both roles in fantasy":[25] "The fantasy of erotic domination embodies both the desire for independence and the desire for recognition."[26] On the one hand, as Benjamin writes of *The Story of O*, the masochist seeks "to be *known*": "The pain of violation serves to protect the self by substituting physical pain for the psychic pain of loss and abandonment. In being hurt by the other, O feels she is being reached, she is able to experience another living presence. O's pleasure, so to speak, lies in her sense of her own survival and her connection to her powerful lover." On the other hand, O also covertly acts out her independent self through the "powerful lover": "her sacrifice actually creates the master's power, produces his coherent self, in which she can take refuge."[27]

In Sabina's case, many of these terms will have to be transposed, since her autonomous side is always in control, her "togetherness" impulses deeply repressed. But the element of playing both roles is clearly present. The theme first enters when Sabina puts on her grandfather's bowler hat in front of Tomas. On the face of it, the hat indicates identification with a male ancestor and, by extension, her "masculine" role of adventuress, libertine. It is, if one likes, a phallic accessory, a fetish. But suddenly Sabina sees it differently, as sexual "humiliation," because Tomas is fully dressed and she is not. "But instead of spurning [the humiliation], she proudly, provocatively played it for all it was worth, as if submitting of her own will to public rape" (87).

But one might wonder whether Sabina is really excited by the "public rape" (after all, it is she who then "pull[s] Tomas down to the floor")— or, rather, by the fact that her masculine side is so in control within the game that she can see herself as feminine, submissive, without loss of self. Later, we are told that at this very moment Sabina has a fantasy of "Tomas seating her on the toilet in her bowler hat and watching her void her bowels" (247)—a drastic example of what Benjamin calls the masochist's wish to be "reached," to be recognized.

With Franz, things become more complicated. Sabina becomes aware of her loneliness. (She has just, like Tomas, distanced herself from the anti-Communist Czechs who are her natural allies, out of distaste for any kind of group identity, group pressure.) For the first time in the book, she is tempted to act out her dependent side: "She had an overwhelming desire to tell him, like the most banal of women, Don't let me go, hold me tight, make me your plaything, your slave, be strong!" (98).

But for her, as for O., such dependence is possible only if the man incarnates autonomy to the point of indifference—treats her as a "plaything," a "slave." So, at this very point, Sabina becomes hypercritical of any impulse toward merging or dependence in Franz. His habit of closing his eyes while making love, which makes him feel "disintegrated and dissolved into the infinity of his darkness," is "distasteful" to her (95). His refusal to "give Sabina orders," as Tomas would, seems to her "noble and just," but "disqualifie[s] him from her love life" (111–12). At this point, Sabina seems to understand the double bind she has put herself in, since she could not tolerate "a man who ordered her about," either (112).

When Franz leaves his wife, Sabina is faced—for the only time in the book—with the possibility of a relationship without a built-in guarantee of distance. Briefly she is tempted, wishing to "summon" back her "long[ing] to come to the end of the dangerous road of betrayals" (115). But, to her, a life publicly connected to another person is, like the surface of her paintings, a falsehood: "instead of being Sabina, she would have to act the role of Sabina, decide how best to act the role" (115). Her hypercriticalness comes to her aid: she sees "[m]uscular Franz in coitus" as "a gigantic puppy suckling at her breasts. . . . The idea that he was a mature man below and a suckling infant above, that she was therefore having intercourse with a baby, bordered on the disgusting" (116).

We might be reminded, here, of Gudrun's revulsion against Gerald in *Women in Love*. But Franz is no Gerald; his dependence is a modulated part of a character capable of both decisiveness and nurturing, not the mere obverse of a brutal rationalism. What is going on here is more complex. I suspect Sabina projectively identifies Franz with the whole dependent side of human nature that "disgust[s]" her, first and foremost, in herself. And so, under cover of the gender stereotype that men should be strong, she reverts to the role of the sadist, thus regaining control. "She longed to ravish his intelligence, defile his kindheartedness, and violate his powerless strength. . . . Once more she heard the golden horn of betrayal beckoning her in the distance, and she knew she would not hold out" (116).

But the book does not allow us to find Sabina's solution any more satisfactory than Tomas's. Wandering in Paris, after she hears of Tomas's and Tereza's deaths, "Sabina felt emptiness all around her. What if emptiness was the goal of all her betrayals?" (122). She remembers that her "parents had died in the same week. Tomas and Tereza in the same second. Suddenly she missed Franz terribly" (124).

Thereafter, Sabina becomes more and more deracinated, moving on to America, eventually to California. But she never entirely shakes the images of "togetherness" she despises. At last, feeling that there is no ground she can belong to, nothing "beneath the surface" that is not "alien," "she composed a will in which she requested that her dead body be cremated and its ashes thrown to the winds. Tomas and Tereza died under the sign of weight. She wanted to die under the sign of lightness" (273).

Tomas and Tereza, have, all too literally, died of letting their commitments become weighty: they are crushed to death under a truck. But the metaphor sums up the unresolved opposites of the book. It is also, interestingly, a metaphor Kerr and Bowen use, though, for good or bad, they seem less critical of the principle of "lightness" than Kundera is. But perhaps, for them, Sabina's lightness would be simply a reactive version of heaviness:

> In a "heavy" atmosphere, family members are prone to feel "crowded" by the intense pressure of one another's needs for contact and reassurance and/or prone to feel "lonely" because of the marked distance created by one another's allergies to too much involvement. . . . Families with a "heavy" atmosphere are poorly differentiated ones. . . . Families with a "light" atmosphere are well differentiated ones. In such families people's thoughts, feelings, and actions are controlled almost entirely by processes internal to each individual. Children growing up in such families develop into what their individuality force propels them to be.[28]

If family-systems theory is right, the polarities in these two novels are in some sense universal in human nature. They complicate, and may even be falsely identified with, polarities of gender. They have the potential, therefore, fruitfully to complicate gender criticism—though not all gender critics may welcome such insights as that Tereza's "weakness" does not automatically make her the "innocent victim," or that Sabina not only has masochistic fantasies but paradoxically uses them to regain distance and control in relation to men. Nor will all gender critics welcome a new assertion of universals. But for me, these concepts of subtle exchange often tell a more complete truth about couple experience, in life as well as in literature, than either male or female blame-placing does.

In my final chapter, I take up, with some trepidation, other complicating perspectives: male critiques of gender relations over the last two centuries, in comparison with those of their feminist contemporaries. Here, too, we will find that the deep issues of separation and merging often run alongside the more evident social and ethical ones. But there is a curious reversal: it is often the women who want to break free from the existing order who care most passionately about autonomy. And the men—worried about being judged or treated coldly by women, either in the market economy of patriarchy or in some putative feminist New Order—suddenly espouse the "togetherness" principle. An irony, indeed; but such ironies of course illustrate Kerr and Bowen's fundamental point—that both impulses belong to all of us, and it is only by a good deal of denial and projective identification that men or women disown either.

Male Sexual Prophecy

Blake to Bly

THERE IS A scene in Lawrence's *Sons and Lovers* that, for me, reverber-
ates with the thousands of quarrels men and women must have had
about feminism, over the roughly two centuries since the redefinition
of gender became a subject of public debate. I don't mean the brutal
quarrels, but the ones that begin in good will, where the two parties
seem to agree, yet end up hating each other. Paul and Clara have gone
to the same suffragette meeting; both apparently have liked it.

> "You were at Margaret Bonford's meeting the other evening,"
> he said to her. Miriam did not know this courteous Paul. Clara
> glanced at him.
> "Yes," she said.
> "Why," asked Miriam, "how do you know?"
> "I went in for a few minutes before the train came," he answered.
> Clara turned away again rather disdainfully.
> "I think she's a lovable little woman," said Paul.
> "Margaret Bonford!" exclaimed Clara. "She's a great deal
> cleverer than most men."
> "Well, I didn't say she wasn't," he said, deprecating. "She's
> lovable for all that."
> "And of course that is all that matters," said Clara witheringly.
> He rubbed his head, rather perplexed, rather annoyed.
> "I suppose it matters more than her cleverness," he said;
> "which after all would never get her to heaven."
> "It's not heaven she wants to get—it's her fair share on earth,"
> retorted Clara. She spoke as if he were responsible for some depri-
> vation which Miss Bonford suffered.
> "Well," he said, "I thought she was warm, and awfully nice—
> only too frail. I wished she was sitting comfortably in peace—"
> "'Darning her husband's stockings,'" said Clara, scathingly.
> "I'm sure she wouldn't mind darning even my stockings," he
> said. "And I'm sure she'd do them well. Just as I wouldn't mind
> blacking her boots, if she wanted me to." (226)

Paul is clearly interested in feminism, even if he must dissemble that interest a little ("I went in for a few minutes before the train came"). Perhaps he needs to defend his masculinity; or perhaps he wants to deflect Miriam's potential jealousy of Clara. (If the latter, the stratagem fails completely: Miriam promptly notices, though Clara cannot, that Paul's demeanor is uncharacteristically "courteous.") But Paul's receptivity depends on the assurance that affectionate relations between the sexes can be maintained; that Miss Bonford is "warm" and "lovable." (I take "lovable" to mean potentially capable of loving *him*—endowed with that charity that, the epistle says, would "get her to heaven.") To Clara, judging Miss Bonford by this quality immediately compromises her freedom and autonomy. It puts her intelligence in question; and may be a subtle plot to put her back "darning her husband's stockings." To Paul, Miss Bonford's "cleverness" is not at issue; and he cannot see, though the reader can, why his protectiveness toward her seems like a power play to Clara—the more so since its original object is probably his mother, who, however "done out of her rights" (69), still seems to him a tower of strength in her domestic solicitude. He honestly feels that he is the true egalitarian here: "Just as I wouldn't mind blacking her boots." Smarting under what he perceives to be an undeserved insult, Paul falls back on a defensive, misogynist explanation: Clara is a "man-hater," or (even more maddening, from the feminist point of view) she only "thinks she is"—that is, she is mainly concerned with disowning her own sexual need (227).

Lawrence's genius, I think, has pinpointed the rawest nerves in both men and women arguing such topics: the man unable to grasp just how threatened the principle of female freedom and autonomy seems, to the woman; the woman, in her turn, failing to grasp the sincerity, and intensity, of his concern not with power but with affection—the residual anxiety of the preoedipal son. These raw nerves, I shall argue, have informed the different ways in which men and women have wanted to reform the existing sexual order of things, and the reasons why, addressing so many of the same issues, they have so often talked past each other.

BUT WHY, ONE might ask, have *men* wished to reform the sexual status quo? Surely we (that is, we *men*) are economically, legally, and in the soothing of our private vanities, its overwhelming beneficiaries. Yet the literature of the last two centuries reveals a long string of male "prophets"

—bitterly angry both *at* women, and *on behalf of* women, as well as men—against existing social and ethical codes. My hope, in this final chapter, is to suggest some reasons, from the object-relations perspective, for this male discontent; and, in the process, to investigate both what such men saw accurately, and what they failed to see, in comparison with their feminist contemporaries—and what common psychological themes run through both the insight and the blindness.

When I was younger, William Blake seemed to many people the archetype of a male sexual prophet, anticipating by almost two hundred years the sexual revolution we still regarded uncritically. "Everything that lives is holy," he proclaimed. "The head Sublime, the heart Pathos, the genitals Beauty." He attacked organized religion for its antisexual, antibodily ethic:

> And priests in black gowns, were walking their rounds,
> And binding with briars, my joys and desires.

He suggested that degraded forms of sexuality were in fact caused by repression and unrealistic idealization: "Prisons are built with stones of Law, Brothels with bricks of Religion." He was tolerant of multiple love affairs. He seemed accepting of female sexual impulse. "How can the Female be Chaste O thou stupid Druid Cried Los"—Los being the embodiment, in the prophetic books, of Blake's imaginative self. He portrayed as foolish and self-tormenting a male character (the suggestively named Theotormon, in "Visions of the Daughters of Albion") who, because his beloved has been raped, regards her as spoiled for him. Finally, like the Norman O. Brown of his day, he championed polymorphous perversity against a narrowly genital definition of "normal" intercourse:

> Embraces are Cominglings: from the Head even to the Feet;
> And not a pompous High Priest entering by a Secret Place.[1]

What, from the 1960s point of view, could be wrong with that?

A good deal, feminist criticism was to respond, over the next two decades.[2] Too often, Blake seems to regard women not as the victims but as the primary agents of moralistic repression:

> Have you known the Judgment that is arisen among the
> Zoas of Albion? where a Man dare hardly to embrace
> His own Wife, for the terrors of Chastity that they call

> By the name of Morality. their Daughters govern all
> In hidden deceit!

$$(E\ 177, J\ 32:\ 44-48)$$

His defense of free love turns out to be, on closer examination, mainly a defense of male polygamy, and, particularly, of the duty of right-thinking wives not to object to it.[3] Finally, in his last major prophecy, *Jerusalem,* Blake elaborates a metaphysics in which women are onto-logically secondary, lacking independent being. "Emanations," created out of men, as Eve was from Adam's rib, women will be absorbed back into men at the Apocalypse, when "Sexes must vanish & cease."

It may be useful to separate out two levels in our investigation of the case against Blake—the cosmological and the ethical or relational. As a metaphysician, Blake shows a marked nostalgia for the fluid conscious-ness of infancy—the flamey, ever-changing Eden, the Beulah of "mild moony lustres"—which he could and did prolong into adult life by hallucinating. His insistence that this condition was psychic health and creativity earned him the reputation of madness, in his time and later. But one might find a defense for it in Winnicott's notion of the "transi-tional" stage, in which one is not allowed to ask where the boundary falls between subject and object, as having a vital relation to culture. Equally, one might point to Hans Loewald's concept of the persistence of primary process in all creative activity. On the purely epistemologi-cal level, Blake's position often boils down to a tolerance for process, a recognition that there can be many truths, many experiences of the same reality, that only the most narrowly scientistic of postromantic philosophers would object to.

Still, it is clear that for Blake the solidity and separateness of the mate-rial world was a trauma; was, in religious terms, the Fall. He describes this experience through many terrifying metaphors—vegetating, condensing, petrifying, freezing; also a resonantly Kleinian imagery of falling into an "Abyss," "an unknown Space / Deep horrible without End" where

> Mans exteriors are become indefinite opend to pain
> In a fierce hungring void & none can visit his regions.[4]

In these visions, he seems to be revisiting infantile states in which the feeling of infinite isolation, loss of human contact ("none can visit his regions") both causes and results from his own "fierce[ness]" and "hung[er]."

Inconsistently, but with a certain psychological canniness, Blake blames this Fall on several characters simultaneously: on figures of patriarchal authority, inducting the psyche into the realms of "measure" and "Law" (Urizen); on uncompliant females (Enion, Enitharmon); and on the fury and greed of the infant himself (Luvah). But the anger at women often has a peculiar bitterness, because Blake seems to believe they could provide access to the original world if only they wanted to. Women, in Jessica Benjamin's terms, "ha[ve] the good things inside," so that when they withhold sexually, they withhold the reunified world itself:

> Three gates within Glorious & bright open into Beulah
> From Enitharmons inward parts but the bright female terror
> Refused to open the bright gates she closd and barrd them fast
> Lest Los should enter into Beulah thro her beautiful gates.[5]

In the light of such a passage, one suspects Blake's doctrine of emanations of being a wishful reversal of what he feared was the actual state of affairs: that men were ontologically dependent on women for the sustenance of their very identities. When, in a curiously Wagnerian passage, Urizen, the forbidding father, encounters his daughters,

> He threw his flight thro the dark air to where a river flowd
> And taking off his silver helmet filled it & drank
> But when unsatiated his thirst he assayd to gather more
> Lo three terrific women at the verge of the bright flood
> Who would not suffer him to approach. but drove him back with storms
>
> Urizen knew them not & thus addressd the spirits of darkness.
>
> . . . .
>
> She answerd not but filled her urn & pourd it forth abroad.
>
> . . . .
>
> They reard up a wall of rocks and Urizen raisd his spear.
> They gave a scream, they knew their father Urizen knew his daughters
> They shrunk into their channels, dry the rocky strand beneath his feet.[6]

Behind or beside these "three terrific women" stand not only the Rhinemaidens but Fates, Furies, the Triple Goddess—all those female Trinities embodying male terror at woman's power to produce, and therefore possibly to reabsorb, life. That they are the guardians of water, the measurers of what is appropriate, what excessive, male thirst—and therefore, in fact, the creators of the "dry," "shrunk[en]" world that male reason must measure—has clear Kleinian reverberations. (Later in the same prophecy we find that the very worst fate, the fate of Satan, "dishumanizd monstrous," is to have no Emanation to turn to for sustenance: "A male without a female counterpart . . . Forlorn of Eden & repugnant to the forms of life.")[7]

Out of this Kleinean image of the bad mother drying up the world comes the association of the feminine with two of Blake's intellectual bêtes noires, a transcendental interpretation of Christianity and eighteenth-century Enlightenment empiricism with its "watchmaker God."

> O Albion why wilt thou Create a Female Will?
> To hide the most evident God in a hidden covert, even
> In the shadows of a Woman & a secluded Holy Place.
>
> . . . .
>
> Is this the Female Will O ye Lovely Daughters of Albion. To
> Converse concerning Weight & Distance in the Wilds of Newton & Locke
>
> (E 175, J 30: 31–40)

As Margaret Storch observes, this is, on the face of it, one of the most peculiar dimensions of Blake's thought: "This association of female influences with abstract empiricism . . . is difficult to align with historical actuality. It is also problematic in that it seems to go against most of the popular and familiar interpretations of culture, according to which the realm of reason and abstract thought is seen as masculine."[8] But from the Kleinian point of view, this position has a compelling logic. The loss of the living presence of the infantile world—which Blake called "Beulah" and "Eden"—is blamed on the mother's "Female Will." This loss takes place again both when the sacred is reserved to an invisible heaven, "a secluded Holy Place," and when deistic empiricism leaves the material world to "Weight & Distance." (The phrase "In the shadows of a Woman" also seems to associate the hidden Ark, the transcendent Heaven, with the dreaded invisibility of female genitals.) Coming on this passage in Thornton's *The Lord's Prayer, Newly Translated*—"Dim at best are the conceptions we have of the SUPREME BEING, who, as it were, keeps the human race in suspense, neither discovering, nor hiding HIMSELF"—Blake scribbles in the margin, "a Female God" (E, 658).

As a social or ethical thinker, Blake has received considerable, and justified, credit for his proto-Freudian understanding of the dynamics of repressed sexuality and its relation to conventional gender roles. As Alicia Ostriker argues in her largely sympathetic essay, Blake understands the role that splitting and projection play in "sexual violence," the condemnation/justification of one's own impulses by attributing them to one's victims. His Bromion, in *Visions of the Daughters of Albion,* is "the racist who rationalizes racism by insisting that the subordinate race is sexually promiscuous, the rapist who honestly believes that his victim was asking for it." But Blake also understands how the hesitant man, Theotormon, is "victimized by an ideology that glorifies male aggressiveness, as much as by that ideology's requirement of feminine purity."[9]

But women, too, Blake points out, gain complex forms of power by suppressing direct sexual expression, "gratified desire," in themselves and in their men. "The elaborate erotic apparatus of . . . coyness, shyness, modesty, jealousy, teasing, luring the man on and then holding him off, concealing and revealing the body at once"—Northrop Frye wrote, at a time when such statements were not yet controversial—"are not to be dismissed as either silly or amusing; they are . . . symbols of a profound imaginative reality."[10] "Profound" and "imaginative" indeed!—since, as we have seen, in Blake's mind they explain the very separateness of the material world.

Blake's understanding of the power women gain by at once flaunting and denying sexuality is both brilliant and, inescapably, another version of the oedipal son's resentment of his mother's unavailability. Consider his analysis of one of the most conventional sexual scenarios—woman loving the brave soldier, who rushes away to die in battle, while idealizing her innocence and chastity. In *Jerusalem,* he has a female speaker say,

> I have mocked those who refused cruelty & I have admired
> The cruel Warrior. I have refused to give love to Merlin the piteous.
> He brings to me the Images of his Love & I reject in chastity
> And turn them out into the streets for Harlots to be food
> To the stern Warrior. I am become perfect in beauty over my Warrior
> For Men are caught by Love: Woman is caught by Pride
> That Love may only be obtain in the passages of Death.

> (E 236, J 81: 1–7)

We have here, I think, a most subtle reworking, or rationalizing, of the oedipal son's fear that he is not "masculine" enough to fit his mother's expectations. For, in this version, the filial poet-figure, Merlin, is

143

rejected not just because he is weak—that is, vulnerable ("piteous")—but because he is open about sexuality. He presents "Images of his Love," which are repugnant to the pretence of "chastity." A parallel passage suggests that women are "[a]shamed to give Love *openly* to the piteous & merciful Man" (E 218, J 67: 19; italics mine). The supposedly "stern Warrior," by contrast, is passive and conventional in relation to woman. He accepts her claims to chastity; and his deeds of blood, his "passages of Death," are a sadistic sublimation of the consummation neither will admit they desire: "I must rush again to War: for the Virgin has frownd & refused" (E 220, J 68: 63). Consciously "ador[ing]" him (E 218, J 67: 21), yet enjoying the "Pride" that comes with her sexual refusal, woman becomes "perfect in beauty *over* my Warrior" (italics mine). But, of course, male sexuality does not vanish in this arrangement; the poet's "Images" of, as Blake would put it elsewhere, "gratified desire" are deflected onto the "Harlots" whom soldiers are famous for frequenting. And a split is introduced into our concept of male character as well. If men are to be strong, they cannot be either sexually candid or preoedipally needy:

> Let us look! let us examine! is the Cruel become an Infant
> Or is he still a cruel Warrior?
>
> (E 236, J 81: 8–9)

But, as Blake correctly intuits, male strength is most likely to turn into cruelty when it is dominated by unacknowledged infantile need.[11]

Blake's account of these matters is clearly self-interested and defensive. Is it entirely wrong? There have, after all, been fierce women militarists, fueled by eroticized identification with "our boys," from the Napoleonic wars to Vietnam. Jessica Benjamin comments on "the most common fantasy of ideal love, the one so frequently found in mass-market romances," in which "a woman can only unleash her desire in the hands of a man whom she imagines to be more powerful, who does not depend upon her for his strength."[12] In this case, repression of female sexuality is hardly the issue, at least in the twentieth century; but the romance model certainly suggests how avowed male vulnerability might render a lover unacceptable. Indeed, many works by women, from *The Mill on the Floss* to *The Story of an African Farm* to *The Bell Jar*, portray women incapable of erotic feeling for the man they perceive as a kindred spirit, but irresistibly drawn to the man they see as dangerous or wholly Other. It could be argued—and Sabina, indeed, tells us as much in *The Unbearable Lightness of Being*—that women (and men) are as much put in a double bind by women's uncertainty whether they want men to be "strong" or "sensitive" as by men's uncertainty whether they want women to be "pure" or indulgent.[13]

But, however accurate Blake's portrait of female elusiveness may be, it is so devastating, and therefore so hateful, to him because of the earlier, more potent terrors it calls up: the internal invisibility of female genitals, the refusals of mothers. (As Storch points out, images of inadequate feeding are a leitmotif of all of Blake's harsh portraits of women.) "Secrecy" becomes the defining trait of female independence, of a female will. And soon enough, as we have already seen, Blake constructs a whole religious and political myth, associating all forms of public mystification with feminine secrecy.

> The Female hid within a Male: thus Rahab is reveald
> Mystery Babylon the Great: the Abomination of Desolation
> Religion hid in War: a Dragon red, & hidden Harlot.
>
> (E 229, J 75: 18–20)

Such passages help to explain the curious secondariness of Blake's anger at male authoritarian figures, in his later work. Urizen himself "suffers," "a victim of the female power that preserves the dread holiness of sexual delight."[14]

Given these accumulating meanings around the image of a "secluded Holy Place," it becomes harder to take a positive view of Blake's distaste for standard heterosexual intercourse. It seems likely, like the later Lawrence's, to be rooted in a fear of woman's independent sexual pleasure. And Blake's insistent proclamation of "the most evident God," moving though it may be as religious thought, cannot help reminding us of that boyish, defiant externalization of male sexuality—and impatience with its frustration—characteristic of Blake's poet figure.

It may be instructive, at this point, to draw back and compare Blake with his greatest feminist contemporary, Mary Wollstonecraft, whom he knew personally (he illustrated one of her children's books) and whose *Vindication of the Rights of Woman* he is likely to have read.[15] Wollstonecraft's diagnosis of female behavior differs from Blake's far less than one might expect, especially on the score of "hidden deceit." But unlike Blake, she is compassionate and realistic about the causes of these traits in women's upbringing and economic situation. "Women are told from their infancy, and taught by the example of their mothers, that a little knowledge of human weakness, justly termed cunning, softness of temper, *outward* obedience, and a scrupulous attention to a puerile kind of propriety, will obtain for them the protection of man; and should they be beautiful, everything else is needless, for, at least, twenty years of their lives."[16] Elsewhere, Wollstonecraft goes so far as to say, "Women, as well as despots, have now, perhaps, more power than they would have if the world, divided and subdivided into kingdoms and families, were governed by laws deduced from the exercise of reason; but in obtaining it, to carry on the comparison, their character is degraded, and licentiousness spread through the whole aggregate of society" (77). And Wollstonecraft, too, like Blake, deplores the "state of warfare" between sexually aggressive men and resistant women, as "contrary to reason and true modesty" (191).

On the other hand, Wollstonecraft, with her attention to root causes, has some sharp replies for those male critiques that, like Blake's, are rooted in oedipal anxiety. Of the complaint that women prefer unworthy lovers, she says: "It seems a little absurd to expect women to be more reasonable than men in their *likings,* and still to deny them the uncontrolled use of reason. When do men *fall in love* with sense? . . . And how can they then expect women, who are only taught to observe behavior and acquire manners rather than morals, to despise what they have been all their lives labouring to attain? Where are they suddenly to find judgment enough to weigh patiently the sense of an awkward virtuous man?" (180). To Blake's particular bête noir, the predilection for soldiers, Wollstonecraft has a surprising answer. Far from being incarnations of paternal fierceness, soldiers are more like women than other men. Sharing a common uselessness, at least in peacetime, they, too, "practice the minor virtues with punctilious politeness" and "are . . . particularly attentive to their persons, fond of dancing, crowded rooms, adventures, and ridicule." Soldiers and women "both acquire manners before morals, and a knowledge of life before they have, from reflection, any acquaintance with the grand ideal outline of human nature" (55–56).

The contrast between Wollstonecraft and Blake becomes more problematic when values beyond the explicitly gendered come into play. One might say that Wollstonecraft's concern for female autonomy pushes her back into the eighteenth century, in considering "reason" the one uniquely human and valuable trait, at the very point where Blake's rash clinging to the preoedipal pulls him forward toward the twentieth.[17] All the qualities that, say, Rilke will wish men could learn from women are treated in the *Vindication* with contempt. If women live more in the moment than men do; if "a man, when he undertakes a journey, has, in general, the end in view," whereas "a woman thinks more of the incidental occurrences, the strange things that may possibly occur on the road," this propensity is no more to be valued than her "care of the finery that she carries with her." "Can dignity of mind exist with such trivial cares?" (104). Again, if women excel in "sensibility"—for which Wollstonecraft borrows Dr. Johnson's definition, "Quickness of sensation; quickness of perception; delicacy"—Wollstonecraft can discern nothing here but "the most exquisitely polished instinct." And "instinct," for her, remains "material"; "intellect dwells not here," and therefore there is "not a trace of the image of God" (108).

In her life, Wollstonecraft seems to have been much more sexually venturesome than Blake. And her book abounds with enlightened pronouncements on sexual issues: condemnation of the double standard, of the social exclusion of "fallen women," and so forth. Nevertheless, Wollstonecraft's rhetoric of the spiritual against the "material" almost inevitably brings puritan moralism in its wake. "Sentiment," she observes, is a "fallacious light," because it is "too often used as a softer phrase for sensuality" (86). Dedicating her book, perhaps ironically, to a French bishop, she does not hesitate to appeal to the arguments that might weigh most strongly with a celibate clergyman: "In France the very essence of sensuality has been extracted to regale the voluptuary, and a kind of sentimental lust has prevailed." She goes on to argue "that to render the human body and mind more perfect, chastity must more universally prevail, and that chastity will never be respected in the male world until the person of a woman is not, as it were, idolized" (24–25). In a later passage, she seems to condemn sexual experimentation even in marriage, referring to "libertines" who "seduce their own wives" (121). And she contends that, in general, "a master and a mistress of a family ought not to continue to love each other with passion. I mean to say that, they ought not to indulge those emotions which disturb the order of society" (64). And so Wollstonecraft's critique of the "idoliz[ation]" of women seems to pass over into a deep distrust of sexual passion itself.

The differences between Blake and Wollstonecraft, I believe, signal a rift between men's and women's thinking that will persist through the next two centuries. Wollstonecraft's pull back toward rationalism is understandable given the simple fact that women were not always acknowledged as rational beings; and rationality is intimately related to autonomous agency. But it places Wollstonecraft in the odd position of resisting a trend, in romanticism as later in modernism, to reassess the value of intuition, primary-process thinking, the thinking of the body, living in the moment—qualities once denigrated partly because they were classed as "feminine." (I wonder if some of the academic feminists in the United States who align themselves so readily with Lacan and/or social constructionism do not share some of Wollstonecraft's reasons for not taking the intuitive at face value.)

The pull toward sexual puritanism is a more complex phenomenon. Realism about the role that mating rituals play in the larger economic order and in family power-dynamics is one of the few weapons women have had against being entrapped in situations where appearance and reality are totally at odds. More sweepingly, as Carole S. Vance has argued, "The tension between sexual danger and sexual pleasure is a powerful one in women's lives. . . . For some, the dangers of sexuality —violence, brutality, and coercion, in the form of rape, forcible incest, and exploitation, as well as everyday cruelty and humiliation—make the pleasures pale by comparison. For others, the positive possibilities of sexuality—explorations of the body, curiosity, intimacy, sensuality, adventure, excitement, human connection, basking in the infantile and nonrational—are not only worthwhile but provide sustaining energy."[18] But, as Vance soon goes on to say, the threat of male violence is not the only source of sexual danger. "Sexuality activates a host of intra-psychic anxieties: fear of merging with another, the blurring of body boundaries and sense of self that occurs in the tangle of parts and sensations, with attendant fears of dissolution and self-annihilation."[19] If women are socially assumed to be—and sometimes experience themselves as being—more swamped by the "togetherness principle" than men, it is surely plausible that those who most value autonomy will fear sexual merging. (Wollstonecraft's own potential for dependency, in her affair with Gilbert Imlay, as recorded in *Letters Written during a Short Residence in Sweden, Norway, and Denmark,* has been documented by Mary Jacobus.)[20] Because women like Wollstonecraft need to defend against love's engulfing power (as opposed to the male sense of lack or, as in Blake, thirst), they may be more prone to take refuge in a justified cynicism.

Be that as it may, as the nineteenth century wore on, as the physical "idol" of Wollstonecraft's dedication gave way to Coventry Patmore's "Angel in the House," the puritanical side of feminism came more and more to the fore, until "Votes for Women and Chastity for Men" could be a public rallying cry.[21] Women had their own reasons for this "social purity" brand of feminism;[22] but men would naturally be more aware of the domestic power women accrued by making themselves representatives of the collective superego. And, as many writers have pointed out, notably Leslie Fiedler in *Love and Death in the American Novel*, this in turn created a new—or restored a very old—theme for misogyny: woman the civilizer, the restrainer of natural male energy.

This resentment in male writers often joined—as in Blake—with irrationalism and sexual liberationism. Later in the nineteenth century, we find another visionary poet, Arthur Rimbaud, writing that "the poet makes himself a *seer* by a long, prodigious, and rational *disordering of all the senses*," and going on to say that "when the unending servitude of woman is broken, when she lives by and for herself, when man—hitherto abominable—has given her her freedom, she too will be a poet! Woman will discover part of the unknown! Will her world of ideas be different from ours? She will discover things strange and unfathomable, repulsive and delicious."[23]

Rimbaud, clearly, is much less threatened by the idea of female agency than Blake is—or by the departure of women into unfeminine, "repulsive" areas of the psyche. But his vision is not altogether altruistic, either; like Blake, he understands what the present system costs men, economically and in their desire for erotic response. In *A Season in Hell*, he justifies his homosexuality as the only alternative to what "marriage" has become. (Presumably, he has his parents' marriage in mind; his father left the family early, and his mother has been described by biographers as cold, materialistic, and puritan, rather like Pavese's.) "I don't like women. Love must be invented afresh, that is sure. All *they* can do is wish for a secure position. Once they have gained it, their hearts and their beauty are put aside: nothing remains but cold disdain, the food of marriage, nowadays." And when Rimbaud does see himself as potentially heterosexual, it is in these terms: "Or else I see women who bear the signs of happiness, and whom *I* could have turned into good comrades, devoured from the start by brutes who are about as sensitive as piles of faggots."[24]

There is something irreducibly appealing, to me, in this image of a heterosexual version of himself and Verlaine, wandering poets together. Of course, feminists might bristle at the unquestioned assumption that the male partner would take the lead, Pygmalion fashion. Behind this surface arrogance, however, may lurk oedipal bravado, and oedipal resentment of the woman who would stay with a "brute." (Although, of course, Rimbaud is no readier than Blake to imagine what it might cost a woman to lead the life of a "good comrade," even supposing that relationship, by itself, were as egalitarian as he fantasizes.)

In both Blake and Rimbaud, one might say, the valuable call for personal courage and sexual liberation, for both sexes—the recognition that, without candor about desire, relationships can only center around power and manipulation—is clouded by acute anxiety that male needs, both oedipal and preoedipal, be met. Blake in particular, I think, exhibits the paradox Nancy Chodorow diagnoses in two later male sexual revolutionaries, Herbert Marcuse and Norman O. Brown. They chafe at the traditional requirements of masculinity, strength and assertiveness, and the lessening of male subjectivity that these requirements entail. Thus they seem basically feminist. "There is little question that Brown and Marcuse reject many of the gender-defined qualities of traditional masculinity. Orpheus and Narcissus oppose the achievement-oriented promethean performance principle with song, contemplation, merging, and beauty, with images of soft receptivity that oppose aggressive mastery of the world."[25] (One might compare, here, Blake's "piteous" Merlin with his "Images of his Love.") But Chodorow cautions that the true "image of the perfect person" here—like Blake's redeemed Albion—is not a woman but a "man . . . who incorporates feminine qualities."[26]

Moreover, such thinkers, in their anxiety that male desire be satisfied without recourse to the soldierly dominating role, and that that desire be allowed its preoedipal, narcissistic, "polymorphous perverse" resonances, cannot help fearing female subjectivity and female sexual agency. Taking their ideal from the experience of earliest infancy, they fail, as Chodorow puts it, to "recognize the contradictions that inhere in the problem of mutual narcissisms" and come to see all women who impose limits, or desire for themselves, as forbidding mothers. "It is of course the mother who is experienced as a narcissistic extension of the child and who imposes drive organization and modification. The mother's subjectivity is the reality principle for the child, and the mother requires that the infant separate from her and give up its primary narcissistic relation to reality. . . . A woman directly enforces the primary restraints that seem to be the essence of unfreedom."[27]

This insight casts a compelling light back on Blake's mythically aggrandized resentment of women. Even his emanation theory, in all its foolish grandiosity, now appears as a desperate attempt to deny "the reality principle" by denying "the mother's subjectivity." And the quarrel we have constructed between Blake and Wollstonecraft comes to sound strangely like the quarrel between Paul and Clara, transposed back through time: the son in panic at frustration, emotional loneliness, and the "reality principle"; the daughter too fragilely established in her own autonomy not to be afraid of mutuality, even if it means being afraid of her own desires.

WITH THE END of the nineteenth century, we see, as Gilbert and Gubar have put it, "a major shift in gender relations," a "brash affirmation of female creative primacy."[28] Partly this is a result of the suffrage movement and the entry of women into the workforce. But it is also a result of intellectual transformations, the work of male as well as female thinkers. In 1861, Bachofen published *Mother Right,* arguing that a worldwide matriarchal social order had preceded the patriarchal one. In succeeding years, Frazer's *The Golden Bough* and Jane Harrison's *Prolegomena to the Study of Greek Religion* unearthed the figures of powerful goddesses, mothers and dangerous consorts, alongside but, ultimately, *before* the male gods. And suddenly, in the writings of both men and women, the "feminine" acquired a positive valence; no longer a set of defects to be apologized for and corrected, it became a radiant source of neglected potential, socially and metaphysically. Thus we find Edward Carpenter, in *Love's Coming of Age* (written in 1896), noting, perhaps for the first time in history, as a *virtue* women's quicker social maturity in "understand[ing]" and "master[ing]" the realm of feeling—the "quickness of perception" Wollstonecraft herself treated disparagingly. Carpenter even suggests, anticipating Benjamin, that male dominance may be "a kind of revenge" for men's relative helplessness before their own feelings "on the affectional plane."[29]

Gilbert and Gubar place more emphasis on the spur images of immensely powerful goddesses could give to male paranoia, in works like Rider Haggard's *She*.[30] But it is equally plausible to suggest that they played a role in the immense positive transvaluation of the "feminine" intuitive unconscious we have already seen in earlier twentieth-century male writers. Rilke spoke approvingly of Bachofen, whose thought also had an enormous influence on the *kosmische Runde* circle in Schwabing, with which Frieda von Richthofen was associated; and thus on Lawrence in the first phase of marital merging and enthusiasm, when he wrote that men need to get "their souls fertilized by the female."[31]

These writers remain, like Blake and Rimbaud, passionate irrationalists; but their irrationalism is now tinged with an intense, defiant identification with the "feminine." I do not want to repeat here what I have said earlier about the two greatest and most complex figures of this phase, Rilke and Lawrence, but it is worth pausing over a later and more drastic male conversion to the implications of the new anthropology: that of Robert Graves. In his sweeping, quirky work of mythography *The White Goddess,* Graves contends that, in "the religious theory of early European society . . . woman was the master of man's destiny: pursued, was not pursued; raped, was not raped. . . . When the victory of the patriarchal Indo-Europeans revolutionized the social system of the Eastern Mediterranean, the myth of the sexual chase was reversed."[32] But, Graves makes clear, this reversal was in almost no way a good thing. The very moral ambivalence of the Great Goddess had saved the ancients from the error of "philosophical dualism with all the tragi-comic woes attendant on spiritual dichotomy," which have afflicted the monotheistic religions (384). Graves even anticipates ecologically oriented feminists like Dinnerstein in suggesting that "the natural resources of the soil and sea" have been "exhausted by man's irreligious improvidence" because of the ascendancy of "the restless and arbitrary male will" over "the female sense of orderliness" (391–92).

Above all, Graves insists, *all* male creativity resides in the acceptance of matriarchal values, including the dark fate ultimately reserved for the sacred King with whom the poet identifies, the son-lover of the goddess: "Poetry began in the matriarchal age, and derives its magic from the moon, not the sun. No poet can hope to understand the nature of poetry unless he has had a vision of the Naked King crucified to the lopped oak, and watched the dancers, red-eyed from the acrid smoke of the sacrificial fires, stamping out the measure of the dance, their bodies bent uncouthly forward, with a monotonous chant of: 'Kill! kill! kill!' and 'Blood! blood! blood!'" (373). This scene provokes none of the horror in Graves that it does in Pavese; indeed, for him it, or the seasonal myth it encapsulates, is "the single Theme" of poetry. All true poetic "original[ity]" is "the poet's inner communion with the White Goddess, regarded as the source of truth," and therefore worthy of any degree of self-sacrifice (370, 373). The other ideal of poetry, the "Classical" or "Apollonian," is blasted throughout the pages of *The White Goddess* as "court-poetry, written to uphold the authority delegated to poets by the King" (368), and as "sentimental homosexuality" (371).

Randall Jarrell—no stranger himself to the dark sides of female identification—wrote a brilliant psychoanalytic essay on the personal background of Graves's system. Graves, he suggests, was attempting to heal a profound sense of self-division; to counterbalance a sterility he sensed in his own very British "dry, matter-of-fact, potboiling, puzzle-solving, stamp-collecting . . . side." "Men," Jarrell observes, "are as dry and as known to him as his own Ego; women are as unknown, and therefore as all-powerful and as all-attractive, as his own Id."[33]

But, Jarrell goes on to say, acceptance of the feminine did not come easily to Graves. He points to two early passages in Graves's autobiography, *Good-bye to All That*, in which experiences of female dominance or sexual initiative so frightened him that "my normal impulses were set back for years."[34] Jarrell might also have pointed to the premonitory wisdom of this apparently unrelated observation: "I have worked hard on myself in defining and dispersing my terrors."[35] Graves portrays himself at the time of the Great War as a puritanical virgin and emotionally homosexual—small wonder he is later so contemptuous of "sentimental homosexuality." It was only as a badly shell-shocked, disillusioned veteran that he, as he poignantly puts it, transferred his "loyalty" from the regiment, first to his vehemently feminist wife, Nancy, and later to his muse, Laura Riding.[36]

Graves's feminism, in short, is counterphobic. Misogynist stereotypes are not rejected or analyzed in his work, they are simply transvalued, as Jarrell says, in a way that recalls the defenses of childhood: "The child should permit against her no conscious aggression of any kind, and intend his *cruel, capricious, incontinent,* his *bitch, vixen, hag,* to be neither condemnation nor invective, but only fascinated description of the loved and worshipped Mother and Goddess, She-Who-Must-Be-Obeyed."[37] To put it differently, Graves, believing women to be all-powerful, adopts the masochistic strategy of incorporating that power by submitting to it. To put it differently still—as Jarrell shrewdly hints, perhaps out of his own experience—Graves projects the "Id" in order not to have to "explain" it; he disowns the negative both in himself and others, displacing it onto cosmic necessity, the unquestioned nature of the Goddess.[38]

Feminist criticism—in keeping, no doubt, with its fierce guardianship of the autonomy principle—has been less concerned with these matters than with Graves's suggestion that only a superwoman should try to write poetry herself, rather than be a muse to men: "A woman who concerns herself with poetry should, I believe, either be a silent Muse and inspire the poets by her womanly presence, as Queen Elizabeth and the Countess of Derby did, or she should be the Muse in a complete sense; she should be in turn Arianrhod, Blodeuwedd and the Old Sow of Maenawr Penarrd who eats her farrow, and should write in each of these capacities with antique authority."[39] Of course, Graves explicitly says he does not mean that "a woman should refrain from writing poems"; he felt he had found his modern Sappho, in the person of Laura Riding. But perhaps Graves's two shortcomings are related: in his concentration on the mythic, he had little to say about the relations, literary or otherwise, between ordinary men and women.

Still, one might have expected the positive transvaluation of the "feminine" in Graves—or Carpenter, or Rilke, or early Lawrence—to have produced some degree of rapprochement in the intellectual battle of the sexes. But the tenor of feminism itself was changing. As late as Olive Schreiner's *Woman and Labor* (1911) there is still the concession, as in Wollstonecraft, that a part of male anger at women is justified—that "sex parasitism," as Schreiner calls it, has given upper-class women an easier life at considerable moral cost to both sexes. (There is also an echo of Wollstonecraft's rationalism not only in Schreiner's ponderous style but her relentless scientism, sometimes relativist, sometimes essentialist, drawing evidence not only from tribal customs but "the little kapok bird of the Cape," who "rear the young with equal care," the male sitting in a "small shelf or basket . . . immediately below the entrance to the cavity in which the little female sits on the eggs.")[40]

Turning to Virginia Woolf's *A Room of One's Own,* eighteen years and a world war later, we are in a different world. First of all, we find Woolf perfectly willing to make a stylistic principle of that feminine attention to "the strange things that occur on the road" rather than the goal of the journey that Wollstonecraft found so undignified. The sight of a tailless Manx cat brings to the surface Woolf's depressed feeling about the Oxbridge luncheon; "drawing cartwheels on the slips of paper provided by the British taxpayer for better purposes," she "unconsciously . . . draw[s] a face" that reveals her true judgment of the male writers she has been reading.[41] There is more than a nod to Freud here (some feminists might want to say, a parody of him). But, beyond this, Woolf is making a serious case for the value of free-associative or intuitive thinking as opposed to schematic thinking: however fecklessly charming it may appear, it is more likely to unearth the unpleasant, the repressed, the socially unwelcome truth. (But what Woolf transvalues here is not the vatic intuition Robert Graves thought he saw in Riding; it is the daily, inconsequential, whimsical kind that male writers often condescend to or find exasperating.)

Wollstonecraft's reverence for reason has not entirely vanished from Woolf's mental framework, though it is treated with irony. Entering the British Museum, Woolf appears pleased to think of herself as "a thought in the huge bald forehead which is so splendidly encircled by a band of famous names" (27). She even reflects that "one needed answers, not questions; and an answer was only to be had by consulting the learned and the unprejudiced, who have removed themselves above the strife of tongue and the confusion of body and issued the result of their reasoning and research in books which are to be found in the British Museum" (27). Of course, this hope is so soon dashed that Woolf might be suspected of introducing it satirically; but is the satire directed only against the British Museum, or against the naïf in Woolf herself, the woman too prone to a quasi-medieval reverence for *auctorite?*

For the question Woolf seeks to answer is pragmatic in the extreme: "Why are women poor?" But what she finds, beyond some "very queer facts about the habits of the Fiji islanders," is a farrago of male opinion, whose very contradictoriness reveals the intensity of emotional fixation —"written in the red light of emotion and not in the white light of truth" (30, 34–35). "Wherever one looked men thought about women and thought differently" (32). With this perception, the battle has already been carried into the enemy's camp. The question is no longer, as for Wollstonecraft and even Schreiner, why women are such-and-such a way; but why men need to perceive them so.

So Woolf poses the further question: why do men find women so important—"the most discussed animal in the universe" (28)—yet seem bent on denigrating them? Why are those who "see[m] to control every-thing" (36) angry? Her diagnosis is harsh, and has been influential. Self-confidence is indispensable to everyone; how much more so to "a patriarch who has to conquer, who has to rule." "And how can we generate this imponderable quality, which is yet so invaluable, most quickly? By thinking that other people are inferior to oneself" (37). Moreover, she goes on to reflect, men's oversensitivity to criticism com-ing from women

> was not merely the cry of wounded vanity; it was a protest against some infringement of his power to believe in himself. Women have served all these centuries as looking-glasses possessing the magic and delicious power of reflecting the figure of man at twice its nat-ural size. Without that power probably the earth would still be swamp and jungle. . . . That serves to explain in part the necessity that women so often are to men. And it serves to explain how rest-less they are under her criticism. . . . For if she begins to tell the truth, the figure in the looking-glass shrinks. . . . The looking-glass vision is of supreme importance because it changes the vitality; it stimulates the nervous system. Take it away and man may die, like the drug fiend deprived of his cocaine. (38–39)

Woolf's metaphors—the mirror, the addiction—are brilliant.[42] Had she intuited their early childhood resonances, her essay would in fact possess the "pity and toleration" it aims for (41). We cannot blame her for lacking this perspective: Melanie Klein did not publish with the Hogarth Press until 1932; Winnicott did not use the metaphor of mater-nal mirroring until 1967; Heinz Kohut was a child in 1928. But, lack-ing this further depth, we get the image of man the abnormal egotist, the conqueror, the warmaker, the schematizer, whose whole business is "giv-ing judgment, civilizing natives, making laws, writing books, dressing up and speechifying at banquets" (38). Woolf begins to attribute toler-ance and negative capability exclusively to women, saying "it is one of the great advantages of being a woman that one can pass even a very fine negress without wishing to make an Englishwoman of her" (54–55). Between Wollstonecraft and Woolf, feminism has passed from refuting stereotypes of women to—however deftly and wittily—creating stereotypes of men.

This is not, of course, where *A Room of One's Own* comes to rest. The later passages about the "androgynous" or "man-womanly mind" (108), the mind of Shakespeare or Jane Austen, which is not angry, but "ha[s] consumed all impediments" (73), are famous and noble, and still too much for many identity-politics thinkers to swallow. But the more satiric passages give us a hint why the, in some ways comparable, transvaluations of the "feminine" in a Carpenter, a Rilke, or a Graves might have seemed too little, too late; more emotion-laden responses to Woman as she impinges on Man, where a little factual candor about the predicaments of actual women would have been infinitely more useful.

THAT WOOLF'S aggressive tone toward masculine assumptions and behavior has become the dominant one, in the last thirty years, hardly needs saying. Feminist anger has transformed language and manners, reshaped the conventions of literature, and given peculiar fault lines, a peculiar sadness, to the inner struggles of marriages. But the "second wave" of feminism has not been monolithic; and its splits have occurred, often, around the old issues of autonomy and sexuality. Radical feminism, Alice Echols reminds us, had its origins in the New Left, and for a time shared its enthusiasm about sexual experimentation. A "natural polymorphous sexuality"—akin to Blake's or Norman O. Brown's—was advocated by American writers like Shulamith Firestone and, in France, by Irigaray. As Echols remarks, "Radical feminists understood that women's sexual inhibition is related in large part to the absence of safe, accessible and effective contraception which renders women sexually vulnerable. They attributed women's attachment to traditional morality not to the innately spiritual quality of women's sexuality, but rather to our socialization which encourages sexual alienation and guilt."[43]

Even in the 1960s, though, there was no perfect unanimity. Writers from the Marxist-patterned Boston group Cell 16, which advocated female celibacy, held that "happy, healthy self-confident animals and people don't like being touched, don't need to snuggle and huggle," and even that lesbianism "muddles what is the real issue for women by making it appear that women really like sex as much as men—that they just don't like sex *with* men."[44]

With the 1970s, the group Echols calls "cultural feminists"—writers like Adrienne Rich, Mary Daly, Jane Alpert, Robin Morgan—distanced themselves from the political Left and reinstated an essentialist claim that women were biologically "closer to nature," more nurturing, less aggressive than men, and so "uniquely qualified to save the planet from nuclear holocaust and ecological ruination."[45] With this move, stereotypes of male and female sexuality came to the fore: "Male sexuality is driven, irresponsible, genitally oriented, and potentially lethal. Female sexuality is muted, diffuse, interpersonally oriented, and benign. Men crave power and orgasm, while women seek reciprocity and intimacy. . . . Women's sexuality is assumed to be more spiritual than sexual, and considerably less central to their lives than is sexuality to men's."[46] As Echols demonstrates, this view could quickly pass from descriptive to prescriptive, in relation to women's sexual behavior. Its apotheosis, in the antipornography movement of Andrea Dworkin and Catherine MacKinnon, stigmatized and alienated not only men but liberal heterosexual women, transsexuals, and even "lesbian feminists experimenting with s/m, butch-femme roles, and bisexuality."[47]

Probably *both* the early feminist interest in sexual experimentation and the later feminist stereotyping have struck a raw nerve in men because of the apparent rejection of mutual need between the sexes. The most petulant pages of Norman Mailer's *The Prisoner of Sex* (1971) have to do with test-tube babies, vibrators, and the incurable alliance, from Mailer's point of view, between feminist independence, technology, and an antiintuitive rationalism.

On the other hand, Mailer's most powerful pages defend—often by simply describing—male experience of heterosexual impulse and the irrational. Answering Kate Millett's *Sexual Politics* (which, of course, had attacked him, along with Lawrence and Henry Miller), Mailer chides Millett for using the term *sexual revolution* to refer only to women's political gains, and therefore not even treating the 1920s as a significant decade.[48] Millett's "counterrevolutionary sexual politician," Henry Miller, is "the true sexual revolutionary" (102) because he considered "lust" a legitimate literary topic, and did not entirely separate it from "love":

Lust is a world of bewildering dimensions, for it is that power to take over the ability to create and convert it to a force. . . . Lust exhibits all the attributes of junk. It dominates the mind and other habits, it appropriates loyalties, generalizes character, leaches character out, rides on the fuel of almost any emotional gas—whether hatred, affection, curiosity, even the pressures of boredom—yet it is never definable because it can alter to love or be as suddenly sealed from love, indeed the more intense lust becomes, the more it is indefinable, the line of the ridge between lust and love is where the light is first luminous, then blinding, and the ground is unknown. (110)

Mailer is willing to concede, finally, that Miller's heroes do often degrade women in their sexual quest, as Millett says, but he argues that "it was man's sense of awe before woman, his dread of her position one step closer to eternity . . . which made men detest women, revile them, humiliate them, defecate symbolically upon them, do everything to reduce them so one might dare enter them and take pleasure of them" (116). This is a risky statement, if it seems to excuse actual humiliation and violence; but it needed to be made, at a time when feminists would soon be calling male sexuality in its essence "the stuff of murder, not love."[49] More recent feminists—notably Susan Bordo—have often concluded, as Mailer does, that a view of women as powerful and unapproachable plays a large role in both rape and pornography. Bordo even goes on to suggest, even, that certain pornographic fantasies, that to female observers convey sadism and domination, for their male audience serve rather to restore a fragile sense of men's physical and sexual acceptableness.[50]

Moreover, Mailer's interest in "the line of the ridge between lust and love" opens the door to *women* who lead their imaginative lives primarily through their sexuality—a controversial category, which "cultural feminism" preferred to condemn or ignore. In this respect, *The Prisoner of Sex* looks forward to what is perhaps the greatest character-portrait in Mailer's later work, that of Nicole in *Executioner's Song.*

I suspect that this need to redescribe male experience from within, after the widely publicized caricatures of masculinity emanating from the cultural feminism of the 1970s, is a lot of the motivation behind the so-called Men's Movement. Certainly some of the most eloquent pages in Robert Bly's *Iron John,* as in Mailer, undertake this work of

renaming. For instance, describing adolescent boys watching a beautiful female contemporary at a summer resort, Bly shows how what is
called "sexual objectification" may, for the "objectifier," be an experience not of exerting control but of being painfully diminished by what,
for him, is a divine visitation.[51] Analogously, Bly's rhetoric of kings and
warriors—while understandably controversial—is on one level making
a rather simple point: a culture loses something if it has no images of
men who are at once good and wise and strong.

Feminists have been a little obtuse in not seeing why men, at this
point, would feel this need to redescribe their own emotional and interpersonal experience in its own terms. It is one thing to point out that
men's descriptions may be defensive or insufficiently exploratory—Susan
Bordo does this quite neatly with Sam Keen in the essay I have cited. But
it is another to say, as so many of the contributors to *Women Respond
to the Men's Movement* do, that "women want a men's movement,"
but only one with an agenda, and assumptions, already dictated by
feminism,[52] to be "less hooked on a spectrum of control that extends
from not listening through to violence," to "come to understand the
evils of patriarchy."[53]

Still, there is something legitimately disturbing in Bly's thought, as in
Mailer's. Where the earlier male "sexual prophets" we have examined
all, in their different ways, tried to find room for aspects of themselves
that their cultures did not consider sufficiently masculine, Mailer and
Bly seem driven to defend male identity at its most traditional. Mailer
—like another of his heroes, Lawrence—contends that men "must work
to become men" and women must "take a creative leap into becoming
women"; therefore the most polarized sexual types are the true
"hero[es]." He cannot believe that to be "some middling mix of both
sexes" could be courageous—as Woolf thought—not just "comfortable"
or "technological" (169). And Bly seems not only to denigrate female-
identified men; as Margaret Randall writes, he "blames women" rather
than the fact that "the male-inherited dominant culture stigmatizes
'soft' men" for their "unhappiness."[54] In its very first pages, *Iron John*
contends that "the strong or life-giving woman who graduated from the
sixties . . . played an important part in producing this life-preserving,
but not life-giving, man" (3).

Bly's case is a more complicated and interesting one than Mailer's
because Bly began as a Jungian/Gravesean defender of the Eternal

Feminine. In his first foray into gender theory, the 1973 essay "I Came Out of the Mother Naked," he wrote: "All my clumsy prose amounts to is praise of the feminine soul, whether that soul appears in men or in women. The masculine soul, which in its middle range is logic and fairness, and at its highest vibrations hurries toward the spirit, also needs praise, but I am not doing that here. . . . We know that the despising of the feminine soul has been the cause of some of our greatest errors and disasters."[55] The essay is filled with references to Bachofen, Neumann's *The Great Mother,* and Graves. "Having gone out into masculine consciousness," Bly says, "a man's job is to return" (29). "All of my poems come from the Ecstatic Mother; everyone's poems do. Men in patriarchy try to deny the truth that all creativity lies in feminine consciousness" (40). Occasionally, as above, there is qualified praise of "father consciousness," but, more often, Bly represents it as linear, imperialistic, "hard." In any case, at our moment in history, "the turn has come. Women want more masculine consciousness, and men want more mother consciousness; they want a balanced consciousness" (49).

Bly's shift away from this praise for balance may have its roots in his changing responses to the collective phenomena we call "the sixties." Bly had been a passionate spokesman for the antiwar movement; his men seeking more mother consciousness clearly include hippies, with "their beads and long hair and ecstasy" (43). After the debacle of the early 1970s, Bly (like others, including some of the cultural feminists) began to feel that the counterculture had undervalued the importance of remaining part of the larger community: "The important thing is the community itself and its continuity, because it is a living forest of people, ecologically sound; that is important, not the flying fragment. The 'prophet' knows this; that is why in such a true community he allows himself to be killed without a lot of self-pity, and without writing 'An Enemy of the People' or 'Crucible.'"[56] In this 1974 essay, 1960s revolutionaries were not willing-enough martyrs; by 1990, they are largely psychoanalytic case histories. "The son's fear that the absent father is evil contributed to student takeovers in the sixties," Bly now pronounces, even if, "the country being what it is, occasionally they d[id] find letters from the CIA" (21–22). Bly also suggests that if women did not, as Blake said, prefer the soldier to the poet (he cites the bumper stickers that read WOMEN SAY YES TO MEN WHO SAY NO), there was was some kind of self-interested, even sinister, power play, "energetic women" choosing "soft men" who could be cast in a filial role (3).

But even in "I Came Out of the Mother Naked," we can already detect a paranoid image of the devouring female. Trying to explain the emergence of the demonic at the end of the 1960s—for example, there was Altamont, and Manson—and drawing on Jung's sense of the necessary moral ambivalence of all archetypal figures, Bly reminds us of Kali with her necklace of skulls and constructs his own myths of the "Teeth Mother" and the "Stone and Death Mothers . . . standing right next to the Ecstatic Mothers" (43). He elaborates: "Whenever a man enters the force field of a Mother, he feels himself being pulled toward mothers and childhood, back toward the womb, but this time he feels himself being pulled *through* the womb, into the black nothing before life, into a countryside of black plants where he will lose all consciousness, both mother and father. The teeth in the vagina strip him as he goes through. He is dismembered while still alive" (41).

Some readers, I suspect, will want to close the book (Bly's, if not mine) at the very evocation of such a fantasy. Yet Jessica Benjamin confirms that such ideas do occur, in the unconscious, and suggests that recognizing them may be a healthy antidote to the Freudian stress on penis envy:

> While the little boy may consciously represent the mother as castrated, clinical evidence reveals that unconsciously the boy sees this mother as extremely powerful. She does not appear lacking a sexual organ; rather her vagina is known and feared for its potential to re-engulf the boy, whose little penis would be far too small to satisfy it. (As an illustration of this fear, consider a three-year-old boy who, shortly after inquiring in detail about his mother's genitals and how babies are born, became panic-stricken at the end of his bath when the plug was pulled: he now feared that he or his toys could be sucked down the drain.)[57]

(If this latter anecdote does not illustrate Bly's hypothesized dread of "being pulled back *through* the womb, into the black nothing before life," it is hard to see what would.)

The question, as we approach the negative treatment of feminine influence (and, particularly, of mothers) in *Iron John*, will be whether Bly maintains the distinction between fantasy and reality, or, in Jung's terms, between the "archetypal" and the "individuated." Does he remain content with recognizing the intrapsychic force of Teeth Mother and

Death Mother fantasies? or do they unconsciously color his judgment of interpersonal situations? Not seldom, in *Iron John*, we come across remarks like the following: "The possessiveness that mothers typically exercise on sons . . . can never be underestimated" (12). Bly cites, approvingly, a passage from Mari Sandoz's *These Were the Sioux* that describes how young Sioux boys were forbidden, after the age of seven, to look their mothers in the eyes. Indeed, so strong is Bly's horror of any "sexual energy" between mother and son that on one occasion he seems to approve of violence as a response to it. The story is attributed to "another woman." (It is noteworthy, but not particularly inspiring of trust, that whenever Bly moves toward a particularly controversial assertion, it is attributed, as with Mari Sandoz, to a female speaker.) This woman's son has just returned to an all-female household, after a long visit with his father. One night, when she tells him to come to dinner, and touches his arm, "*he* exploded and *she* flew against the wall. . . . We notice no intent of abuse . . . and no evidence that the event was repeated. . . . The psyche or body knew what the mind didn't" (18–19).

But how does Bly know there was "no intent of abuse"? (As my friend Elizabeth Tallent has pointed out, the verbs he uses prejudge the case: "exploded" excludes agency from the son's experience; "flew" excludes damage or injury from the mother's.) In a culture where male violence toward women is common, we cannot so simply rule out the darker, earlier sources of rage that Klein, Dinnerstein, and Benjamin chart so powerfully, or be sure that the boy's psyche (or Bly's) so know-ingly distinguishes the Teeth Mother from a flesh-and-blood woman behaving with simple affection.

Not surprisingly, boys who do remain female-identified get the brunt of some of the most brilliant and hostile rhetoric in Bly's book. The "naive man" (as Bly calls him) particularly tends to sympathize with women, beginning with his mother. He feels "flattered" to share her confidences, even if they enlist him in a conspiracy against his father. Later, he is drawn to women who similarly "share their pain." He will often accept mistreatment from such women, using the word *special* to exempt himself from "examin[ing] the dark side of the person." Perhaps —Bly shrewdly suggests—in failing to examine their dark side, he is hoping "they will not investigate his," since he retains, unexamined, "a secret and special relationship with a wounded little boy inside him-self" whose "self-pity" he avoids questioning (63–64). By paying too much attention to the woman's pain, he does not have to come to terms with his own.

Naive men, finally, overvalue "ecstasy" and (as Bly himself tended to in his earlier essay) "ignor[e] all masculine sources of it" (65–66). They have all the qualities of the figure the Jungian theorist Marie-Louise von Frantz calls the *puer aeternus*: "flying people, giddily spiritual," who "do not inhabit their own bodies well, and are open to terrible shocks of abandonment . . . are unable to accept limitations, and are averse to a certain boring quality native to human life." Female identification, it would seem, goes with excessive spirituality, ungroundedness, excessive vulnerability, and a "grandiose" conception both of the self and its appropriate mate, "mak[ing] love with invisible people at high altitudes" (57).

When I read these paragraphs, I cannot help seeing the protagonists of my own book rising before me in a kind of ghostly procession. The portrait of men who almost professionally "pick up women's pain" calls up Lawrence's Paul Morel, the Rilke of the unrequited lovers, the Jarrell of the monologues. When I read about men who consider their women "special" and do not protect themselves against their dark side, I see Pavese, Graves, and the Jarrell persona of "Hohensalzburg"— who, clearly, is also finding a way not to criticize his own "self-pity." When I read about "flying people, giddily spiritual," who are "averse to a certain boring quality native to human life," I think of the Jarrell who felt "like an angel" while skiing, of Rilke and Blake with their own angelic companions. What this portrait leaves out, of course, is the genius of these men, their compassion, their emotional flexibility, the positive "trickster" quality that gets them around the limits that our culture sets to how men can feel, can create.

Of all the writers we have discussed, Bly seems closest to Lawrence in his two-sidedness. It is enlightening, then, to look at Bly's own account of Lawrence, for what it leaves out as well as what it includes. As an adolescent, Bly says, Lawrence "wanted the 'higher' life, and took his mother's side." Only when he was dying in Italy did he "notice the vitality of the Italian workingmen," and "begin to feel a deep longing for his own father." He came to feel, then, "that his mother's ascensionism . . . had encouraged him to separate from his father and from his body in an unfruitful way" (20). This is of course factually wrong: Lawrence began to take his father's side much earlier, in the Baxter

Dawes sections of *Sons and Lovers*. But it is also spiritually wrong, in suggesting that the turn to male identification was simple and happy.

For me, one of Bly's most sympathetic psychological insights is his idea of *katabasis*—that it is necessary to descend from angelic heights to live with ashes, depression, the knowledge of one's own dark side and of other people's. There is no one, I think, this is truer of than Lawrence; but what he must come to terms with are the consequences of his masculinist "resolution," no less than those of his female identification. We have seen, in Nixon's *Lawrence's Leadership Politics and the Turn Against Women*, the struggles with paranoid rage, homosexuality, and fascism that accompanied the "turn" to the masculine. We see in *Kangaroo* Lawrence's own, perhaps more creative, descent to ashes, as Somers must look at the fissures in his "ideal" marriage, the brutality of the actual male supremacists he has fallen in with, the gap between his grandiose image of himself as a leader and his withholding, rather pusillanimous behavior.

And yet, Bly's (and Lawrence's) diagnosis that much male unhappiness derives from absent fathers and seductive mothers—and that such family configurations are typical in the late twentieth century—receives some unexpected corroboration in recent feminist literature. Witness Nancy Chodorow, summarizing earlier research:

> In the absence of men, mothers, cross-culturally, may early sexualize their relation to sons. Bibring argues that this is indeed the case in many mid-twentieth-century nuclear family households, where there is a strong, active mother who runs the household and exhibits other traits of superiority to her husband (e.g., in cultural or social spheres) and a father who, for a variety of reasons . . . is uninvolved in and unavailable for family life. In these situations, she suggests, there is too much of mother: "the little boy finds himself . . . faced by a mother who appears to be as much in need of a husband as the son is of a father." The mother, then, sexualizes her relationship to her son early, so that "Oedipal" issues of sexual attraction and connection, and jealousy, become fused with "pre-Oedipal" issues of primary love and oneness.[58]

If this is true, then the fusion of preoedipal needs with masculine love needs—an enormous source of problems, as we have seen throughout —might be alleviated, as Dinnerstein and Benjamin have said, if fathers took a larger, more openly affectionate, role in their sons' upbringings.

So I am left with a question about how to end this book. Neither masculinism nor feminism saves, it would seem. Should I regard my writers as tragic failures, in a way Bly would diagnose, in one sense, only too accurately—all with missing or unsatisfactory fathers, all, as Lawrence said, with "sad fates"? Or should I see them, as I would like to, as heroes, restoring to the male psyche what Auden called "the mother's richness of feeling"? Some of Jessica Benjamin's recent writings suggest a middle way of approaching this difficulty. Drawing on Fast's work, she posits an early "overinclusive phase" in which children, though nominally aware of their biological sex, continue to believe that "they can have or be everything."[59]

> Now recognizing certain basic distinctions between masculinity and femininity, children continue to try, through bodily mimesis, to imaginatively elaborate both options within themselves. A thirty-month-old girl may imitate her older brother's play with action figures in order to assimilate symbolic masculinity, the phallic repertoire of colliding, penetrating, invading and blocking. A boy of twenty-four months may insist that he has a vagina, but at three years, more aware of external anatomy, he might instead claim to have a baby inside his tummy. . . . To the extent that the child imaginatively identifies without yet realizing the impossibility of acquiring certain capacities and organs, envy is not a dominant motive. But gradually the over-inclusive period becomes characterized by envy and ongoing protest. . . . At this point, castration represents for both sexes the loss of the opposite sex capacities and genitals. . . . The sexes are parallel in their insistence on being everything, their elaboration of complementarity as opposites held within the self, and their protest against limits.[60]

In terms of this early childhood experience, there is a tragic dimension both to life-careers that adopt narrowly prescribed gender identities and to those that defy them. Both give up something, in terms of concrete social possibilities and of a fundamentally human "protest against limits."

But, Benjamin goes on to argue, our notion of the desirable or "normative" outcome need not be the most rigidly monosexual. It can be, rather, a kind of Winnicottian play, the retention of a transitional space in which the old overinclusiveness is kept alive without seeming a threat to literal sexual identity:

I believe it is possible to recuperate the overinclusive without losing differentiation. . . .

The claim that the oedipal division institutes the renunciation
of omnipotence, an acceptance of limits—being only the One or
the Other . . . misses the dimension of bridging difference through
symbolic forms that depend on identification. Such forms give
depth to the delineation of difference.[61]

(An earlier, more explicitly Winnicottian version of this essay speaks of
"creativity . . . reestablished at the level of play and imagination" after
the "successful mourning of the loss of omnipotence.")[62]

People with this capacity, as Benjamin implies, will not distinguish
"identificatory love" and "object love" as clearly as traditional psychoanalysis does, to the greater "depth" and "empathy" of human relationships.

Robert Bly himself has moved back toward allowing female identifi-
cation a positive role in male development in his most recent book, *The
Sibling Society.* He writes here of an intrapsychic figure he calls the
"Lofty Companion" and distinguishes from the more paternally toned
Freudian "Superego": "When latency is over . . . the boy and girl will
have two constructed figures or companions inside, if all goes well.
One, wisely or unwisely, will apply standards, . . . tell you what not to
do, and in general lower your self-esteem for the sake of standards.
The other, the agency of aspiration, works to lift you out of the moral,
intellectual, and feeling shortages that your family has always lived
with, and helps you become one of the better ones, or wiser ones, or
deeper ones, or nobler ones."[63] Though Bly says, at first, that this
Companion "can be male or female in tone," he soon suggests that, for
him, it was basically feminine—thus, in a way, coming full circle to his
earliest position. "It was my mother who liked poetry, and it's often the
feminine that has such a deep passion for beauty and what is fine. The
Lofty Companion, then . . . is considered, rightly, I think, as springing
from the feminine side of the psyche." Aside from autobiography, it is
feminine, I think, because it restores the dimension of innerness, the
inner "good object," which, Benjamin suggests, boys often lose in the
oedipal crisis. Bly no longer sees its dreaminess as a primarily negative
quality: "The Lofty Companion wants a tensionless state and so is given
to daydreaming, and 'out of the family' experiences. It holds itself
aloof from vulgar folly and whispers, 'You can do it all alone.'" This

grandiose sense of superiority, this tendency "to isolate you from others" no longer incurs any of the negative rhetoric of "flying people, giddily spiritual." Such ascension is now the prologue to a legitimate "life's work" in which the sense of distinction, or distinctness, will be grounded in "success, authenticity, and achievement."[64]

Bly's "Lofty Companion" involves, I think, both the transitional space in which overinclusive identifications continue to occur and the cross-gender identification itself. His ceasing to fear it is, I think, in the essence of Winnicottian play—a recognition that imagination is, finally, not reality, that identity can be fertilized by the Other without becoming the Other.

Human beings, after all, do inherit from both a father and a mother; and they like, and love, in the image of both. If the gender wars become less bitter in the twenty-first century, the delicate complexities of this seemingly simple situation can only become more evident. And if we do not try to make any one resolution of them "normative," we can perhaps see the range of imaginative identifications as neither a threat to our own gender identity nor a cooptation of that of others, but as an intrinsic aspect of human creative play. And we can then see that the love that identifies, and the love that desires, are far less distinguishable than we once believed.

Notes

Introduction

1. Kirk and Raven, *The Presocratic Philosophers* (Cambridge: Cambridge University Press, 1957), p. 238.

2. Wendy Lesser, *His Other Half* (Cambridge: Harvard University Press, 1991), pp. 4, 10.

3. Adrienne Rich, *The Fact of a Doorframe: Poems Selected and New, 1950–1984* (New York: Norton, 1984), p. 249.

4. Sandra M. Gilbert, "Purloined Letters: William Carlos Williams and 'Cress,'" *William Carlos Williams Review* 11 (2) (1985): 5–15.

5. Kaja Silverman, *Male Subjectivity at the Margins* (New York: Routledge, 1992), p. 3.

6. Robert Bly, *Iron John* (New York: Vintage, 1992), p. 2 (page numbers subsequently cited in text).

7. Silverman, *Male Subjectivity,* p. 354.

8. Jessica Benjamin, *The Bonds of Love* (New York: Pantheon, 1988), p. 161 (page numbers subsequently cited in text).

9. Dorothy Dinnerstein, *The Mermaid and the Minotaur* (New York: HarperCollins, 1976), pp. 164, 106.

10. Jessica Benjamin, *Like Subjects, Love Objects: Essays on Recognition and Sexual Difference,* (New Haven: Yale University Press, 1995), p. 13.

1. Jarrell, the Mother, the Märchen

1. All quotations follow the text of *The Complete Poems* (London: Faber & Faber, 1981).

2. Dinnerstein, *Mermaid and Minotaur,* p. 97.

3. See Melanie Klein, "The Origin of Transference," in *Envy and Gratitude and Other Works* (London: Hogarth, 1975), p. 49; and "On Mental Health," ibid., p. 273.

4. Letter to Sister Bernetta Quinn, December 1951. *Randall Jarrell's Letters,* ed. Mary Jarrell (Boston: Houghton Mifflin, 1985), p. 303.

5. Richard Flynn comes closer to my sense of the poem when he says that the boy's feelings for his mother are "complicated, uncomfortable, sexual." But he goes on to suggest that the mother's "solicitous caresses . . . contai[n] a hint of sexual abuse"—a hint I cannot find in the poem. See Richard Flynn, *Randall Jarrell and the Lost World of Childhood* (Athens: University of Georgia Press, 1990), pp. 54–55.

6. See D. W. Winnicott, "Ego Distortion in Terms of True and False Self," *The Maturational Processes and the Facilitating Environment* (New York: International Universities Press. 1965), pp. 140–52.

7. It will be obvious that here I am giving a mere gist of the arguments of some very complex thinkers. See Melanie Klein, *Envy and Gratitude and Other Works, 1946–1963* (London: Hogarth, 1975); Alice Miller, *The Drama of the Gifted Child* (New York: Basic, 1981); and Benjamin, *Bonds of Love,* esp. chapter 1, "The First Bond."

8. Miller, *Gifted Child,* p. 11.

9. Randall Jarrell's Letters, p. 303.

10. William H. Pritchard, *Randall Jarrell: A Literary Life* (New York: Farrar, Straus & Giroux, 1990), pp. 12–13.

11. Ibid., p. 17.

12. "Randall Jarrell: 1914–1965," in Robert Lowell, *Collected Prose* (New York: Farrar, Straus & Giroux, 1987), p. 91.

13. Mary Jarrell, "Ideas and Poems," *Parnassus: Poetry in Review* 5 (1) (1976): 219.

14. Pritchard, *Randall Jarrell,* pp. 201, 226.

15. Flynn, *Randall Jarrell and the Lost World of Childhood,* p. 8.

16. Benjamin, *Bonds of Love,* p. 147.

17. See ibid., chapter 4, pp. 133–81.

18. On the "infinity" of infant despair, see Dinnerstein, *Mermaid and Minotaur,* p. 165 n.

19. See Benjamin on Winnicott's concept of "destruction," *Bonds of Love,* pp. 38–41.

20. See Dinnerstein, *Mermaid and Minotaur,* esp. chapter 6, "Sometimes You Wonder If They're Human."

21. Randall Jarrell, *The Animal Family* (New York: Knopf, 1965), pp. 51–52 (page numbers subsequently cited in text; all are to this edition).

2. Rilke's Solitude

1. *Letters of Rainer Maria Rilke, 1892–1910,* trans. Jane Bannard Greene and M. D. Herter Norton (New York: Norton, 1969) [hereafter *Letters of Rilke*], p. 181.

2. I owe this objection (to "Antistrophes" and to Rilke's stance generally) to Sandra Gilbert.

3. "Antistrophes," *The Selected Poetry of Rainer Maria Rilke,* trans. Stephen Mitchell (New York: Random House, 1984), p. 221 (all subsequent quotations come from this translation, unless otherwise noted).

4. Adrienne Rich, "Mother and Son, Woman and Man," *American Poetry Review* 5 (5) (1976): 7.

5. Rilke, *Letters to a Young Poet,* trans. Stephen Mitchell (New York: Random House, 1984), pp. 68–73.

6. *Letters of Rilke,* p. 112.

7. *Rilke and Benvenuta: An Intimate Correspondence,* trans. Joel Agee (New York: Fromm International, 1987), pp. 77–78.

8. Magda von Hattingberg, *Rilke and Benvenuta,* trans. Cyrus Brooks (London: Heinemann, 1949), p. 6.

9. Ibid., pp. 9–10.

10. Ibid., p. 10.

11. In conversation.

12. *Letters of Rilke,* p. 114.

13. Von Hattingberg, *Rilke and Benvenuta,* p. 13.

14. *An Intimate Correspondence,* p. 109.

15. Von Hattingberg, *Rilke and Benvenuta,* p. 133.

16. "Oh, misery, my mother tears me down," in *An Unofficial Rilke,* selected, introduced, and trans. Michael Hamburger (London: Anvil, 1981), p. 65.

17. Robert Hass, introduction to *The Selected Poetry of Rainer Maria Rilke,* pp. xxii–xxiii.

18. *The Freud Journal of Lou Andreas-Salome,* trans. Stanley A. Leavy (New York: Basic, 1964), p. 182.

19. D. W. Winnicott, "Creativity and Its Origins," in *Playing and Reality* (London: Tavistock, 1971), pp. 74, 78.

20. Von Hattingberg, *Rilke and Benvenuta,* p. 87.

21. Ibid., p. 19.

22. Ibid., p. 131.

23. D. W. Winnicott, "Transitional Objects and Transitional Phenomena," in *Playing and Reality,* p. 14.

24. Rilke, "Some Reflections on Dolls," *Selected Works,* vol. 1: *Prose,* trans. G. Craig Houston (London: Hogarth, 1954), p. 45.

25. Winnicott, "Transitional," p. 12.

26. *Selected Works 1,* p. 45.

27. See Winnicott, "Transitional," p. 15.

28. *Selected Works 1,* p. 48.

29. Ibid., pp. 46–47.

30. Von Hattingberg, *Rilke and Benvenuta*, p. 131.

31. *Letters of Rilke*, p. 113.

32. Letter to Emil von Gebsattel. *Letters of Rilke*, pp. 42–43.

33. *Letters of Rilke*, p. 49.

34. See Donald Prater, *A Ringing Glass: The Life of Rainer Maria Rilke* (Oxford: Oxford University Press, 1986), pp. 206–7.

35. *Letters of Rilke*, p. 41.

36. Leavy, trans., *Freud Journal of Andreas-Salome*, p. 183.

37. See Klein, *Envy and Gratitude*, esp. p. 185.

38. See Leavy, *Freud Journal of Andreas-Salome*, pp. 168–69, 181–85.

39. Ibid., p. 182.

40. Ibid., p. 183.

41. There is no absolutely conclusive evidence that Rilke knew *Totem and Taboo* when he wrote the Third Elegy. However, Lou Andreas-Salome records a conversation with Freud about "a 'fantasy'. . . about the meaning of parricide for the development of civilization" in February 1913, seven months before her vacation with Rilke in the Riesengebirge, when they discussed psychoanalysis exhaustively (Leavy, *Freud Journal of Andreas-Salome*, p. 104). It seems unlikely she would not have shared this "'fantasy,'" which she considered the most "ingenious" work Freud had ever done, with Rainer.

42. Von Hattingberg, *Rilke and Benvenuta*, p. 190.

43. *Letters of Rilke*, p. 114.

44. Hamburger, *An Unofficial Rilke*, p. 59.

45. See Wolfgang Leppmann, *Rilke: A Life* (New York: Fromm International, 1984), p. 310.

3. Lawrence and the "Oedipal Riddle"

1. Other critics contemporaneous with Mailer did see that gender polarity is a fundamental theme in Lawrence, but managed to square this with more conventional readings; H. M. Daleski, for instance, did this by the tortuous maneuver of concluding that "his father is associated with the female principle and his mother with the male." See Daleski, *The Forked Flame*, Madison: University of Wisconsin Press, 1987, p. 63.

2. Norman Mailer, *The Prisoner of Sex* (Boston: Little, Brown, 1971), pp. 151–52.

3. Ibid., pp. 152–53.

4. Carol Siegel, *Lawrence among the Women* (Charlottesville: University Press of Virginia, 1991), esp. chapter 1, "'Those Who Washed Dishes with Lawrence.'"

5. D. H. Lawrence, *Sons and Lovers* (New York: Signet Classics, 1985), p. 41 (all subsequent references are to this text, unless otherwise noted).

6. See, for instance, Dinnerstein, *Mermaid and Minotaur,* p. 103: "The boy's restitutive urges toward the early mother—as echoed in later relations with her and with other females—are less tinged than the girl's with fellow-feeling. For him, the mother to whom reparation must be made is mainly an idol that has been flouted and must now be mollified lest she exact vengeance, a natural resource that has been assaulted and must now be restored lest it cease to provide."

7. *The Letters of D. H. Lawrence,* ed. Aldous Huxley (London: Heineman, 1932), p. 76.

8. Marguerite Beede Howe, *The Art of Self in D. H. Lawrence* (Athens, Ohio: Ohio University Press, 1977), pp. 10–11.

9. D. H. Lawrence, *Sons and Lovers* (Cambridge: Cambridge University Press, 1992), p. 232.

10. Dorothy Van Ghent, *The English Novel: Form and Function* (New York, Evanston: Harper Torchbooks, 1961), p. 247.

11. Howe, *Art of Self,* p. 14.

12. See Benjamin, *Bonds of Love,* pp. 38–41.

13. This line of reading was first set forth by Daniel A. Weiss in *Oedipus in Nottingham* (Seattle: University of Washington Press, 1962, pp. 29–37), though in more classically Freudian terms.

14. *Sons and Lovers,* Cambridge edition, p. 320.

15. Weiss, *Oedipus in Nottingham,* pp. 34–35.

16. Cornelia Nixon, *Lawrence's Leadership Politics and the Turn against Women* (Berkeley: University of California Press, 1986), p. 15. See *Letters,* p. 218.

17. John Middleton Murry, *Son of Woman: The Story of D. H. Lawrence* (New York: Jonathan Cape & Harrison Smith, 1931), p. 51.

18. "Wedlock," in *The Complete Poems of D. H. Lawrence,* ed. Vivian de Sola Pinto and F. Warren Roberts (New York: Viking, 1971), p. 246.

19. *Complete Poems,* p. 214.

20. Murry, *Son of Woman,* pp. 50, 54.

21. *Complete Poems,* pp. 124–25. See Murry, *Son of Woman,* pp. 46–47.

22. "Lady Wife," in *Complete Poems,* pp. 234–35. See Murry, *Son of Woman,* pp. 52–53.

23. *Complete Poems,* pp. 254–56.

24. Murry, *Son of Woman,* p. 57.

25. Ibid., pp. 34–35.

26. Lawrence, *Psychoanalysis and the Unconscious and Fantasia of the Unconscious* (New York: Viking, 1960), p. 138.

27. D. H. Lawrence, *Women in Love* (New York: Penguin Classics, 1986), p. 188.

28. Robert Langbaum, *The Mysteries of Identity* (New York: Oxford University Press, 1977), pp. 333–35.

29. Daniel Albright, *Personality and Impersonality: Lawrence, Woolf, and Mann* (Chicago: University of Chicago Press, 1978), pp. 44–45.

30. See Nixon, *Lawrence's Leadership Politics,* p. 201.

31. See D. W. Winnicott, "The Location of Cultural Experience," in *Playing and Reality* (London: Tavistock, 1971), pp. 95–103.

32. Howe cites a passage from "The Crown," contemporaneous with *Women in Love,* in which Lawrence explicitly specifies that what our "disintegration" takes us back to, out of "our completeness," is "the states of childhood" (20).

33. For Nixon's definitive reading of this aspect of the book, see *Lawrence's Leadership Politics,* pp. 113–30.

34. The long-suppressed "Prologue" to *Women in Love* was published in D. H. Lawrence, *Phoenix II* (New York: Viking, 1970). While the "Prologue" is usually remembered for its vivid acknowledgement and evocation of Birkin's homosexual side, it actually draws a more complex picture, concluding, "But it was not so, that he always loved men." It triangulates three kinds of love: the compulsive attraction to men; the identificatory love of women Lawrence's early life predisposed him to ("he was always terribly intimate with at least one woman, and practically never intimate with a man. . . . He studied the women as sisters, knowing their meaning and their intents"); and the "violent excess with a mistress whom, in a rather anti-social, ashamed spirit, he loved," and with whom "he forgot about this attraction that men had for him" (*Phoenix II,* pp. 104, 106).

35. Charles Ross, introduction to D. H. Lawrence, *Women in Love* (London: Penguin Classics, 1986), pp. 24–26.

36. 43. See Sandra M. Gilbert and Susan Gubar, *No Man's Land,* vol. 1: *The War of the Words* (New Haven: Yale University Press, 1988), esp. pp. 37–40.

37. Benjamin, *Bonds of Love,* p. 164.

38. "Dignity and Impudence" are of course Victorian clock-figures; but they have a nice aptness to Gudrun's perpetual concern with how she is outwardly perceived.

39. See Nixon, *Lawrence's Leadership Politics,* pp. 209–14.

40. Eliseo Vivas, for instance, takes the scene unambiguously this way. See *D. H. Lawrence: The Failure and the Triumph of Art* (Evanston: Northwestern University Press, 1960), pp. 240, 242. See also Daleski, *Forked Flame,* pp. 153–54.

41. Benjamin, *Bonds of Love,* p. 172.

42. D. H. Lawrence, *Kangaroo* (London: William Heinemann Ltd., 1955), p. 94.

43. D. H. Lawrence, *St. Mawr,* in *St. Mawr and The Man Who Died* (New York: Vintage, 1960), p. 147.

4. Pavese's Despair

1. See Benjamin, "Woman's Desire," *Bonds of Love,* chapter 3.

2. Ibid., p. 163.

3. Dinnerstein, *Mermaid and Minotaur,* p. 43.

4. Benjamin, *Bonds of Love,* p. 170.

5. Ibid., p. 163.

6. Ibid., p. 164.

7. Dinnerstein, *Mermaid and Minotaur,* p. 50.

8. Davide Lajolo, *An Absurd Vice: A Biography of Cesare Pavese,* trans. and ed. Mario and Mark Pietralunga (New York: New Directions, 1983), pp. 22–23.

9. Lajolo, *An Absurd Vice,* pp. 62–63, 88, 113, 136.

10. Ibid., p. 69.

11. Cesare Pavese, *This Business of Living: Diaries 1935–1950,* trans. A. E. Murch, with Jeanne Molli (London: Quartet Books, 1980), p. 49.

12. At least one diary entry, 25 April 1946 (*This Business of Living,* p. 276), implies sexual satisfaction on the woman's side: "When passion has left her exhausted . . ."

13. "I mattini passano chiari," Cesare Pavese, *Poesie* (Milan: Oscar Mondadori, 1987), p. 206. Here, and in all subsequent citations from Pavese's poetry after *Lavorare stanca,* I quote my own translations, published in *American Poetry Review* 26 (5) (1997): 35–39.

14. *This Business of Living,* p. 345.

15. Ibid., pp. 38, 78, 281.

16. Ibid., p. 82.

17. Lajolo, *An Absurd Vice,* p. xiv.

18. *This Business of Living,* p. 344.

19. Ibid., p. 98.

20. See Lajolo, *An Absurd Vice,* pp. 165–68, 172–76.

21. Ibid., p. 4.

22. Cesare Pavese, *Dialogues with Leuco,* trans. William Arrowsmith and D. S. Carne-Ross (Boston: Eridanos, 1989), pp. 58–59.

23. *Dialogues with Leuco,* p. 45.

24. Joanne Feit Diehl, unpublished paper, "The Prodigal's Return: 'Infantile Anxiety Situations' and Elizabeth Bishop's Long Journey Home."

25. All quotations from *Lavorare stanca* come from William Arrowsmith's translation, *Hard Labor* (New York: Ecco Press, 1979). Where Arrowsmith's renderings differ significantly from the Italian, it will be discussed in the text.

26. William Arrowsmith, introduction to *Hard Labor,* p. xxiv.

27. *Hard Labor,* pp. 208–9.

28. Dinnerstein, *Mermaid and Minotaur,* p. 95.

29. Ibid., p. 164.

30. Ibid., pp. 106–7.

31. In *The Smile of the Gods,* trans. Yvonne Freccero (Ithaca: Cornell University Press, 1968), Gian-Paolo Biasin devotes several pages to the identity of landscape and woman in Pavese, offering this extraordinary quotation from *A Great Fire:* "I found again my childhood memories, as of someone who dreams of a destiny and a horizon which is not hill or cloud but blood, woman of whom clouds and hills are only a sign" (194).

32. *Dialogues with Leuco,* p. 45.

33. Dinnerstein, *Mermaid and Minotaur,* p. 112.

34. *Dialogues with Leuco,* p. 46.

35. Dinnerstein, *Mermaid and Minotaur,* pp. 126, 124, 130.

36. Ibid., pp. 124–30 passim.

37. *Dialogues with Leuco,* pp. 5–7.

38. Ibid., pp. 104, 102.

39. See Dinnerstein, *Mermaid and Minotaur,* pp. 61–62, esp. footnote.

40. *Dialogues with Leuco,* p. 56.

41. Ibid., pp. 59, 58.

42. Ibid., pp. 59, 60.

43. Again, I quote from my own translations. For the originals, see *Poesie,* pp. 181–94.

44. *This Business of Living,* p. 266.

45. *Dialogues with Leuco,* pp. 22–23.

46. Ibid., pp. 23–24.

47. See *Poesie,* pp. 197–210.

48. *This Business of Living,* p. 344.

49. Lajolo, *An Absurd Vice,* p. 69.

5. Questions of Autonomy: Two European Novels

1. Dinnerstein, *Mermaid and Minotaur,* p. 38.

2. Ibid., p. 42.

3. Michael E. Kerr and Murray Bowen, *Family Evaluation* (New York: Norton, 1988), p. 59.

4. Maggie Scarf, *Intimate Partners* (New York: Ballantine, 1987), p. 22.

5. Kerr and Bowen, *Family Evaluation,* pp. 74–75.

6. Ibid., p. 64.

7. There are, of course, exceptions; e.g., Robert Greer Cohn's "Man and Woman in Gide's *The Immoralist,*" *Romanic Review* 80 (3) (1989): 419–33. In its rather free-form but illuminating, half-Freudian, half-Jungian way, this article does acknowledge the centrality of male/female dynamics in the book.

8. Andre Gide, *The Immoralist*, trans. Dorothy Bussy (New York: Vintage, 1958), p. 9 (all subsequent references are to this translation).

9. Jeffrey Meyers, *Homosexuality and Literature, 1890–1930* (London: Athlone, 1977), p. 35.

10. Kerr and Bowen, *Family Evaluation*, p. 181.

11. Ibid., p. 265.

12. Cf. ibid., p. 129: "The occurrence of symptom exchanges means that the basic level of chronic anxiety or emotional problem in a family has not changed; the anxiety or undifferentiation has simply become 'agglutinated' or bound in a new place."

13. See Silverman, *Male Subjectivity*, pp. 366–73; also Sigmund Freud, *Three Essays on the Theory of Sexuality* (New York: Basic, 1962), 11 n.

14. Cf. Kerr and Bowen, "Triangles," *Family Evaluation*, chapter 6.

15. It is, of course, possible to read this episode in many different ways. According to Meyers, p. 36 "the scissors in the folds . . . are symbols of copulation that reveal Michel's homosexual attraction." But, as Joseph Aimone points out, the scissors, belonging to Marceline, might better be seen as a "sign of the castrating phallic mother," a power the son attempts to repossess from her (letter to author).

16. Meyers, *Homosexuality and Literature*, p. 39.

17. Lesser, *His Other Half*, p. 6.

18. John Updike, *Rabbit at Rest* (New York: Fawcett Crest, 1990), pp. 191–92.

19. Lesser, *His Other Half*, p. 7.

20. Milan Kundera, *The Unbearable Lightness of Being* (New York: Harper Colophon, 1985), p. 10.

21. Lesser, *His Other Half*, p. 8.

22. Kerr and Bowen, *Family Evaluation*, p. 172.

23. Lacanians, I suspect, would be fascinated with the "crack," as associating female sexuality with a void, a between-space. They would not be wrong; though I suspect the issue is more how Sabina experiences her existential in-betweenness in her sexual life than anything essential about female sexuality.

24. Benjamin, *Bonds of Love*, p. 80.

25. Ibid., pp. 69–70.

26. Ibid., p. 52.

27. Ibid., pp. 60–61.

28. Kerr and Bowen, *Family Evaluation*, pp. 194–95.

6. Male Sexual Prophecy: Blake to Bly

1. *The Poetry and Prose of William Blake*, ed. David V. Erdman (Garden City: Doubleday, 1965), "Jerusalem": plate 69, lines 43–44, p. 221 (all citations

from this prophecy will take the following form: E [page number], J [plate number]: [line number].

2. Of the feminist critiques, the most psychoanalytically enlightened are Margaret Storch, *Sons and Adversaries: Women in William Blake and D. H. Lawrence* (Knoxville: University of Tennessee Press, 1990), and Brenda S. Webster, "Blake, Women, and Sexuality," in Miller, Bracher, and Ault, *Critical Paths: Blake and the Argument of Method* (Durham: Duke University Press, 1987), pp. 204–24. I draw on both, explicitly and implicitly, throughout this discussion. A less psychoanalytic but unusually fair-minded treatment is Alicia Ostriker's "Desire Gratified and Ungratified: William Blake and Sexuality," *Blake: An Illustrated Quarterly* 16 (3) (1982–83): 156–65.

3. See Webster, "Blake, Women, and Sexuality," p. 205; Storch, *Sons and Adversaries*, p. 21.

4. Blake, "The Four Zoas: Night the First," in Erdman, *William Blake* p. 308.

5. Ibid., p. 308.

6. Ibid., p. 338.

7. Blake, "The Four Zoas: Night the Eighth," in Erdman, *William Blake*, p. 363.

8. Storch, *Sons and Adversaries*, p. 6.

9. Ostriker, "Desire," p. 157.

10. Northrop Frye, *Fearful Symmetry* (Boston: Beacon, 1962), p. 74.

11. Robert Bly makes the same point in *Iron John* (New York: Vintage, 1992), pp. 84–86.

12. Benjamin, *Bonds of Love*, p. 120.

13. See my discussion of Sylvia Plath in *Introspection and Contemporary Poetry* (Cambridge: Harvard University Press, 1984), esp. p. 35.

14. Storch, *Sons and Adversaries*, p. 81.

15. A number of scholars have gone further and suggested that Blake was actually influenced by the *Vindication*. See Michael Ackland, "The Embattled Sexes: Blake's Debt to Wollstonecraft in *The Four Zoas*" (*Blake: An Illustrated Quarterly* 16 (3) (1982–83): 172–83); G. E. Bentley Jr., "'A Different Face': William Blake and Mary Wollstonecraft," *Wordsworth Circle*, 10 (4) (1979): 349–50); Judith Lee, "Ways of Their Own: The Emanations of Blake's *Vala, or The Four Zoas*," *ELH* 50 (1): 131–53. But, as Ackland himself observes, our knowledge of how much of Wollstonecraft Blake actually read, and how seriously he absorbed it, is "frustratingly incomplete."

16. Mary Wollstonecraft, *A Vindication of the Rights of Woman* (New York: Norton, 1967), pp. 49–50.

17. An intriguing article by Orm Mitchell suggests that the only works of Blake's known for certain to be responses to Wollstonecraft subtly criticize her, on exactly these grounds. Orm Mitchell, "Blake's Subversive Illustrations to Wollstonecraft's *Stories*," *Mosaic* 17 (4) (1984): 17–34.

18. Carole S. Vance, "Pleasure and Danger: Toward a Politics of Sexuality," in Carole S. Vance, ed., *Pleasure and Danger* (Boston: Routledge & Kegan Paul, 1984), p. 1.

19. Ibid., pp. 4–5.

20. Mary Jacobus, *First Things* (New York: Routledge, 1995), chapter 4, esp. pp. 66–73.

21. Alice Echols, *Daring to Be Bad* (Minneapolis: University of Minnesota Press, 1989), p. 13.

22. For a detailed and nuanced account, see Ellen Carol DuBois and Linda Gordon, "Seeking Ecstasy on the Battlefield," *Pleasure and Danger*, pp. 31–49.

23. Arthur Rimbaud, letter to Paul Demeny, May 15, 1871; *Collected Poems*, trans. Oliver Bernard (London: Penguin Classics, 1986). pp. 10, 13–14.

24. Rimbaud, *A Season in Hell, Collected Poems*, p. 320.

25. Nancy J. Chodorow, *Feminism and Psychoanalytic Theory* (New Haven: Yale University Press, 1989), p. 143.

26. Ibid., p. 144.

27. Ibid., pp. 140–41.

28. Sandra M. Gilbert and Susan Gubar, "Turn-of-the-Century Literature," in *The Norton Anthology of Literature by Women* (New York: Norton, 1985), p. 948.

29. Edward Carpenter, *Love's Coming of Age* (New York: Mitchell Kennerley, 1911), pp. 32–33.

30. See Sandra M. Gilbert and Susan Gubar, *No Man's Land*, vol. 2: *Sexchanges* (New Haven: Yale University Press, 1989), esp. pp. 33–34.

31. See Carol Dix, *D. H. Lawrence and Women* (Totowa, New Jersey: Rowman & Littlefield, 1980), pp. 8–11. For Rilke on Bachofen, see Prater, *A Ringing Glass*, p. 308.

32. Robert Graves, *The White Goddess* (New York: Creative Age, 1948), pp. 332–33.

33. Randall Jarrell, "Graves and the White Goddess," *The Third Book of Criticism* (New York: Farrar, Straus & Giroux, 1969), pp. 108–9.

34. Robert Graves, *Good-bye to All That* (New York: Doubleday, 1985), p. 19.

35. Ibid., pp. 34–35.

36. Ibid., p. 280.

37. Jarrell, "Graves and the White Goddess," p. 107.

38. Ibid., p. 110.

39. Graves, *The White Goddess*, p. 372. This is the only passage from Graves referred to in the whole of Gilbert and Gubar's vol. 1 of *No Man's Land* (see pp. 148–49, 152).

40. Olive Schreiner, *Woman and Labor* (New York: Frederick A. Stokes, 1911), p. 193.

41. Virginia Woolf, *A Room of One's Own* (New York: Harcourt Brace Jovanovich, 1929), pp. 29, 32.

42. Oddly, Edward Carpenter also uses the "mirror" image, though in a much more balanced, even-handed context (*Love's Coming of Age*, 86–87).

43. Alice Echols, "The Taming of the Id," in Vance, *Pleasure and Danger*, p. 56.

44. Echols, *Daring to Be Bad*, p. 162; Echols, "Taming of the Id," p. 55.

45. Echols, "Taming of the Id," p. 51.

46. Ibid., pp. 59–60.

47. Ibid., p. 62.

48. Mailer, *Prisoner of Sex*, p. 101.

49. Andrea Dworkin, quoted in Echols, "Taming of the Id," p. 59.

50. See Susan Bordo, "Reading the Male Body," *Michigan Quarterly Review*, 32 (4) (1993): esp. 706–8. See also Miller, *Gifted Child*, pp. 89–90.

51. See Bly, *Iron John*, p. 135.

52. Of course, "men's movement[s]" being as various as feminisms, some men have willingly accepted this agenda; see John Stoltenberg, *Refusing to Be a Man* (Portland: Breitenbush Books, 1989).

53. Kay Leigh Hagan, ed., *Women Respond to the Men's Movement* (San Francisco: Pandora [Harper Collins], 1992), pp. 5, 14. The contributors quoted are, respectively, Gloria Steinem and Rosemary Radford Ruether.

54. Margaret Randall, "'And So She Walked Over and Kissed Him,'" *Women Respond to the Men's Movement*, p. 144.

55. Robert Bly, "I Came Out of the Mother Naked," *Sleepers Joining Hands* (New York: Harper & Row, 1973), p. 49.

56. Robert Bly, "The Network and the Community," *American Poetry Review* 3 (1) (1974): 19–21.

57. Benjamin, *Bonds of Love*, p. 94.

58. Chodorow, *Feminism and Psychoanalytic Theory*, p. 72; Chodorow references Philip Slater, *The Glory of Hera: Greek Mythology and the Greek Family* (Boston: Beacon Press, 1968); John W. M. Whiting, Richard Kluckhohn, and Albert Anthony, "The Function of Male Initiation Rites at Puberty," in Eleanor Maccoby, T. M. Newcomb, and E. L. Hartley, *Readings in Social Psychology* (New York: Holt, Rinehart & Winston, 1958); Grete Bibring, "On the 'Passing of the Oedipus Complex' in a Matriarchal Family Setting," in Rudolph M. Loewenstein, *Drives, Affects, and Behavior: Essays in Honor of Marie Bonaparte* (New York: International Universities Press, 1953).

59. Benjamin, *Like Subjects, Love Objects*, p. 126.

60. Ibid., pp. 63–64.

61. Jessica Benjamin, "Constructions of Uncertain Content," *Shadow of the Other* (New York: Routledge, 1998), p. 74.

62. Copy of earlier version supplied to the author by Jessica Benjamin.

63. Robert Bly, *The Sibling Society* (Reading, Mass.: Addison-Wesley, 1996), p. 124.

64. Ibid., pp. 122–24. For Benjamin's in some ways remarkably parallel discussion of how the "ego ideal" is intertwined with the ideal maternal recognizer, see her "What Angel Would Hear Me? The Erotics of Transference," *Like Subjects, Love Objects*, pp. 143–74.

Index